D1567995

The World and Ideas of Ernst Freund

ERNST FREUND

OSCAR KRAINES

The World and Ideas
of Ernst Freund:

THE SEARCH FOR GENERAL PRINCIPLES
OF LEGISLATION AND ADMINISTRATIVE LAW

THE UNIVERSITY OF ALABAMA PRESS

University, Alabama

Copyright © 1974 by
The University of Alabama Press
ISBN 0-8173-4819-0
Library of Congress Catalog Card Number:
73-22719
All rights reserved
MANUFACTURED IN THE UNITED STATES OF AMERICA

Contents

Contents

Preface

Forty-one years have passed since Ernst Freund's death, and in the interval no biography or comprehensive study of the man and his influence appeared. Only three articles were published which could be characterized as biographical and analytical accounts, and all were short and sketchy. The first of these appeared in 1933 in the *Journal of Political Economy* as a seven-page obituary authored by Arthur H. Kent. The second, in 1962, was a twenty-seven page unsigned comment in the *University of Chicago Law Review;* and the third was Francis A. Allen's forty-page preface to the 1965 edition of Freund's *Standards of American Legislation.* Together, however, they form a useful foundation for any full-length study of Freund's ideas and achievements, and this writer acknowledges his debt to these authors.

There is much of the prophet in the pioneer, and Freund was a practical combination of the two. A major concern of his, from the 1890's on, was the subject of administrative powers and discretion, which today is a primary study area in law, public administration, and political science. Foreseeing many of the great problems we now face, he warned of their inevitability and aggravation if popularly elected legislatures failed to set and clearly define standards and limits of legality, particularly in civil liberties and civil rights; and he correctly foretold of the turning to and reliance on a judiciary remote from the electorate which would fill the gap but often too late, haphazardly and unevenly. His efforts to attain uniform state laws on marriage and divorce, guardianship, rights of illegitimate children, child labor, working conditions, narcotics and drug addiction were far ahead of his time and point up some of the major failures of our legislatures.

Freund introduced the study and teaching of bill-drafting, and was the first to delve deeply into the regulatory process and to evaluate its various devices, especially licensing and the dispensing power. So exhaustively penetrating were his analyses that the few later investigations into the police power, standards and principles of legislation, and administrative powers and discretion, while timely and updating, have hardly carried the depth of inquiry beyond him. He was among, if not, the first to recommend that legislative committees hire staffs of experts in political science, economics, sociology, and management, and to campaign for an improved selection of legislators. He was a key consultant to legislative and judicial bodies, constitutional commissions, law schools, administrative agencies and private social service associations, drafting many constitutional changes, legislative bills and municipal charters.

In Freund's concept of the American dream, individual citizens were free to learn and think for themselves, to choose and change their employment and residence, and to judge for and express themselves; and consequently, they were capable of governing themselves. Freund equated social justice with the American ideals of equality—equal opportunity and equal treatment under the law. However, in order to preserve the dream, he spent a lifetime of teaching, writing, and practical action aimed at creating the restraints which would curb the excessive acquisition and use of executive and administrative power. Just as he courageously and eloquently criticized the unconstitutional, illegal, and unethical activity of government officials in the name of national security during the "Red Raids" of the early 1920's so would he have castigated the behavior of executive and administrative officials in the "Watergate Affair" of the early 1970's. "Watergate" would have been a prime example of his fears and justification for the restraining and standardizing of unguided and uncontrolled executive and administrative authority and discretion.

It is the hope of the author that the present generation see Freund as relevant, and that he—and also Frank J. Goodnow—be read. It is regrettable that the former when identified is associated primarily with the police power and the latter is described as the one who separated politics and administration. A far better niche in American legal and administrative history is deserved by both.

Freund was one of those rare thinkers who spoke and wrote epigrammatically. A treasure of keen, quotable observations on law, politics, sociology, public administration and a variety of other subject areas awaits the reader. Permit several examples to illustrate: "An unjust law sustained is perhaps even a little worse than a just law declared unconstitutional." "Not every standard of conduct that is fit to be observed is also fit to be enforced." "What is needed is not merely an open mind, but some theory of education and action." "The strongest sympathy . . . cannot be a substitute for thorough understanding."

The many reforms urged by Freund, reflecting his enduring goal of making democracy effective primarily through legislative action, are as timely today as during his lifetime. In such context it is the aim of this study to provide an introduction to Freund with the hope of inspiring deeper and more comprehensive research into the many realms of interest and concern of one of America's profoundest and most creative and influential thinkers and men of action.

The author gratefully acknowledges the sharing by U.S. Senator Abraham Ribicoff of Connecticut of his personal recollections of Freund, and the assistance of the Department of Special Collections, Joseph Regenstein Library, University of Chicago, in making the Ernst Freund Papers available and permitting their quotation.

The World and Ideas of Ernst Freund

Introduction:

Freund and Law in a Changing America

In 1927 Felix Frankfurter, who became interested in administrative law early in his career, wrote in an article on "The Task of Administrative Law":

> In the United States, the pioneer scholarship of Frank J. Goodnow and Ernst Freund long remained caviar not merely to the general. Their work was for many years unheeded by bench and bar, a fact which is not too surprising when it is recalled that legal education hardly took note of it. But the prophetic scholar has his amused revenge when practice propounds theory. Necessity *is* the mother of discovery. And so, this illegitimate exotic, administrative law, almost overnight overwhelmed the profession, which for years had been told of its steady advance by the lonely watchers in the tower. Hardly a volume of bar association proceedings is now without some reference to this new phenomenon.[1]

To the names of Goodnow and Freund must be added that of Frankfurter. "It is to American scholars," remarked Arthur T. Vanderbilt in 1937, ". . . that the credit for the investigation, analysis, and presentation of the principles of administrative law, simultaneously with their development in actual practice, must go." The pioneer work, Vanderbilt asserted, "has been done, by and large, by three men, successively—Goodnow of Columbia, Freund of Chicago (himself a student under Goodnow), and Frankfurter of Harvard—and their disciples." [2]

1

FREUND'S BACKGROUND

Ernst Freund was born in New York City on January 30, 1864 while his German parents, Ludwig A. and Nannie Bayer Freund, were visiting America. Brought back to Germany, Ernst grew up in a middle class Jewish environment. He attended the Kreuzschule at Dresden from 1875 to 1877 and the Gymnasium in Frankfort-on-the-Main from 1877 to 1881 and upon graduation studied at the Universities of Berlin and Heidelberg from 1881 to 1884, the latter awarding him the degree of Doctor of Canon and Civil Law in 1884.

Preferring to assert his American citizenship, Freund settled in 1884 in New York City where he attended Columbia College from 1884 to 1885 and practiced law from 1886 until 1894. For two years, in 1892 and 1893, he taught public law at Columbia University while doing graduate work. In 1894 he left to join the faculty of political science at the University of Chicago. Three years later Columbia granted him the degree of Doctor of Philosophy in Public Law. At Chicago Freund rose rapidly from instructor to associate professor.

On October 1, 1902 the University of Chicago Law School was opened under the plan recommended by the University's first president, William Rainey Harper. In the latter's view the law school was to be more than a training institution for admission to the bar. Following suggestions presented by Freund, who joined the Law School at its creation, Harper asserted that an education in the law implied a scientific knowledge of law and of legal and juristic methods which cannot be understood in their entirety without a clear comprehension of the historic forces of which they are the product, and of the social environment with which they are in living contact. A scientific study of law involved the related sciences of history, economics, philosophy—the whole field of man as a social being. Harper at first felt the new law school should be an institute for legal research; but as Frederic Woodward, vice president of the University of Chicago, observed in 1933, "Freund was instrumental in convincing him that the more urgent need was for a professional school of high standard and that emphasis on research would naturally develop in such an institution." [3]

In June, 1932 Freund reminisced about the creation of the Law School before a convocation of graduates of the professional schools of the University of Chicago:

> There was quite a demand at the time that the school should not be "merely professional," but should set itself up as a school of jurisprudence; but those who made the issue were not entirely clear as to its implications. President Harper wisely concluded that the vital thing was the establishment of the highest professional standards, leaving the question of jurisprudence in abeyance.[4]

At the time, questions arose as to whether the new Law School should devote itself to jurisprudence or the teaching of students to become practicing attorneys. After three decades had passed, Freund in his reminiscenses remarked:

> To my question: Is jurisprudence something better than law? Is scientific different from professional law? Should scientific law be merged in the social sciences? I suggest a demurrer rather than an answer. I do think that if we had established a school of jurisprudence we should have been disappointed in our expectations. As a professional school we have not failed, but it may well be that the task of the professional school has been conceived too narrowly. Unless, within the limitations of time and equipment, a university law school explores all the resources of law, learns from history, and inspires itself by university ideals, it does not do its full duty to the legal profession; but if, inspired by these ideals, it succeeds in broadening and deepening the law-consciousness of the legal profession, and indirectly thereby, of the community, that will also be the most valuable contribution that a university can make to law and to legal science.[5]

The first faculty of the new Law School included James Parker Hall, Ernst Freund, and Floyd R. Mechem; and it was not long before these scholars attracted a body of students that became famous as independent thinkers in the law, political science and sociology. Among the teachers at the University of Chicago at the time were John Dewey, Charles E. Merriam, Robert Morss Lovett, James Henry Breasted, Herbert J. Davenport, Robert A. Millikan, John F. Jameson, and Thorstein B. Veblen.

Freund's interests were broad and leaned greatly to the political science area. So much so that in 1903 Freund played a major role in forming the American Political Science Association and served as its president in 1916, succeeding such colleagues and friends as Frank J. Goodnow, James Bryce, Frederick N. Judson, Woodrow Wilson, Albert Bushnell Hart, W.W. Willoughby and John Bassett Moore. Freund took a particularly active part in the political life of Chicago and the State of Illinois. "Many of the statutes in Illinois are the result of his work," noted the *American Bar Association Journal* in its obituary on Freund in 1933.[6] Freund was one of the drafters of Chicago's revised Charter in 1906 and 1907, and represented the Chicago City Council at the Illinois Constitutional Convention from 1920 to 1922 which created a new state constitution. For the former he drafted provisions which granted home rule to the City; and for the latter he drafted provisions which enlarged the home rule powers of Chicago. These provisions were adopted by the Constitutional Convention after Freund defended himself and his draft against bitter attacks by politicians and special interest groups. The electorate approved the new constitution on December 12, 1922.[7]

Freund's active participation in reform began at the turn of the century when Theodore Roosevelt was President and Melville Weston Fuller was Chief Justice of the Supreme Court. It was then that a group of "Young Turks" in the law were professing ideas which rejected the social, economic and legal theories of Herbert Spencer, William Graham Sumner and Thomas M. Cooley. Freund, with his study of *The Police Power* in 1904, felt himself linked to Justice Oliver Wendell Holmes' promotion of experimentation with social and economic legislation by the states.[8] He further allied himself two years later with Roscoe Pound when the latter shocked the American Bar Association at its annual convention in St. Paul with his paper on "The Causes of Popular Dissatisfaction with the Administration of Justice". The new sociology, evolving as a defense against the effects of the industrial and technological revolutions, was likewise advanced by Louis Dembitz Brandeis with his brief on behalf of the state in *Muller v. Oregon* [9] in 1908 advocating limitations on working hours for women, particularly mothers, engaged in unhealthful employment, such as in laundries. Brandeis argued that the survival of the human race depended on the health of women, especially mothers. At the root of this reformation in the law was the industrial and technological revolutions brought on, as Felix Frankfurter often later pointed out, by the steam engine. It was James Watts who, in effect, became the most important law reformer of modern times.

Freund and Brandeis were active together for many years as officers of the American Association for Labor Legislation. Brandeis served as a vice-president; and Freund was a member of the executive committee and was elected also its president and secretary in 1908. In November of that year Freund organized the Illinois State Branch of the Association and served as its first and long-time president. Both helped the Association draft its legislative programs, while Freund regularly prepared its summaries and studies of workmen's compensation legislation. Brandeis was particularly concerned with hours of labor legislation, and Freund combined the same concern with the issue of workmen's compensation. Governor Charles S. Deneen of Illinois recognized Freund's expertness and appointed him one of two legal advisers in 1905 to a special state commission to study and recommend legislation for workmen's compensation in Illinois. This broad interest in labor legislation brought Freund into national legal circles; and in 1912 he was elected by the American Bar Association to its Committee on Compensation for Industrial Accidents and Their Prevention.

With Julius Rosenwald and Judge Julian William Mack, Freund was a founder in 1908 of the Immigrants' Protective League and for several years was its president and for twenty-four years was a member of its board. He drafted the statute which created the Illinois State Immigrants' Commission of which Grace Abbott was secretary. When the Cable Act providing independent citizenship for married women was being debated in 1921 and 1922, Freund formulated a set of principles to guide Congress and the administration in the legislation's effects on both foreign-born and native American women.

From 1908 to his death in 1932, Freund was also a member of the National Conference of Commissioners on Uniform State Laws representing Illinois and serving as its president in 1920. He framed model statutes relating to marriage, divorce, illegitimacy, guardianship, child labor, workmen's compensation, and working conditions which many state legislatures enacted into law. Freund participated actively in nearly all of the Commission's meetings and served as chairman of a number of its committees, particularly the committees on scope and program, legislative drafting, and social welfare. The rules adopted by the Conference and printed annually to this day in its handbook for the guidance of legislative draftsmen were formulated by Freund.

In 1919 Freund wrote the first comprehensive study of illegitimacy laws of the United States and the major foreign countries. His draft of a uniform law for states on the legal rights of illegitimate children was adopted by the Conference in 1922 and has been enacted, with minor changes, by many of the states. He worked closely with the United States Children's Bureau and other social agencies on this and other programs. His draft of a divorce jurisdiction act was likewise approved by the Conference and adopted by several states. In addition, he served for years as a member of the Illegitimacy Conference of the Chicago Council of Social Agencies.

Freund took a leading part in founding the University of Chicago's School of Social Service Administration, the first graduate school of its kind in the United States. His courses at the Law School on administrative law, domestic relations, municipal corporations, and statutes were as popular with social service as well as law students. "He had great respect for social workers and thought that their experience should be drawn upon in framing programs for legislative action".[10] He contributed articles and money to various social service journals, and attended many conferences of social workers where he read papers and sat on committees.

In 1915, Freund was chairman of a committee of the American Institute of Criminal Law and Criminology which prepared the first study on the classification and definition of crimes in the United States. From 1916 to 1921 Freund was a member of and prime mover on the American Bar Association's Special Committee on Legislative Drafting which produced a *Legislative Drafting Manual* whose basic assumptions and outlines are still in effect today. In 1917, Freund's *Standards of American Legislation* was awarded Harvard Law School's James Barr Ames medal. Three years later the Commonwealth Fund established a Special Committee on Administrative Law and Practice with the aim of sponsoring a series of comprehensive studies on administrative powers and procedures. Freund was its chairman; and the three other members were Walter L. Fisher, Felix Frankfurter and Frank J. Goodnow. The first of the studies, Gerard C. Henderson's *The Federal Trade Commission,* appeared in 1924. Freund's *Administrative Powers Over Persons and Property* was published in 1928.

When the John P. Wilson, Sr. professorship in law was established in 1929 at the University of Chicago Law School Freund was selected as the first holder of the chair by unanimous consent. That same year he served as an editorial consultant in the preparation of the *Encyclopaedia of the Social Sciences,* which appeared in 1930; and for it he contributed the articles on administrative law, legislation and licensing. In 1931 Freund was awarded an LL.D. by the University of Michigan.

Freund had held the position of professor of jurisprudence and public law at Chicago from the establishment of the Law School until his death. He was active in law, politics, labor, and social work; and, in addition to a full academic workload, he carried on an almost superhumanly ambitious writing and lecturing program. His published writings number twenty books and pamphlets and ninety articles. A leading member of at least five major organizations, he presented papers before scores of local, national, and international societies; and he served as director and guiding mind of many large-scale study projects in a variety of legal, political and social fields.

Fairly tall, about 5 feet 10 inches, Freund stood straight and dressed neatly and modestly. He was a scholars' scholar as well as a students' teacher; and both faculty and students respected and liked him. He spoke with a slight German accent and in a low, soft voice.

Freund married late in life on May 13, 1916 when he was fifty-two years old. His wife was Harriet Woodworth Walton of Chicago, the daughter of Lyman A. Walton, a retired banker. The couple adopted two daughters. On October 20, 1932 Freund died of a heart ailment in Chicago at the age of sixty-eight. Death came suddenly in the evening while he was asleep at the Billings Me-

morial Hospital. He had been stricken in his office two days
earlier and was taken to the hospital where his wife was recovering
from a serious eye operation to save her sight.[11]

FREUND AND CHANGING AMERICA

The industrial and technological revolutions in the United
States were transforming the country from a rural to an urban
society. In the rural areas the farmers organized into granges
demanding governmental protection against domination by the
railroads. This resulted in the creation of state regulatory commissions. In the urban areas industrial workers formed unions,
whose ranks were augmented by many immigrants from European
countries with histories of administrative agencies, demanding
the establishment of local, state, and federal regulatory commissions to provide protection against domination by many branches
of industry. These pressures, likewise, led to the creation of regulatory commissions at various levels of government.

Freund saw the growth of administrative law spurred on by two
major movements occurring in the latter half of the nineteenth
century. One was "the prohibition legislation of the fifties" and
the second was "the Granger legislation of the seventies." The
latter he characterized as "the first great attempt to control the
traditional economic freedom." [12]

As America's predominantly rural agricultural society changed
to a predominantly urban industrial society, it became increasingly
complex in character and tended toward greater centralization in
all spheres of governmental activity, particularly in the area of
administrative action. The abuses of power by private industry led
to public demand for economic regulation by government, "a
demand," Edward L. Metzler characterized, "which in some of its
features has been erroneously denounced by its opponents as the
philosophy of socialism." [13] This expansion of government at all
levels into economic regulation was further extended into the field
of social welfare, a movement provoking even greater denuncia-
tion by opponents of centralization and socialism. In fact, op-

ponents of centralization bitterly assailed centralization *per se* as socialism. Furthermore, the entry of government into the areas of economic regulation and social welfare contributed largely to the growth in public expenditures and accordingly to increased taxation—an additional source of bitterness for opponents of centralization and socialism. To add still another point of vexation, Freund observed, the expansion of administrative power, based on the enactment of administrative law and discretion, stressed the subordination of private interest to the general welfare leading to the erosion of the solid protections of the common law with its emphasis on individual and property rights.[14]

What was occurring, observed Leo M. Alpert, was "the increasingly more pronounced shift from the state as a sovereign power issuing its commands to a state fulfilling public services." "The implication from such a shift is that administrative action is no longer an expression of the sovereign state oppressing individuals through 'bureaucratic' action, but is the characteristic expression of the modern state seeking the welfare of the individual and of the society of which he is a component part." [15]

Forrest Revere Black saw the change of American society after the Civil War, with regard to government, as follows: "The multiplication of administrative officers (commissions, boards, and bureaus) has challenged and cut deep inroads into many well-established doctrines. Old landmarks in the law are crumbling before this new assult." [16] This was vaguely foreseen by Woodrow Wilson who observed in 1887: "It is getting to be harder to *run* a constitution than to frame one." [17]

Wilson's foresight was elaborated on by Roscoe Pound in 1924 when, addressing the American Bar Association, he stated: "Perhaps in such an era of transition the hegemony of the executive is inevitable." As the eighteenth century and the first half of the nineteenth century relied upon the legislature and the last half of the nineteenth century relied on the courts, the twentieth century is no less clearly relying on the administration.[18]

Not until the early part of the twentieth century was administrative law written up or taught at all as a distinct part of the legal curriculum, and much later in the field of political science. As late as the last decade of the nineteenth century, as James Willard

Hurst observed, "it was the exceptional school that offered any course in legislation." "The law curriculum did not bring administrative law into distinct focus until past 1900. And except for Ernst Freund's pioneering, for twenty years, administrative law was restricted almost entirely to the problems of judicial review of administrative action." [19] "The two earliest writers in America to recognize the growing importance of administrative law," wrote William Seagle in *The Quest for Law,* "were Frank J. Goodnow and Ernst Freund. Both did pioneering work." [20] Joseph P. Chamberlain described Freund as "the first of the teachers of legislative law in American schools." [21]

Administrative law is not one of the traditionally recognized parts of the Anglo-American legal system. The law which controls the administrative agencies and their officials has never been accorded a distinct legal existence but rather a case existence, fitted into whatever branches of the law under which the particular cases arise. Moreover, law produced by the administrative authorities, as James Hart aptly pointed out, "was until recently scarcely admitted to exist, and, when actually met in the course of adjudication, was, in the words of Mr. Justice Holmes, 'softened by a quasi.' " [22]

However unacknowledged and indistinct in form, administrative law has existed as long as there have been administrative agencies and administrators. The American pioneers who saw this clearly and endeavored to develop the subject were Frank J. Goodnow, Ernst Freund, Floyd R. Mechem, Montgomery H. Throop, Bruce Wyman, and Felix Frankfurter. Greatest credit for establishing the place of administrative law in American law and political science must be given to Freund and Goodnow. It was Freund who prepared the first systematic casebook in administrative law published in the United States in 1911.

Felix Frankfurter described Freund as "one of the most distinguished of all legal scholars in the whole history of the legal professoriate." [23] "Ernst Freund is one of the great and distinctive figures in the history of American legal scholarship," wrote Francis A. Allen in the opening sentence of his preface to the 1965 edition of Freund's *Standards of American Legislation.*[24]

If Frank J. Goodnow is properly called "the father of American administration," then Ernst Freund may be called "the father of

American administrative law." Whereas the former stressed organization and personnel, the latter almost ignored these and emphasized individualism, private rights, principles of effective legislation, legislative and administrative standards, and the reduction of administrative discretion. Frankfurter, the third in this great triumvirate of builders and interpreters of American administrative law, stressed constitutionality and administrative procedures.

In Vanderbilt's assessment: "Goodnow viewed administrative law from the standpoint of the State," while "Freund on the other hand, was concerned primarily with the effect of administrative action on private rights" and "due doubtless to his Continental background, he has stressed the importance of legislation in its bearing on administrative law. Frankfurter and his school, with the exception of [John] Dickinson, have contented themselves in the main with intensive studies of particular agencies or problems rather than general treatises." [25] Vanderbilt aptly observed that Frankfurter and Davison were alone among these pioneers who emphasized the constitutional aspects of administrative law and the interrelationship of constitutional and administrative law.

In short, a proper understanding of administrative law required: in Goodnow's approach, a knowledge of politics and its relationship to public administration; in Freund's outlook, a recognition that private rights and problems of legislation were inseparably involved in administrative action; and in Frankfurter's viewpoint, a grasp of the interrelationship of administrative law with the issues of constitutional law and public law in general.

Freund's interests and concerns were much broader than Goodnow's and Frankfurter's. Freund immersed himself in the entire range of human behavior as it related to government. Consequently, he found himself much sought after to write and lecture on administrative management, criminal law, international law, civil rights and liberties, and social services in addition to his basic specialty—administrative law. He innovated laws on workmen's compensation, limitations on working hours, minimum wages, child labor restrictions, domestic relations, co-guardianship rights for women, and the status of illegitimate children. Freund was equally concerned with the problems of racial discrimination;

and from the very beginning of his career he maintained "it is extremely difficult to reconcile race distinctions with the principles of our constitutional law." [26] Freund played a significant role in shaping the important body of commercial law which emerged from the National Conference of Commissioners on Uniform State Laws.

Freund's life exemplified, as Felix Frankfurter noted, "the preoccupation with the validity of economic legislation." [27] From the very beginning, Freund devoted himself to the development of general principles of law and administration and their relation to broad social theory. In his first book, *The Legal Nature of Corporations,* which was his doctoral thesis and which was published in 1897, Freund stated in the preface that the essay's subject "belongs to a field of study and investigation that has been comparatively little cultivated in this country: the analysis and nature of legal conceptions without immediate or exclusive reference to practical questions." [28] It was this devotion to general principles and broad social theory rather than to practical concerns of the legal profession that made Freund's influence with the bench and bar "less striking than that of certain other legal scholars of his generation." [29]

Felix Frankfurter in 1936 remarked: "Frank J. Goodnow and Ernst Freund, as early as the '90's, saw general tendencies towards an Administrative Law in what the profession and the courts treated as unrelated instances." [30] In that early period Freund saw as "one of the most important political problems of the present day" "the problem how to combine bureaucracy and self-government." [31] As Albert Langeluttig pointedly observed in his review of Freund's *Legislative Regulation* in 1933: "With the reading of this volume comes, for the first time, the realization that every rule promulgated, whether by legislator or bureaucrat, sets up in the social structure a changing of relationships whose ultimate effects can rarely be anticipated." [32] Actually, this approach of Freund's can be traced back to his earliest writings in the 1890's.

Freund often referred to his teacher Frank J. Goodnow as the grand père of administrative law and to himself as the petit père. He recognized Goodnow as the true initiator of the subject as a separate branch of the law. However, as Langelutting noted in 1933: "If Goodnow was the founder of the study it is to Goodnow's student that the profession is indebted for the great development of investigation in this field." [33] Langeluttig, assessing Freund's role in the study of legislation as a science, here called Freund appropriately the grand père.

FREUND'S COMPREHENSIVE APPROACH

Freund's approach, from the early 1890's on, was deeper and more comprehensive than that of most of the commentators of the late 1930's on. His viewpoint was that the increasingly growing industrial and technological revolutions were so greatly and rapidly transforming our society that government inevitably had to respond to these huge, profound pressures both by encouraging and directing their beneficial effects and by discouraging and preventing their evil results. This governmental response was viewed by Freund as two-pronged: (1) legislative and (2) executive or administrative. In our system of separated powers, the legislature and executive would naturally be the forces to act. The legislative response was initially and primarily characterized by the resort to the police powers. Consequently, Freund's first major, full-length study was on the subject of the police powers of the federal and state legislatures.

The executive or administrative response involved administrative powers delegated to the executive by the legislatures and also administrative discretion exercised by the executive and by administrators independently of the legislatures. The delegation of administrative powers to the executive and administrators did not disturb Freund. This was inevitable, for the legislatures lacked the technical expertness. However, the discretionary authority of administrators troubled him. At best this new phenomenon was a necessary evil that needed controlling by the legislatures and as a last resort by the courts, and had to be gradually reduced by legislative standards that would become increasingly more precise as legislatures would hire experts in drafting, investigating, and auditing. This generalized view of the legislative and administrative responses offers an approach to an analysis of Freund's thinking.

It was on the matter of administrative discretion with respect to individual rights that Freund's essential humanity and deep regard for the individual person showed up boldly and aroused differences among other leading legal thinkers, particularly John H. Wigmore. Freund clearly pointed out that he was not opposed to administrative discretion *per se,* but only that which impinges on and restricts private rights. As for the latter type of discretion, he sought to devise principles, standards and guidelines for legislators and administrators to follow, especially legislators, so as to reduce such discretion to a minimum.

In this connection, Freund opposed Wigmore's reliance on benevolent administrators; and in a debate in 1925, discussed in detail in a later section of this study, Freund took sharp issue with Wigmore on this point and rejected the trusting of private rights and liberties to the vague, uncertain, unguaranteed, and nebulous benevolence of administrators.

While Freund contributed greatly in his time to the subject areas of legislation, police power, administrative powers, and administrative law, it may well be that his ideas and warnings on administrative discretion will constitute his most significant contribution to our times. For, it appears now to be generally agreed by experts in public law, political science, and public administration that the main problem in judicial review today is the control of administrative discretion. Two recent events support this view. In 1970 the Firearms Division of the Internal Revenue Service, without court order, checked into the public libraries of Atlanta, Georgia to gather data on individuals who borrowed books on firearms, explosives, or subversive subject matter. The other is the "Watergate Affair" in which executive and administrative officials sanctioned, participated in, or covered up illegal break-ins and burglaries, the use of electronic surveillance domestically against American citizens without court orders, the engagement in mail thefts, perjury and the obstruction of justice, including destruction of evidence, particularly incriminating governmental documents, and the direction of the Internal Revenue Service to harass certain individuals regarded as unfriendly to the President. These events would not be unknown to Freund. He railed against similar illegal behavior of executive and administrative officials and law enforcement personnel during the "Red Raids" of the early 1920's.

The Legislative Response

THE POLICE POWER

Coordinating political science and sociology with the law, and recognizing that new conditions call for the application of old concepts in new form, Freund at the age of forty plunged into what Leo F. Wormser described as "a field of the law that was still unplowed and unsettled"—police power. "Little wonder," noted Wormser of Freund's first major book, "that the Supreme Court of the United States and other courts frequently cited it, for through the tapestry that he wove from legal principles runs the golden thread of statesmanship." [34]

Freund titled his study *The Police Power: Public Policy and Constitutional Rights*. Published in 1904, it created a great stir in-legal circles and earned him national fame as a leading authority on administrative law and "one of the most eminent authorities on constitutional law." [35]

There have been many definitions of the legal term "police power" ranging from broad to narrow interpretations since its introduction in 1827 by Chief Justice John Marshall. Acknowledged as the most accurate is Freund's definition. Police power, he observed, is the power used by the government for the promotion of the public welfare through the establishment of restraints and regulations on the use of liberty and property. "The police power restrains and regulates, for the promotion of the public welfare, the natural or common liberty of the citizen in the use of his property." [36]

In *Brown v. Maryland*,[37] Chief Justice Marshall's meaning appeared to be synonymous with "police laws" or "regulations of the police"; but it was not used in any other case until ten years later in *City of New York v. Miln,*[38] when the controversy over abolition of slavery popularized the term. Its use popularly expressed the "residuary sovereignty" of President James Madison. In the following decade, Chief Justice Roger B. Taney declared in the *License Cases,*[39] that "the police power of a state" is "nothing more or less than the powers of government inherent in every sovereignty to the extent of its dominions . . . ; that is to say, the power of sovereignty, the power to govern men and things within the limits of its dominion." Justice John M. Harlan in 1906 in *Chicago, Burlington & Quincy Railway v. Drainage Commissioners* [40] declared that "the police power of a State embraces regulations designed to promote the public health, the public morals or the public safety" and that such power's validity depended "upon the circumstances of each case and the character of the regulation, whether arbitrary or reasonable and whether really designed to accomplish a legitimate public purpose." Five years later, Justice Oliver Wendell Holmes contended in *Noble State Bank v. Haskell,* "It may be said in a general way that the police power extends to all the great public needs. . . . It may be put forth in aid of what is sanctioned by usage, or held by the prevailing morality or strong and preponderant opinion to be greatly and immediately necessary to the public welfare." [41]

If these definitions do not clarify the term's use as we now know it, it is because so many different meanings were given to it since Marshall's time. "The confusion in the use of the term has never been cleared up by the text-writers" asserted the *Harvard Law Review* in 1904 in reviewing Freund's *The Police Power.* "The nearest approach is made in the present work by Professor Freund." [42] I.L. Sharfman noted in his comprehensive study of the Interstate Commerce Commission in 1931: "While there have been numerous instances of narrow construction of the police power, the conception which is coming to prevail is that of . . . Ernst Freund. . . ." [43]

Defining police power as "the power of promoting the public welfare by restraining and regulating the use of liberty and property," [44] Freund conceived it "not as a fixed quantity, but as the expression of social, economic and political conditions. As long as these conditions vary, the police power must continue to be elastic, i.e., capable of development." [45] Public welfare included "primary social interests and economic interests." "The former constitute the undisputed field of the police power, in which state control is universally regarded as legitimate. These interests are peace and security from crime, public safety and health, public order and comfort, and public morals . . ." [46] On the other hand, "the economic interests relating to the conditions of production and distribution of wealth constitute the debatable field of the police power." [47]

Freund recognized that "certain rights yield to the police power while it respects and accommodates itself to others." [48] While the prevention of fraud generally was conceded to be a legitimate function of the police power, the prevention of economic oppression split interested parties and the experts into opposing, unyielding camps. Assertions of constitutional right of liberty of contract were made to counter the invocation of authority under the police power.[49]

The police power in the United States practically began in the last quarter of the nineteenth century. Few, if any, of the thousands of statutes and decisions to which Freund referred had their origin prior to the Civil War. There could be little doubt, he predicted, that the growth of the police power, as reflected in legislation and judicial interpretation relating to public health, safety, and morals and social and economic regulation, would enormously increase as industrialization and urbanization expanded.

While the framers of the Constitution believed that the individual states should regulate the social and economic interests of their inhabitants, changing times, however, have made it impossible for the Federal Government to avoid exercising a considerable police power of its own.[50] Freund critically noted that the police power not expressly granted to the Federal Government by the Constitution was assumed by the Federal Government and approved judicially on the basis of its regulative power over interstate commerce. While the latter power was intended primarily to be exercised with relation to economic interests, it has been employed, and judicially authorized, for the protection of the public safety, health, comfort, and morals. The very meaning of the regulation of commerce has vastly changed since the time of John Marshall and his interpretation of this power as simply the power to prescribe rules.

As to what constitutes the essence of police power, Freund remarked that no community confined its care of the public welfare to the enforcement of the principles of the common law. The state employs its corporate and proprietary resources in the interest of the public to provide improvements and services of various kinds; and it asserts its compulsory powers to prevent wrongs by reducing common law rights through normal conventional restraints and positive regulations that are not restricted to the banning of wrongful acts. Here, for Freund, was the essence of the police power. In his own words:

> The state places its corporate and proprietary resources at the disposal of the public by the establishment of improvements and services of different kinds; and it exercises its compulsory powers for the prevention and anticipation of wrong by narrowing common law rights through conventional restraints and positive regulations which are not confined to the prohibition of wrongful acts. It is this latter kind of state control which constitutes the essence of the police power.[51]

Freund excluded from the police power all state activity which did not operate by compulsion and restraint. He classified state police power activity into three spheres: (1) a conceded sphere affecting safety, health, and morals; (2) a debatable sphere concerned with the proper production and distribution of wealth, public convenience, and advantage; and (3) an exempt sphere dealing with moral, intellectual, and political movements. It was the first sphere that Freund regarded as constituting the police power in its primary sense; and in this area was to be found an ever increasing amount of restrictive legislation. In the second sphere the police power, Freund asserted, was not a fixed quantity and was viewed as an expression of political, economic and social conditions. The third sphere, involving individual rights and constitutional guarantees, was with few exceptions, generally exempt from state police power interference. Perhaps, the greatest confusion existed when attempts were made to extend the police power into the second, or as Freund characterized it, the debatable sphere.

"But if the popular misuse of the term has become too deeply engrafted in legal works and opinions," concluded the *Harvard Law Review*'s review of Freund's book, "to allow a more restricted use of the phrase, then the careful and definite division, now made prominent for the first time in a text-book, is absolutely essential to clearness." "The author is to be congratulated on producing what is perhaps the best work on the subject." [52]

Freund divided "the great objects of government" into three groupings: (1) those involving the maintenance of national existence; (2) those concerned with the maintenance of right, or justice; and (3) those dealing with the public welfare.[53] By the late 1920's these classifications no longer fully held. John Dickinson, for example, in 1927 criticized the inclusion of the functions pertaining to the supply of public services as part of the third category rather than treating them as a separate group. Moreover, the exercise of the police power was restricted by Freund to the third category whereas Dickinson pointed out that the police power was actually being exercised with regard also to the second category.[54]

Freund's distinction between the second and third categories was based on a procedural line separating those matters for the courts to regulate between individuals and those matters in which the state injects itself, as an interested party, either by administrative regulation or criminal action. Dickinson aptly commented: "Procedurally such a line can be drawn, coinciding, except as to criminal action, with the distinction taken above between regulation by law alone and regulation by government. This seems to be the distinction Professor Freund has in mind when he says that 'no community confines its care of the public welfare solely to the enforcement of the principles of common law.' " However, the procedural line in the 1920's was no longer as rigidly fixed as Freund found it to be in 1904. Functions that are in substance the same may travel from one side of the procedural line to the other. "Every matter of private law," Dickinson asserted, "may, and generally does, involve some issue of public policy. There is merely a difference of remoteness. In considering Professor Freund's classification it must therefore be kept in mind that in many fields of regulation public welfare or policy first makes its appearance in common-law adjudications of differences between individuals. This policy in the course of time may come to be enforced directly by an administrative agency or by criminal proceedings. But it would seem that the function of government performed is in both instances the same, namely, 'that of promoting the public welfare by restraining and regulating the use of liberty and property.' " [55]

Freund limited his conception of the police power to the group of activities which were designed to promote the public welfare through restraints on liberty and property. Referring to a mass of court decisions on the subject, he showed that the police power was not a fixed, permanent entity but was the reflection and expression of political, social and economic conditions at a given time. Consequently, the police power must be elastic and capable of development, particularly since the shifting of population from rural to congested urban areas and the complexity of modern life will inevitably increase.

Freund showed that, despite the intention of the framers of the Constitution to leave to the individual states the regulation and care of economic and social interests, there was a large and increasing sphere of federal administrative activity in such functional areas. This federal activity within the domain described as "police power" may be classified into two divisions. One, which Freund labels "positive," emanated from the power of Congress to regulate interstate commerce, and included such legislation as relating to navigation, shipping, combinations in restraint of trade, suppression of traffic in lottery tickets, and banning or destruction of diseased and harmful, adulterated foods. "Professor Freund correctly affirms," wrote James Wilford Garner in 1904 reviewing *The Police Power,* "that it is impossible to deny that the Federal Government exercises a considerable police power of its own, and asserts that it must also be regarded as firmly established that the power over commerce while primarily intended to be exercised in behalf of economic interests may be employed for the protection of the public safety, comfort and morals." [56]

The second division of federal power, described as "negative" by Freund and viewed by him as more important than the positive activities, was the power of control exercised by the Supreme Court, under the Fourteenth Amendment, over the police powers of the individual states. Freund saw how the Supreme Court interpreted the Fourteenth Amendment so as to apply not only to discriminating legislation against Negroes but also against all matters of police power applying to all persons and to corporations. In fact, a large percentage of the cases then decided by the Supreme Court originated in the police powers of the states.

When Morris Raphael Cohen in the 1930's was discussing the place of logic in the law, he was fond of saying: "The consequent difficulties are amply illustrated in the chapters of Professor Freund's book on the *Police Power.*" [57] The court-found device of a police power inherent in the states to protect the public health, morals, and safety enabled government to function under a system in which the combination of the doctrine of natural rights and the traditional theory of a separation of powers limited by a written constitution otherwise would have been severely disruptive. However, the questions of what is and what is not within the police power, as Cohen pointed out in 1937 in a sketch on legal philosophy in America included in *Law: A Century of Progress 1835-1935,* have "never been definitely determined, being in fact largely dependent on the personal opinions of the judges about what states and municipalities should or should not do." [58]

Assessing Freund's approach, Cohen stated:

> Professor Freund, however, has dealt with this problem in a courageous, scholarly manner and has sought to clarify the actual body of American decisions in some rational way. Despite a good deal of natural revulsion against the nebulous speculation that often passes as legal philosophy, he was never quite satisfied merely with digesting the actual decisions but always sought to find a genuinely rational pattern which should aid us not only to harmonize the actual decisions but to supply illuminating ideas on the direction in which the law can wisely be pushed.[59]

Freund's study covered the late nineteenth century and the very early years of this century. No comparable work on the subject dealt with the period 1904 to 1922, the year that the coverage of Thomas Reed Powell's *The Supreme Court and State Police Power, 1922-1930* began.[60] An attempt was made in 1957 by Ruth Locke Roettinger [61] but her volume was not in the class of either Freund or Powell. However, Powell produced a volume which stressed constitutional law rather than administrative law.

Freund never viewed himself as a prophet. He knew that his definition and concepts of the police power would become obsolete. Yet, he seldom hesitated making predictions. He gave special consideration to the Fourteenth Amendment and its probable future significance. He saw in the negative power of control over the police activities of the states by the Supreme Court, under this Amendment, a greater importance than in the positive police power legislation of Congress. Correctly evaluating the Amendment's new significance, Freund pointed out that its original, intended application to prohibit discriminatory legislation against the Negroes no longer was so limited, but now could and would apply with equal, if not more, force to individuals and corporations to prevent economic and social regulation. Regrettably, Freund did not live to see the New Deal era and an even greater expansion of the police power than he had predicted.

PRINCIPLES AND STANDARDS OF LEGISLATION

"The science of legislation," asserted Joseph P. Chamberlain in 1933 reviewing Freund's *Legislative Regulation,* "probably owes more to Professor Freund than to any other American writer and teacher." [62] To discover and devise principles and standards of legislation in order to improve the quality of legislation was Freund's preoccupation his entire professional life. In 1908 he felt a little hopeful that the subject was "beginning to arouse popular attention and interest." [63] Contrasting us with France and Germany where "important legislation . . . is prepared by high officials, trained and experienced jurists and economists, who work under the guidance and advice of practical administrators with all the official information of a centralized bureaucracy at their command," the United States "is the only country in which this work is left entirely to a large political body possessing no particular qualifications." [64]

Acknowledging that our political system was so different from the European parliamentary systems that for us to adopt their methods would involve a revolution in the relations of the executive toward the legislature, he maintained, nevertheless, that certain reforms could be instituted without nessessitating fundamental changes in our system of government. The shortcomings which require remedying and which may be corrected in consonance with our system "may be said to be lack of responsibility, lack of expert advice, and lack of principle." [65]

Concerning responsibility, Freund advocated the strengthening of the executive at all levels of government and urged them not to yield to the legislatures in matters of policy. Since 1908 the executives have gone far in not only reaching Freund's objective but have surpassed it to the point where legislatures frequently trail behind. As for expert advice for the legislatures, Freund included both the content and legal form of legislation in that order. The passing years have seen the legislative committees hire staffs of experts of various specialties to advise and assist in investigations, research, and drafting of bills.

With regard to the third defect, the lack of principle, Freund defined principle as "the permanent and non-partisan policy of justice in legislation, the observance of the limits of the attainable, the due proportion of means to ends, and moderation in the exercise of powers which by long experience has been shown to be wise and prudent, though it may be temporarily inconvenient or disappointing in the production of immediate results." Constitutional limitations, he contended, constitute "a most valuable body of principles of legislation, but they are not . . . adequate for that purpose." "A rule of law must be rigid and unbending, while at least some principles should be flexible and capable of yielding in an emergency." Transforming such essentially elastic principles of policy as liberty and equality into rules of law "has undoubtedly enabled the courts to exercise a salutary censorship over immature and ill-considered legislation, but in so far as the courts have sought to enforce them as hard and fast rules, the result has been unfortunate for our jurisprudence." "The separation of powers, the non-delegability of legislative powers, the avoidance of special and local legislation, are all according to their nature principles, which under circumstances may be legitimately departed from, and which it may therefore be unwise to set up as absolute rules of law." [66]

Unlike Felix Frankfurter, Freund viewed constitutional law as narrow and limited; and as he was searching for a body of princi-

ples of legislation he saw in the combination of legislative, administrative, and judicial experiences the possibility of extracting and
developing such a body of principles. In his own words, written in
1919:

> But above all it is necessary to realize, not only that con-
> stitutional law as represented by judicial decisions does not
> furnish us with a body of principles of legislation, but that it does
> not even indicate fully and clearly the nature and scope of these
> principles. It is, indeed, from the combined legislative, adminis-
> trative, and judicial experiences that we gather the problems of
> legislation and their solution, but the solution does not proceed
> from or rest upon judicial authority, but must be worked out
> upon the basis of a discipline hardly recognized either in England
> or in this country—an independent science of jurisprudence.[67]

Where the subject of legislation concerns important economic
or social interests, principles of legislation are most significant
and can be applied. "But when it comes to the legal or judicial as-
pect of legislation, to that part of it which relates to its operation
upon technical rights, or to means and methods of execution and
enforcement, there is no such body of principles worked out in a
scientific manner." Consequently, a new kind of expert is needed
to help legislators in drafting legislation. Here, Freund advocated,
is where the universities must enter, train and provide the personnel.
"In the past, departments of political science have regarded the
work too technical and legal, the law schools as not sufficiently
professional. In consequence it has been unduly neglected. The
increasing number and complexity of legislative problems pressing upon the country cannot fail to bring a change of attitude in this
respect." [68]

Freund did not look to the courts for positive regulation; "the
judicial process cannot produce the rule that is regulative in character." [69] The courts are limited in their legal capabilities to set
and enforce standards.

> The courts which can control legislation only by annulling it
> are powerless to enforce the requisite standards, and they can
> deal effectually only with cases of gross abuse of the legislative
> power of classification.[70]

It is the legislature, in Freund's opinion, however, which can set and enforce standards; but to do so effectively requires the professionalization of drafters of legislation. What is needed in the legislatures and their committees is the combination of lawyer and social scientist.

Concerned more with the quality of legislation in a rapidly changing America and with the development of a system of positive principles that should guide and control the making of statutes than with the organization and procedures of legislatures, Freund in 1917 published *Standards of American Legislation*. The book was originally written as a series of lectures for presentation at the Johns Hopkins University in 1915. Particularly involved with the conflict between courts and legislatures and pointing to the constitutional "due process" clause as the source of most of the trouble, Freund contended that due process did not proclaim an immutable cardinal principle of justice but rather asserted a policy likely to be changed by the progress of economic and social conditions and thought.[71] The vague standard of "reasonableness" imposed by the courts in the struggle for supremacy between legislative and judicial discretion had resulted in gradual victory by the legislatures.

Freund noted two major tendencies in the evolution of legislative policy concerning individual personal and property rights: "the steady growth in the value placed upon individual human personality and the shifting of the idea of the public good from the security of the state and established order to the welfare of the mass of the people." [72] Anticipating the awakening of the "social conscience" of America, Freund predicted a basic change in the courts' conception of the "due process" clause leading to eventual legislative promotion of economic and social policies.

In a chapter on the common law and public policy, Freund demonstrated that the common law was "a system of justice rather than of policy, and its policy is not always easy to discover." Moreover, "Most of the common law was developed in that atmosphere of indifferent neutrality which has enabled courts to be impartial but also keeps them out of touch with vital needs" of society.[73] While the common law may have served adequately to adjust and reconcile the narrow, specific conflicts between individual litigants, it failed to perform effectively with regard to the broad, general social needs and the controversies between large sections of the population in modern technological societies. Accordingly, the modern legislature had to step in to create standards conforming to the changed concepts of public interest. The obstacles, however, were great, such as the absence of a clear understanding of the legislative tasks and the opposition of powerful corporate economic interests and their lobbies.

Freund was correct in concluding that the constitutional doctrines aimed at restraining the legislature in the economic and social arena did not contribute materially to the principles of American public law; nor did judicial doctrines provide principles of legislation or even delineate the type and parameters of such principles. Although the common law itself derived its primary authority from principle based on reason, logic and accepted policy, principle in connection with legislation "does not form a sharp contrast to either constitutional requirement or policy, for it may be found in both; but it rises above both as being an ideal attribute demanded by the claim of statute law to be respected as a rational ordering of human affairs." [74] Freund was boldly asserting that our legal system was guaranteed mainly by due process of law but that did not mean America had developed an adequate system of legislative principles. To this end he proposed a science of legislation based generally on such principles as: (1) correlation of statutory provisions, which would assert the interdependence of right and obligation and which would provide a more carefully measured justice; (2) standardization, which would involve conformity to undisputed scientific data and conclusions, formulation of juristic principles, adherence to an intelligible method of making determinations, and avoidance of excessive or purposeless instability of policy, and which would provide certainty, objectivity, stability, and uniformity; and (3) protection of vested rights and equality, which would ensure individual rights and liberties.

Noting that "judge-made law is ill-suited for guiding legislation, and we should not look to the courts for the development of rules of legislative justice," [75] and drawing on his study of European systems, Freund suggested that the executive branch increase its participation in legislation and train staffs of professionals in this activity. Seeing such a step as voluntary and relatively remote, he presented four concrete, immediate plans for establishing a constructive and effective body of legislative principles: (1) preparation of bills by special commissions; (2) delegation of rule-making power to administrative commissions; (3) organization of bill drafting bureaus; and (4) codification of standing clauses. To aid the legislators, administrators and hired experts in improving the quality and direction of legislation, the American law schools should include appropriate courses in their curricula and discard "the common-law attitude toward legislation, looking upon it as an inferior product of the non-legal mind to be tolerated and minimized in its effects." [76]

Freund realized that people identify with a popular assembly more readily than with an appointive judiciary, and also that people will more readily accept restrictive legislation and regulation which they feel they have a part in formulating than they will decrees and orders imposed by despots. "Living under free institutions we submit to public regulation and control in ways that would appear inconceivable to the spirit of oriental despotism." [77] However, he opposed legislative regulation the objection of which was to stamp out an evil but did so under the guise of regulating commerce. "A legislative policy can hardly be worked out in a satisfactory manner if it has to sail under a false flag." [78] In general, Freund opposed the resort by legislatures to the criminal law to enforce private morality and business ethics. He was especially appalled by the large-scale deployment of police and courts in enforcing laws against abortion, drunkenness, gambling, and prostitution on both grounds of principle and practicality, and warned of the jamming of court calendars with needless delay and waste.

Aware of the political nature of the legislative process, Freund, nevertheless, urged legislatures to write laws explicitly. He conceded that statutes are subject to judicial interpretation even when they appear to be clear; but what he aimed at eliminating was inept and ambiguous terminology and structure. As for interpretation, he wrote in 1917, it is "part and parcel of our law," and "in cases of genuine ambiguity courts should use the power of interpretation consciously and deliberately to promote sound law and sound

principles of legislation." This, to Freund, was far more important than "a painstaking fidelity to the supposed legislative intent,"
which he felt was "in reality often a fiction." The legislatures are
fully aware that "any but the most explicit language is subject to
the judicial power of interpretation." Consequently, that power
might be used "as a legitimate instrument of legal development and
of balancing legislative inadvertence by judicial deliberation;"
but English and American legal sentiment, however, "is decidedly
against the exercise of such judicial power, which is strongly
advocated by new schools of jurisprudence in France and
Germany." [79]

In discussing the application of the test of reasonableness as a
development of natural law, Charles Grove Haines asserted in the
Yale Law Journal in 1916 that the judiciary in the United States
introduced the reasonableness test as a part of the doctrine of
judicial review of legislative acts, "particularly with respect to the
police power and to industrial legislation." "Notice and hearing,
the fundamental conditions of due process, according to Professor
Freund, would be without value if it did not assure a just cause
for proceeding against the individual; the essence of due process
then is just cause, and this must underlie every act of legislation." [80]
Freund maintained that "the just cause of legislation is the performance of some legitimate function of government." "It thus becomes
a requirement of the constitution that every statute should be the
exercise of some recognized power justified by the reason and
purpose of government." [81]

In his "masterly treatise," *Standards of American Legislation,*
Freund, remarked Arthur N. Holcombe in 1929 in his review of a
later book by Freund, "gave a strong impetus to the growing interest in and respect for the science of legislation." [82] In this
volume he studied the results of judicial review of legislation with
special reference to the application of reason, and concluded that
the courts had failed to help establish adequate principles and
standards of legislation. Disappointed also in the legislatures and
executive departments, Freund suggested the greater delegation
of powers over persons and property to administrative agencies.

Underlying Freund's views on legislative principles and standards
in a federal, constitutional system was the basic idea that the con-

stitutions should be general and brief and that the legislatures should work out the details. In an article in the *American Bar Association Journal* in 1921, Freund discussed various contemporary amendments to the United States Constitution and remarked:

> There is a good deal of unnecessary detail in constitutions that hampers and embarrasses legislation; but when the people desire to accomplish through the constitution a direct result independent of legislative assistance, they overlook the fact, more potent than the constitution itself, that there are few propositions of law that can be made sufficiently brief for constitutional formulation, and at the same time self-executing.[83]

Freund maintained that a constitution is not a fit instrument to reform complex civil relations. It can proclaim a principle of equality, but it ought to leave it to the legislature to work it out. On the other hand, all law cannot be reduced to writing and included in legislation. In fact, the unwritten elements frequently determine the ultimate application of legislation as it affects human action. Interpretation necessarily arises and gives direction to the legislation. These points were continually stressed by Freund. The simple resort to declaratory rules, he observed, testified to the inability of the written law to foresee the future and provide for the contingencies to come.

"Legislation," Freund insisted, "cannot claim to be an expression of pure principle, but of necessity embodies a considerable amount of discretion, expediency and compromise."[84] More than this, though, Freund aimed at legislation based on justice. As Leo F. Wormser observed of Freund's approach to legislation: "In drafting legislation, he surveyed the relation of law to individual rights from a point of view broader than precedent or abstract formula. His retrospect of historic changes afforded him a fairer basis for evaluating proposed statutory policies. . . . Legislation, drafted by him, often established new norms to meet the altered conceptions of right and wrong and of the public good. . . . His keen discernment pierced loosely reasoned statements and sought, above all else, to found legislation upon justice."[85]

While recognizing the need for legislation to reflect social change, flexibility for its own sake—the use of flexible terms and general phrases—in statutes was not necessarily good. In fact, where competing jurisdictions may be involved, "flexibility is of evil, because it results in confusion." "Flexible terms . . . are even in the grant of official power undesirable where the risk of error is a choice between penalties." As a principle of legislation, Freund recommended in 1921: "where the legislative policy is to confer specific benefits and not merely benefits of a very general public character, and the corresponding detriment or prejudice to interests is vague and speculative, general phrases are to be preferred; where, on the other hand, the policy is primarily restrictive or one of grudging concession, fixed and definite terms should be chosen."[86] Generally, he saw flexible terms to be more appropriate to civil than to criminal legislation.

Freund was among the first to observe that "one of the most striking cases of almost inevitable ambiguity is presented by the word 'shall' " in statutes. Provision for official action "even if intended as a duty, calls for the creation of the appropriate power, which is indicated by 'may'; and in a great many cases, the power having been created to aid some other interest, its exercise becomes a duty by implication. 'Shall' is thus included in 'may'." [87] While this observation is taken for granted in our day, it was relatively new when he proclaimed it. Similarly, Freund differentiated between the declaratory rule and the regulative rule. The former he defined as "a rule of decision, . . . the expression of justice, and, as such claiming rational validity," and the latter as "an expression of government in the nature of a rule of conduct." [88] This, too, has been generally accepted the past three decades.

Underlying all these observations was Freund's central theme that due process and constitutional government can be attained and assured only by a system of principles of legislation. This conviction remained with Freund from the late 1880's to his death. In 1916, he concluded his presidential address to the American Political Science Association in the following words:

> No great nation, nor for that matter, any live community, can afford to be tied by dead hands, or to have its policies mapped out generations ahead; but however great the emergency, a free people may well insist that whatever changes may be necessary shall be brought about under observance of that order and with that respect for right and justice which the world knows as law

and which we happen to call due process. This is what constitutional government ought to mean, and this can be accomplished only, by a system of principles of legislation.[89]

Deeply concerned with the relationship between legislation and liberty and justice, Freund had posed in 1904 several basic questions, vexing even to this day: "What does it mean, to say that the fundamental law secures a certain amount of liberty, if it is not said how much, or that it forbids unjust discrimination, if the injustice is not defined?" For Freund it was the merest commonplace that some restraint of liberty of contract and business, some discrimination, was not merely valid but essential to the interests of society. "Can the fundamental law be satisfied with the proclamation of rights of absolutely indeterminate content, directly contrary to other recognized principles, or is not limitation and definition of some sort absolutely essential to an intelligible rule of law?" The courts have criticized, denounced and condemned, but have given no positive guidance. The course of adjudication is marked by divided jurisdictions and divided courts, "resulting in a lamentable uncertainty as to the limits of legislative power." [90]

For the vast majority of the acts on the statute books of the states, the reasons or considerations inducing their adoption have not been formulated. Often, no discussions arose in the legislatures; and if debates occurred, only incomplete accounts were preserved in the daily press. With regard to administrative rules and decisions, "The whole amount of this source material is poor as compared with what the official publications of England, France and Germany afford." As for the history of the operation of statutes, "there has never been any systematic observation of the working of the laws of persons, property, or contracts." Except for the subjects of bankruptcy, divorce, and to some extent personal injuries, "there are no civil judical statistics, still less, of course, any information regarding the legal relations that do not reach the courts." In codifying the German civil code, Freund explained, use was made of data collected by the government regarding the prevalence of certain forms of marital contracts and testamentary dispositions. Nothing of this kind "would be available in the United States." Freund hoped that someday the Census Bureau would be assigned the task of collecting judicial statistics. As a consequence of this void: "General impressions instead of exact and systematic observations will, for a long time to come, be the basis upon which the policy of our civil legislation will be built, and there is no promise of any radical advance of jurisprudence in this respect."[91]

Freund was more optimistic with regard to revenue and police legislation. Here he considered that a considerable amount of information was even then available in the official reports of the authorities. Anticipating the growth and multiplication of regulatory agencies, he urged that comprehensive records be kept and made public of their activities. "All this material ought to be collated and digested in the same manner as is now done with judicial decisions, and the result should be the construction of a body of principles of legislation to supplement the existing body of principles of law. Both in its material and in its method this branch of legal science must differ considerably from the judicial jurisprudence with which we are most familiar; but it is a department of our science equally legitimate and valuable, and destined to grow in importance with the increasing legislative activity of the modern state." [92]

In Freund's time American administrators played a relatively minor role in recommending and drafting legislation affecting their own agencies. In England, France, and Germany, however, since the Governments introduced all important bills, administrative agencies maintained staff for ascertaining the facts underlying proposed measures and commanded the services of highly qualified officials to act as draftsmen. "These conditions cannot be easily reproduced in a country in which the government has no initiative in legislation, and in which it is often very difficult to place the responsibility for the framing and the introduction of a measure." Some states here, though, had made provision for officials to aid in the drafting of bills and for the systematic collection of information regarding legislation and legislative problems. Also, a great deal of valuable statistical work was being done for the first time by official bureaus in a number of states and by the federal government in Washington. "It is to be hoped that these efforts in the direction of improving and harmonizing methods of legislation will, in the near future, be further extended and especially that they will receive the active support of legislative bodies." [93]

In line with Justice Holmes, Roscoe Pound, and Louis D. Brandeis, Freund was critical of the refusal of the courts to look beyond the particular litigation and seek out the social issues that gave rise to the legal controversy. Freund sought to measure the extent to which social policy worked itself gradually into the common law. In his *Standards of American Legislation,* Freund wrote:

> Most of the common law has developed in that atmosphere of indifferent neutrality which has enabled courts to be impartial, but also keeps them out of touch with vital needs. When interests are litigated in particular cases, they not only appear as scattered and isolated interests, but their social incidence is obscured by the adventitious personal factors which color every controversy. If policy means the conscious favoring of social above particular interests, the common law must be charged with having too little policy.[94]

Freund's criticism of the courts took a different design from Holmes, Pound and Brandeis, for he felt that the judiciary was unable to create the principles and standards to guide social policy, and that only the legislature could fulfil this mission. Freund emphasized legislative principles and standards in all of his varied interests throughout his life. For example, although he was a strong supporter of granting zoning boards power to grant variances, he was opposed to their exercise of such power totally on their "own uncontrolled discretion." [95] His reaction to the decision of the Supreme Court of Illinois in the case of *Welton v. Hamilton* [96] in April, 1931 was thus easily predictable. The Court held that since no rule or standard had been provided by the legislature for the guidance of the newly created zoning board of appeals this constituted an invalid delegation of legislative power. "The decision in *Welton v. Hamilton*", wrote Freund in the *National Municipal Review* for September, 1931, "will thus at least have the beneficial effect that a less satisfactory will be replaced by a more satisfactory procedure." [97] However, Freund was critical of the court in that it confused arbitrary power with the arbitrary exercise of that power. The court, he insisted, could have struck down the latter while sustaining the former and thereby "saved the power with a view to its legitimate application." [98]

Freund's *Standards of American Legislation* was very well-received. It won the coveted James Barr Ames Medal awarded by the Harvard Law School. As J. Van der Zee remarked in his review in 1917 in the *Iowa Law Bulletin,* "the student of law, whether in the law school or the practice, will be greatly stimulated by Mr. Freund's study of a subject which is only beginning to receive the attention it deserves." [99]

To Freund, as to many of the judicial philosophers of the period, legislation constituted much more than law. They saw in legislation the whole of human experience. In one of his last articles, written in 1932 for the newly published *Encyclopaedia of the Social Sciences,* Freund stated:

> So far as statutes give authority and direction for carrying on the complex business of government, they constitute law in the sense that law may be identified with the orderly adjustment of human affairs; but the foundation of experience and information underlying most statutory provisions is primarily political, social, economic, financial, technical or administrative, and not legal. [100]

To achieve the best in possible legislation was unrealistic to Freund. Politics would prevent such attainment. One must adjust to settling for "second-best" or get "nothing at all":

> The political character of legislation must be constantly borne in mind in judging statute law. Thus juristic imperfections not only are explained but appear as inevitable. The choice between the second best and nothing at all is the normal situation. [101]

Freund recognized the need for flexibility and the practical impossibility of totally standardizing legislation: "Perfectly standardized legislation is a counsel of perfection." This was especially true for legislation dealing with administrative powers. With regard to codes of civil and criminal procedure, legislation could very well be nearly wholly standardized, but "the exercise of administrative powers is prescribed by provisions scattered through a large number of statutes creating these powers." [102]

Freund differentiated between legislative and judicial law in the article on "Legislation" in the *Encyclopaedia of the Social Sciences* as follows:

> Legislation moreover is a political act in that it rests upon the voluntary choice of the legislature. It is true that under democratic government public opinion may tend to force considera-

tion of certain matters by the legislature, but considerable scope is nevertheless left the legislature as to the time, extent and details of action. Judge made law, on the other hand, is the by-product of litigation, so that the tackling and settling of a legal problem become an inescapable duty.[103]

To the very end, Freund, striving a lifetime for principles of legislation, consistently rejected "constitutionality" as the basis for formulating such principles:

> Since American doctrines of constitutional law are almost entirely based on judicial decisions, they fail to emphasize principles and relations which lie at the threshold of legislative consideration and which consequently determine the source and structure of written law without giving rise to litigation.[104]

While hopefully relying on the legislatures, Freund recognized the reluctance of Congress and state legislatures to formulate clear and definite standards governing administrative action. "It may well be that this reluctance to prescribe ultimate standards is more significant than judicial theories of constitutional power." [105]

Two years earlier, John B. Cheadle of the University of Oklahoma Law School, aware of Freund's lifelong mission, remarked in the *Cornell Law Quarterly* in 1930 that "Professor Freund has faith in the ultimate value of legislation as a unifying, coordinating, and developing agency; and it is not a dead faith." [106] At memorial services for Freund in 1933 Frederic Woodward noted that Freund "chose as his field the borderland between law and political science and beginning as a pioneer he rapidly became a widely recognized authority, particularly in what may be called the science of legislation." [107]

Freund had concluded his *Standards of American Legislation* with the hope that even if the "legal science of legislation. . . . cannot be carried to the plane of an exact science," it should arouse competent people to involve themselves in statute-making and attract legal scholars and political scientists to study and develop "this rich and practically unworked field." His wish was that the book "would stimulate interest in the subject and its possibilities." [108] The following year Nathan Isaacs bemoaned: "Still the need of a study of statutory interpretation is already foreseen here. . . . Prof. Ernst Freund has taken the lead in this work." [109]

Freund had truly taken the lead, but there were no followers. Twenty-seven years later, in 1944, Judge Charles E. Wyzanski, Jr., of the United States District Court in Massachusetts, assessing in the *Harvard Law Review* the status of law school courses in legislation and administrative law, observed: "The . . . need for developing standards of legislation has long been apparent. Twenty-nine years ago the late Professor Ernst Freund discussed *The Meaning of Principle in Legislation*. That lecture would still serve as an admirable prolegomenon for a course in legislation. And such a course would serve the uses not only of those who were drafting or interpreting statutes but of those who were concerned with the preparation of any sort of document that was to govern on a large scale the relations of numerous persons, private or public. We have been much too slow to admit that a definite part of legal science is the study of the nonlogical aspects of regulatory schemes, the aspects which are sometimes treated as though they were the exclusive province of psychology, or semantics, or philosophy." [110]

LEGISLATIVE REGULATION

Freund's last book, published in 1932, the year of his death, was *Legislative Regulation: A Study of the Ways and Means of Written Law*. Written as a logical complement to his *Administrative Powers Over Persons and Property* which appeared in 1928, it was sponsored by the Commonwealth Fund but undertaken on Freund's own initiative. His primary purpose was to study regulative legislation producing legal rules, legislation that "transforms freedom which is subject to necessary law, into freedom directed by rules of law which are adventitious and not absolutely necessary." "Since this law is the practically exclusive product of legislation, we may expect to find it controlled by conditions and limitations inherent in the legislative process. This, in any event, is the dominant thesis of the present study, which is consequently described as a study of legislative regulation." [111]

With an eye to practicality, Freund aimed the book at those concerned with the functions and tasks of legislation, with the hope of assisting in phraseology and style, forms and methods, and technical details of penal and civil regulation. He recognized that those concerned with case law could avail themselves of elaborate digests while those concerned with examining statutes lacked similar aids and would have to search into mountains of scattered, uncorrelated statutes without even skimpy indices. It was to meet this need that Freund wrote the book. Yet, this first attempted systematic presentation of the subject could hardly be more than "fragmentary and sporadic",[112] as Freund conceded. Realistically, he stated in the book's preface:

> . . . an exhaustive presentation of material, if possible, would serve no purpose: legislative technique is not, like judicial doctrine, a matter that can be established by preponderance of argument or authorities; it is essentially a matter of judgment and expediency. But precedent plays as important a part in legislation as it does in judicial decisions, though in a different sense: legislators do not like to use new methods of expression, but a form once used has considerable persuasive effect. And, of course, if it can be shown that forms that have been used are undesirable, it is not necessary to prove that they have been authoritatively condemned.[113]

Freund's intention was to show for what purposes written, or statutory, law was best suited and for what purposes unwritten, or decisional, law was preferred. He posed and examined into the various problems requiring attention in the event one or the other law was determined by the legislature to regulate the given situation. Alternatives were presented with recommendations for selecting the most feasible choices. Some of the most vexing problems were analyzed, such as: Should registration or licensing be applied? Should penal provisions or publicity alone be relied on for sanctions? Should standards be spelled out in general or specific terms? Should statutes be so drafted as to permit broad or narrow administrative discretion?

Freund divided his study into five parts: "Legislation as a Form of Law"; "General Legal Aspects of Regulation"; "Phraseology and Terms"; "The Technique of Penal Regulation"; and "The Technique of Civil Regulation." In the first part, he distinguished between unwritten or declaratory and regulative law, with the former he described as the province of the judiciary and the latter he assigned to the legislature. Part two was concerned with the

general legal aspects of regulation; and parts three, four, and five
dealt with the mechanics and techniques of legislation, particularly
phraseology, terms and style, and the application and effect of
statutes. In general, two classes of legislation were contrasted:
one, government legislation, such as administrative organization,
police, public services, and revenue; and the other, law-legislation,
which includes criminal law and private law, and legal procedure.
The former is concerned also with the declaratory law that is incident to it; and the latter deals with the regulative rules promulgated in aid of such legislation.

Freund divided law into three types: regulative, declaratory,
and interpretative.[114] Regulative law appears [115] to be defined as
"the expression of government, in the nature of a rule of conduct,
imposed upon rather than implicit in a situation, conventional in
character, and generally operating with form requirements, precise
quantities, or administrative arrangements." [116] On the other hand,
declaratory law is "in the nature of a rule of decision . . . . the
inevitable product of default or controversy . . . . implicit in a given
situation . . . . the expression of justice and, as such, claiming rational validity." [117] Interpretative law is the adaptation of a declaratory or regulative rule of decision to particular cases usually
exercised by the courts but not infrequently also by the legislature
especially in enactments of codes. These three classes of law are not
distinctly delineated and may so shade one into another that it
could easily become debatable into which class a given statute or
decision may fall.

Always mindful of the demands on the legal system by a rapidly
changing society, Freund saw that the slowness of the judicial
process would enhance the role of the legislature as the organ for
making declaratory law. This legislative development was best
exemplified by the modification of the law of torts concerning
workmen through the Employers Liability Acts. The relation of
master and servant was so changed that the rule of negligence was
set aside and absolute liability of the employer was substituted.

For regulative law, Freund maintained, legislation was necessary
since "normally speaking, the judicial process cannot produce the
rule that is regulative in character." [118] This was particularly
true for the fixing of time periods as found in statutes of limitation,

and for the establishment of administrative machinery to regulate interstate common carriers with regard to fair and equal rates and service.

While Freund understood and considered what could be classified as preventive law, he did not assign it a separate classification. Although here the courts possessed certain instruments of preventive law such as writs of injunction and the abatement of nuisances, the powers of the legislature in this area far exceeded those of the judiciary. This was most notably true in legislative and administrative fixing of rates and service conditions to prevent unfairness and inequality, rather than allowing such happenings with redress through suits for damage.

Freund viewed regulative law as being characterized by conventionality in contrast to the rationality of declaratory law. Furthermore, declaratory law, he held, had a superior ethical base. Critically observed Edwin W. Patterson, in 1933 in a symposium on administrative law in the *Iowa Law Review:* "It thus appears that regulative law is framed in *terms* which do not refer to recognized ethical categories. A rule prescribing 'just and reasonable' hours of labor is declaratory; a rule fixing an eight-hour day is regulative. Each may be ethically justifiable".[119]

In an article on "Legislation" that appeared in the *Encyclopaedia of the Social Sciences* shortly after his death, Freund made an attempt further to delineate and elaborate on his definition of regulative legislation as follows:

> The term regulative, or regulatory, legislation is commonly used to designate a distinct species of legislation. The differentiation is based upon a somewhat inarticulate recognition of the fact that regulation transcends the bounds of necessary law. The underlying thought may be expressed in this way: human relations involve the possibility of controversy concerning reciprocal rights and obligations and concerning the line between permissible conduct and punishable or remediable wrong. The peaceful settlement of these controversies calls for the impartial arbitrament of some authority, and the province of these arbitraments constitutes the province of necessary law. Rights, however, involve managing and disposing powers of varying scope, and reciprocal relations involve the possibility of contractual adjustment. From this results a province of freedom within the law. Considerations of policy may lead the state to restrict this

freedom and to subject it to conventional rules. Where the state instead of dealing with private rights deals with official powers of its own creation it may recognize, in analogy to the freedom of private management and contract, the freedom of official discretion or, on the other hand, it may bind official action by conventional rules. Since these conventional rules impinge upon a possible legitimate freedom of private or of official action, they may be regarded as adventitious (not inescapable) law, and it is convenient and appropriate to speak of this type of law as regulation.[120]

Relying more heavily on the legislature than the administrative departments, agencies and regulatory commissions to consider the rights of individuals, Freund asserted that the legislature "may give added protection to private right by throwing safeguards around the administrative process itself, both by circumscribing the substance of discretion and by prescribing appropriate forms for its exercise." "In these respects the development of regulative legislation has incidentally brought in its wake also a development of administrative law." [121]

Freund's views as expressed in *Legislative Regulation* were consistent with his long-held opinion that all government could be divided into "control" and "service." [122] As he stated in the *Encyclopaedia of the Social Sciences* published after his death:

> If official power serves as an instrument for controlling private conduct, regulation which checks its exercise may be looked upon as a safeguard of individual liberty. Again, if official power is an instrument of governmental service and that service directly affects private property interests, specific regulation is equivalent to enforceable private right. In the carrying on of those governmental services, however, which do not involve normal private rights, an excess of regulation may have the same disadvantage as excessive regulation of private conduct—it may purchase regularity at the cost of initiative and effectiveness.[123]

Where the governmental service calls for development and progress, "official discretion is the equivalent of individual liberty; and it may be as legitimate to recognize it in the organization of the service for this purpose as to set up detailed regulations for functions of routine and of conservation." However, how do you choose between discretion and regulation? Freund left this as "a matter of policy, to be determined from case to case." [124]

Legislative Regulation was published several months before Freund's death. In a sense, it represented a bridge between his two greatest studies—*Standards of American Legislation* and *Administrative Powers Over Persons and Property*—showing the relation between legislation and administration insofar as law was concerned. *Legislative Regulation* was acclaimed as one of the outstanding contributions to American juridical literature and received many more reviews than any of his previous books. Reviewing the book in the *American Political Science Review* in October, 1932, Joseph P. Chamberlain remarked that it "is obviously the product of a long period of experience and study. It collects and organizes an astonishing variety of material on legislative regulation." [125]

Yet, this was not Freund's best work. It had many weaknesses and left much unsaid. For example, it did not include in its scope an inquiry into the legislative process as such, nor a study of the techniques of legislation not simply as related to the problems of regulation but also as a means of presenting statutory data to the legislature for facilitating its consideration of and action on public policy issues. This was noted most sharply by George A. Shipman in 1933 in his review in the *West Virginia Law Quarterly*.[126] Also, Freund failed to evaluate the different techniques and devices to promote effective regulation. This was pointed out by Edward S. Corwin in the *Columbia Law Review*. Corwin observed that, despite the "immense amount of authoritative information drawn from a vast body of material chiefly statutes" and the logical arrangement and clarity of presentation, Freund had omitted "to evaluate the various techniques and devices for their regulatory effectiveness." Nevertheless, Corwin acknowledged that the study was "a monument to the scholarly thoroughness and intellectual clarity which one associates with all of Professor Freund's work." [127]

Frederick K. Beutel in the *Tulane Law Review* began his review by asserting: "It is almost impossible to review a book which is itself a review of the statute law of the world." "The fact that so great a scholar as Mr. Freund admits the necessity of choosing his materials at random speaks eloquently of the need of systematization of Anglo-American as well as world legislative material." "The author should be especially complimented on the fact that he has searched for general principles not only in Anglo-American legislation but throughout the laws of the world." [128]

If the book's value is to be judged on its most lasting contribution, it would appear to be the techniques for drafting improved legislation, particularly style and phraseology. Freund's tendency to introduce volume often led to extraneous inclusions. Accordingly, the sections on legislation as a form of law and the general legal aspects of regulation were not highly pertinent. Furthermore, as Beutel perceived, Freund assumed that interpretation of statutes by analogy in the United States was impossible, and in his discussion of analogy he failed to distinguish between the general and special statutes. [129]

Beutel sensed Freund's importance not as a builder but as the breaker of new ground and the layer of foundations. This is what Freund essentially was. It was on Freund that Frankfurter built. As Beutel remarked, Freund's book "represents excellent spade work and should be an inspiration to others to advance much farther in the field of legislation, which has been so badly neglected by Anglo-American students." [130]

Some reviewers felt Freund's book was geared to the law school professor rather than the practicing attorney. For example, Andrew A. Bruce in the *Journal of the American Institute of Criminal Law and Criminology* found it "somewhat difficult to read"; and while recognizing that all of it was "worthy of considered thought," he questioned whether it would "be read, except in the classroom." Yet, it was undeniable that the study was the product of "profound scholarship and the analytical instinct of a really great mind." [131] Contrast this review with that of Samuel Feldman in the *Temple Law Quarterly:* "Professor Freund's study should be of profound interest to every practicing lawyer who seeks to acquire a comprehensive survey of the nature of legislative enactments. To those who are concerned with the drafting of state statutes and municipal ordinances, it is particularly instructive and elucidating. This book will indeed occupy a prominent niche in law libraries and law schools among our leading text books." [132] Further, note the remark of Justive Evan A. Evans of the Seventh United States Circuit Court of Appeals in the *American Bar Association Journal* characterizing the book as "a revelation and a guide to the thinking lawyer and layman." [133] Also, the statement of J.O. Muus in the *Indiana Law Journal:* "Professor Freund's book contains valuable suggestions for the lawyer as an aid in the reading and interpretation of statutes and for the legislative draftsman as a manual of practical guidance." [134]

The reviews in foreign legal periodicals, likewise, praised Freund's study. W. Ivor Jennings in the *Law Quarterly Review* called it "the greatest contribution to English legal science since Bentham." "Freund has written a book which need never be attempted again. It is indeed unlikely that anyone will possess the knowledge of the administrative law in many jurisdictions which is necessary for the purpose." [135] Sidney Smith in the *Canadian Bar Review* commented on the need for such a study particularly because "in the curriculum of Canadian Law Schools no place is given to a study of the possible objects of legislation and the effectiveness of the various types of statutory enactments." Noting that the chapter on "Policies and Standards" was "the most suggestive one in the book, "he recognized Freund's single-most emphasis on standards and his search for a scientific set of principles which would harmoniously unite legislation and administration. . . . The author points a moral which is true in Canada as in the United States, when he contrasts the standard of a statute and the standard of administration of it. A variance between the two spells failure for the hopes of reformers who regard more legislative action as a panacea for mal-adjustments in society." [136]

Not all the reviewers saw Freund's contribution for what it really was. Freund had argued for years that the legislator, executive, administrator, political scientist, and social reformer in general must search for and assess not only all possible alternative policies but also all possible choices of methods for accomplishing the goals selected. Even when the right or good ends are chosen they may be subverted by the wrong methods. One of the keenest reviewers, in this connection, was Oliver P. Field, who wrote in the *Minnesota Law Review:* "The central theme of this book is that of determining the types of situations, to which law is applied, for which written law should be utilized, and the types for which the unwritten law should be developed. . . . The great value of

Professor Freund's book is that it puts the draftsman, the social reformer, and the legislator upon notice that the choice of a particular method of regulation involves other choices as well, and the book also puts them all upon notice that if the wrong method be chosen the ends sought to be attained may never be realized. This, to the reviewer, is the great moral of the book." [137]

Perhaps George A. Shipman summarized in one sentence what all the reviewers thought of Freund's contribution to understanding the fundamentals of legislative government: "In the study of American legislation as a means for the effectuation of state policy, the late Professor Freund was easily the pioneer."[138] It was on legislation that Freund generally relied most of his life to carry out governmental policy within a framework of principles and standards which would ensure effectiveness and at the same time guarantee individual liberties and private rights. His *Legislative Regulation* was not a rigid book. While it revealed his fears of administrative hearings and preference for judicial review on the merits, these were not as fully asserted as in his early writings; and his reliance on legislative standards appeared to give way a bit to the extent of a broad statement of objectives by the legislature and of leaving the standards to be developed through trial and error by administrative action.[139]

A full discussion of Freund's views on administrative powers and discretion and on administrative law is contained in the next part of this study. Suffice it is to mention at this point that Freund's book on *Administrative Powers Over Persons and Property,* dealing wholly with the encroachment of administrative powers on individual liberty and private property, appeared in 1928, four years before *Legislative Regulation.* The reader should bear in mind that the latter study complements the former by concern with the effectiveness of regulative legislation to achieve social objectives.

LEGISLATIVE DRAFTING

From 1916 to 1921 Freund served as a member of the American Bar Association's Special Committee on Legislative Drafting and was the prime drafter of the Association's *Legislative Drafting Manual,* which contained "a selection of directions, or suggestions, for drafting laws and model clauses for constantly recurring provisions and problems." [140] Felix Frankfurter also was a member of this committee at the time. Said Arthur H. Kent in 1933 of Freund's work in this area: "His contributions to the development of a science of legislative draftmanship in this country are of the first order." [141]

"It is impossible," wrote Bertram M. Gross in 1953, "to devise any rigid set of rules to guide the drafting of legislative proposals." [142] Referring to Freund's manual on drafting, Gross observed that legislative drafting was an art and could not be formalized. Freund had acknowledged the practical necessity of ambiguity in legislative drafting resulting from politics, but would not condone it resulting from inefficiency and incompetency. He compared statutes to contracts as follows:

> As a legal act a statute, like a contract, must be adjusted to possible controversy—it must avoid inconsistency and where it cannot avoid ambiguity the statute must accept it with open eyes.
>
> Ambiguity whether avoidable or inevitable calls for interpretation; this is a lawyer's task and one upon which lawyers are apt to look as the specifically legal work in connection with legislation. There is perhaps some inclination to look upon the framing or drafting of a statute as a legal task mainly in so far as it anticipates and by anticipation solves problems of interpretation. From that point of view drafting is largely controlled by judicial decisions, but greater familiarity with drafting problems will disclose the inadequacy of mere subserviency to judicial decisions. Risks of interpretation will have to be accepted or expedients discovered which will avoid or minimize such risks; and situations will have to be foreseen and dealt with which will make or mar the success of the statute before it ever comes into court. Skilled performance of this kind is likely to be of greater importance than adequate adjustment to judicial interpretation and constitutes an essential phase of the science of legislation.[143]

The draftsman, Freund insisted, was extremely important, for once the legislature approved then the statute's language might affect not only the other branches of government but also all of society.

> The phrasing of a statute has its ultimate test in administrative or judicial interpretation, the expectation of which (particularly of the latter) stamps upon it its legal character; but the draftsman must be aware that his success from the point of view of subsequent interpretation counts for nothing unless he can first win the approval of the legislature.[144]

Ironically, the draftsman's real hurdle is the legislature. Once
drafted and approved, the statute leaves his realm and, unless returned for amendment, he can only watch its travels through the
executive and judicial branches and in society.

One of the most vexing questions faced by legislative draftsmen is the choice between discretion and regulation, "inasmuch
as the vesting of discretion can be accomplished by simple forms
of expression." [145] Simplicity and flexibility should be combined
with preciseness and clarity. In Freund's words:

> Specific regulation may involve an elaborate technique, but the
> technique is a matter of legislative science only in so far as the
> choice of terms should avoid undue rigidity and obvious diffi-
> culties of interpretation; otherwise the details of the regulation
> of official powers belong to administrative science.[146]

Generally, "legislative style is a matter of custom and tradition,"
Freund asserted in 1932; and in the United States bills are prepared by members of the legislatures, in contrast to Europe where
bills are drafted by the administrative departments. However, the
beginnings of change were noticeable by that year. The legislatures
were beginning to hire staffs of experts to conduct legislative research and draft bills; and administrative departments were occasionally asked to review draft and pending bills and in certain
instances even to submit recommended legislation. Freund had
sought for over forty years to professionalize legislative drafting.
"The placing of the preparation of bills upon a professional basis
is an important step in the evolution of a scientific technique of
legislation." [147]

A promoter of legislative reference services when Charles
McCarthy started the movement in Wisconsin at the turn of the
century, Freund saw the need for an even more intensive, sys-
tematized and continuous gathering of information by the executive and judicial branches of government. While such services
were hardly developed by the legislatures and the executive agencies, he wrote in *State Government* in 1931, "For such important
matters as civil and criminal justice it is entirely undeveloped
owing to the fact that our judicial system lacks administrative
supervision." [148]

Information gathering, to Freund, was only the beginning of a series of processes by which policies are legislated into law, transformed into administrative action, or subjected to judicial interpretation. Particularly concerned with the legislative process, Freund urged the sharp separation of the fact-finding function of a legislative reference service and the advisory function of experts on problems of sociology or political economy from the legislative drafting operation. "The problem of drafting relates to the formal side of legislation. The draftsman should not be called in until the social and economic issues have been disposed of and a policy has been agreed upon. It then becomes a distinct function to translate the legislative policy into the terms of a statute, and the question is what an expert service can contribute to the successful accomplishment of this task." [149]

Freund decried the lack of "a sufficiently differentiated branch of jurisprudence dealing with the form of legislation" and the draftsman's art being "but slightly developed." Yet he felt that in time, after years of systematic study of the principles of drafting and the creation of drafting bureaus, "the specialist in substantive law or procedure will certainly find the specialist in legislation as indispensable as is now the case vice versa." The result will be the evolution of "a formal science of legislation as a recognized branch of jurisprudence which will command the respect of lawyers, courts, and legislators." [150] This science of standards, or legislative standardization as Freund preferred to describe it, involved standardization *of* not *by* legislation. Elaborating, he asserted:

> When we consider the effect to be produced by law upon private action or even upon public institutional management, a dead level of standards is not an unqualified ideal. But so far as it is wise to displace either individual liberty or official discretion by statutory rule, there can be little question that needlessly variant rules are undesirable. Variety lends a touch of picturesqueness to life, but picturesqueness is not what we look for in the statute book. . . .
>
> That the ideal of even justice is not altogether utopian appears from the fact that procedural or remedial law is largely standardized in the sense indicated. Every statute ultimately depends for its effectuation upon remedial processes, civil or criminal; but these do not vary from statute to statute. The rules of law governing their application are prescribed by general codes of

procedure, which every statute incorporates by reference. Because it is the product of historical evolution, we accept this
standardization as a matter of course.[151]

Needless diversity, particularly in the law of administrative
action, provoked Freund. The volume of legislation operating
through the exercise of administrative powers dealing with in-
spection, licensing, rule-making, and issuance of orders was
constantly increasing. "As distinguished from judicial power, administrative power has no common law basis, but is of purely
statutory creation, and is created, as occasion arises, from statute
to statute." [152] The terms and conditions of administrative power
vary from state to state due not only to differences in policy but
also to differences in drafting styles and techniques. As a result,
there are variations in organization, jurisdictional prerequisites,
scope of discretion, procedural requirements, promulgation of
rules, issuance of orders, granting of licenses, revocation powers,
and remedial provisions.

Still timely is Freund's description of variations in the penal
and enforcement area:

> A great deal of diversity is also presented by the penal and
> enforcement provisions of regulative legislation. Commonly
> these are treated as routine matters, copied somewhat at random
> from such precedents or other sources as are available. Some-
> times, on the other hand, the desire to "put teeth into the law"
> leads to drastic or even draconic penalties, without any realiza-
> tion of what their enforcement would mean, or that they are
> likely to remain unenforced.[153]

This diversity was especially true of the anti-trust legislation
in the last two decades of the nineteenth century. "Scattered
through the American statute books we find informers' shares,
multiple damages, cumulation of offense units, and similar expe-
dients, which have long since been discarded in other countries.
These are small credit to our legislative morale, and while generally vegetating in our innocuous desuetude, are apt to burst
occasionally into scandals." [154]

For Freund the ideal situation would have been for the legislature to indicate its policy in the form of resolutions and to rely
on experts for the legal formulation. That such reliance presup-

posed a high degree of standardization—not reached even in our own times—was acknowledged by Freund. Equally recognized was the opposition of legislators to surrendering such power to the experts. To this Freund countered that the legislators exercised the final check and say and could make changes and corrections. However, the truth was, Freund maintained, that "Constructive and well phrased statements in the Statutes are not usually the product of collective legislative wisdom, but originate in the closet of some draftsman. Unaided by professional guidance, legislative practice may produce a routine and a style; it will never produce adequate standards of legal draftsmanship." [155]

In view of Freund's repetitive arguments on the need for legislative clarity in setting standards, guidelines, intents and limitations, how inappropriate, if not inaccurate, was Alfred F. Conard's remark in 1947: "Eminent writers like Freund and Horack have pleaded for a simpler style, but have not said why they want it." [156] Yet, the various reports of the American Bar Association's Special Committee on Legislative Drafting and the *Legislative Drafting Manual* itself explicitly gave reasons for the need of improved legislative drafting. Apparently, Conard was not aware of these activities and works of Freund.

Leo F. Wormser in 1932 pointed out that Freund's "handbook of rules for drafting uniform statutes may well be the teacher of all draftsmen of legislation"; and his various guide materials on legislative drafting could help "as a comforting compass" to steer draftsmen away from "piecemeal or haphazard legislation" and from "sporadic enactment of disassociated statutes." [157]

Arthur H. Kent was fully aware of Freund's efforts when he evaluated the *Legislative Drafting Manual* in 1933:

His handbook of rules for drafting uniform statutes may well be a guide for every legislative draftsman. But he did not stop with insistence upon due observance of niceties of legislative form and style. Nor was it enough that legislative precedents and rules of statutory interpretation established by judicial decision should be taken into proper account, disastrous as ignorance or disregard of these too often has been. . . .

His work as a legislative draftsman shows that he practiced the principles which he preached. . . . [and] he never permitted his emotional attitudes to cloud his practical judgment or distort the objectivity of his attitude toward his task. Scientifically drafted as are these statutes from the point of view of form and style, they are grounded upon a solid basis of fact, and show an accurate perception of how far it is feasible for legislation under given conditions to go. In the preparation of them, he worked in close co-operation with social workers and experts in the allied fields. This same well-rounded mastery of his subject was displayed in his draftsmanship and defense in the Illinois Constitutional Convention of 1919-20 of those sections which would have given to Chicago real autonomy in local affairs.[158]

Apparently Conard had relied on Freund's *Legislative Regulation,* published in 1932, as the key to Freund's views on legislative drafting. Insofar as that particular book was concerned, as George A. Shipman asserted in his review in 1933: "The draftsman, moreover, will be disappointed for no complete solution of his difficulties will be found." [159] Nevertheless, Joseph P. Chamberlain, reviewing the book the same year, pointed out that it was in "aids to draftsmen with which the book abounds," and aptly acknowledged Freund to be "not solely a teacher" but also a practitioner in the public interest, a draftsman of statutes." [160] Yet, even here Conard might find opposition, particularly from Albert Langeluttig who, reviewing *Legislative Regulation* in 1933 wrote with regard to the sections on drafting: "Sources of error, inaccuracy and futility in legislation throughout the world are referred to in the development of principles for the avoidance of legislative mistake." "The volume is a store house of information and suggestion for lawyers and legislative draftsmen." [161] This opinion was echoed by Andrew A. Bruce writing of Freund's *Legislative Regulation* in the *Journal of the American Institute of Criminal Law and Criminology* in 1933: For the professional legislative draftsmen "it will be a mine of information and suggestion and a useful guide." [162]

LABOR LEGISLATION

A special cause of Freund's was the improvement of the working conditions of men and women employed in industry. Of particular interest were the limitation of hours of labor, workmen's compensation, industrial hygiene, and health insurance. Equal rights for women but with certain protections for women's special needs constituted one of Freund's key objectives.

Limitation of Hours of Labor

Freund was probably the first law school professor to advocate special regulation by government of women's hours of labor in factories. Such "discrimination between men and women cannot be condemned as arbitrary," he wrote in *The Police Power* in 1904. "It is clear that some special provisions regarding women's labor are justified by their greater physical weakness." However, he did not believe that such regulation should apply to all fields of employment, contending that "a separate rule for all women for all purposes hardly represents a reasonable classification, for in the effort to make a living men and women have a right to the greatest possible equality before the law." [163]

Anticipating the growth of the labor movement and the ultimate legalization and governmental regulation of the collective bargaining process, Freund commented prophetically in the *Journal of Political Economy* shortly after the United States Supreme Court decision in *Lochner v. New York* [164] in 1905:

> Lochner vs. New York will undoubtedly be cited as a leading case in labor legislation. It will be relied on by all who are opposed to state interference with labor relations. But they will probably find that the decision will not greatly embarrass the Supreme Court, if at any time, it should be inclined to take a more liberal view of the legislative powers of the state. . . . There is nothing in the law, as now established, which makes the outlook for increased regulation of labor relations hopeless.[165]

The Court had invalidated a New York State law which prescribed maximum hours of labor for men working in bakeries. Such work was not unhealthful, the Court held, and therefore no maximum hours could be fixed by the state legislature. Freund aptly pointed out in the *Green Bag* that "the liberty of contract may not be impaired by limitation of hours of labor, where health and safety are not in question." This was the first time that the Supreme Court had overturned a state's protective labor legislation; and Freund hoped that "a change in public opinion sufficiently strong and widespread would eventually compel judicial acquiescence, even without a change of the Fourteenth Amendment." It cannot be denied, he said, that "agitation for labor or social legislation of an advanced type, has suffered a serious check through the decision in *Lochner v. New York*." [166]

The following year when the Illinois courts granted injunctions restraining labor unions from committing any acts which would in effect force employers into signing closed-shop agreements, Freund observed in the *Journal of Political Economy:*

> Assuming (though the point is by no means settled) that it is beyond the power of the legislature to secure to laborers fair conditions of employment, such a limitation of the police power demands logically that laborers should be allowed to secure these conditions for themselves by their combined efforts, and it can be justified, if at all, only by the existence of the widest possible power of organization and association. . . . The judicial opposition to interference in the relation between employer and employee, both on the part of the legislature and on the part of labor unions, results in an undue curtailment of the rights of organized labor. The recognition of an adequate measure of this right, if it is to come at all, must come from a legislative regulation of the right of combination, and of privilege, as distinguished from unlawful, interference.[167]

In 1909 Illinois passed a law limiting the number of hours women were permitted to work in a day to ten hours. A paper box manufacturer brought suit and the lower courts declared the law unconstitutional. Freund rallied support for an appeal to the Illinois Supreme Court. In addition to writing a number of special bulletins for the Illinois Bureau of Labor Statistics and articles for law and labor journals and giving interviews to the press, in all of which he asserted the law's constitutionality, Freund enlisted the aid of Louis D. Brandeis and William J. Calhoun. Brandeis presented a brief on behalf of the National Consumers' League, and Calhoun assisted Attorney General William H. Stead of Illinois in arguing the appeal. Stead pointedly cited Freund's *Police Power;* and in April, 1910 the Court declared the act of 1909 constitutional.[168]

As president of the Illinois Branch of the American Association for Labor Legislation, Freund in 1909 decried in an article in *Survey* that "Among the important federal states of the world, the United States is conspicuous for its almost total lack of power to enact social legislation." He contrasted our condition with that of Austria, Germany, and Switzerland, where limitations on hours of labor, accident and sick insurance, invalid and old age pensions, and industrial conciliation were all provided for in the nineteenth century. Almost always positive, Freund sought methods and techniques which would circumvent constitutional, sectional or economic obstacles to compulsory legislative action. Voluntary interstate agreements, he suggested, could help achieve the desired social legislation; and to implement such agreements, joint bureaus and commissions could be established, especially with regard to labor regulation. In the article in *Survey* Freund further stated:

> All legislation tends to become more and more technical and scientific. Much of the regulation of labor reduces itself to questions of classification, of devices, of standards, of statistical facts, of dangers, risks, and tendencies capable of more or less accurate measurement. Why should not the elaboration of such matters be committed to boards of experts maintained by a number of states in common, thus securing a higher grade of service and authority at reduced expense? The data thus worked out and laid down from time to time would then furnish standards to which the legislation of the several states might advantageously refer with resulting uniformity.[169]

Seeing little hope for uniformity of labor legislation policies on a national scale "for a considerable time to come," Freund urged "the exertion of proper efforts to secure uniformity of policy for sections or groups of states with similar industrial conditions and a similar state of public opinion." "It is possible that we have offset excessive separation in legislation by excessive nationalism in the work of agitation and initiation." Acknowledging the basic conservatism of the United States at that time, Freund continued:

> Many of the tentative solutions offered for labor problems are untried in this country, and viewed with suspicion or alarm. A great subject like industrial insurance must be brought and kept before the public mind for years until public opinion is educated up to it.[170]

Again seeking solutions, Freund recommended that this matter could be given momentum through a conference of governors of the states within a given section of the country. In time, the governors' conference became a nation-wide affair at which such problems were considered.

Freund felt that the demands for social legislation would grow as the public becomes more educated. "The demands of the public welfare change and rise with a growing knowledge of dangers and of the means of counteracting them." "The point at which the detriment to the public welfare is sufficient to overbear the liberty of the individual varies according to the physical conditions; an intelligent realization of these conditions is the prerequisite of the exercise of the police power." [171]

Foreseeing the growth of the labor movement and its spearheading the demand for a higher standard of living for workers, Freund wrote in the *Illinois Law Review* in 1910:

> Our views on social relations and public control may undergo considerable changes. A certain standard of living may come to seem as important as the preservation of health; industrial employment may become affected with a public interest, and regulation may supersede contract, as contract has superseded status.
>
> And it is quite possible that after another quarter of a century the limitations which our courts treat today as fixed and essential requirements of American institutions, will appear to have been an interesting, perhaps an inevitable, but after all a merely passing phase of our constitutional development.[172]

In 1914 Freund outlined in the *American Labor Legislation Review* a draft of proposed legislation limiting the workday of men to ten hours. Such legislation he argued, "would not make impossible demands upon legislative foresight and circumspection," but it "would require a somewhat higher type of administrative organization than most states have as yet developed for dealing with labor problems, yet the time is rapidly approaching when additional administrative organization and power will be called for in any event for the handling of other phases of labor legislation." [173]

Workmen's Compensation

When a workmen's compensation law was proposed by Massachusetts in 1906 which would have placed an undue financial hardship on the small employer, despite his support of such legislation in general. Freund argued that the bill went "beyond the rule of liability recognized in any other country" and decried its impracticability. There was "no good reason why the first American movement in the right direction should not be of a more conservative character." [174]

In 1911 the New York State Court of Appeals in the case of *Ives v. South Buffalo Railway Co.*[175] held the New York State Workmen's Compensation Law of 1910 unconstitutional. The decision, Freund commented in *Survey*, "cannot fail to cause widespread disappointment and regret." New York's compulsory law "was the fruit of the most careful study and consideration, such as lie back of few of our laws." It was enacted "to remedy the grave defects of the present law concerning industrial accidents, which had produced a general sentiment, shared alike by employee, employers, and the general public, in favor of a radical reform along the lines adopted in European countries." [176] The Court had professed sympathy with the law's purpose but found that the proposed method of relief was so revolutionary that it violated the ancient and fundamental principles which were in existence when our constitutions were adopted, and these principles were linked by the guarantee of due process of law.

To Freund the question reduced itself to the following:

> Can the employer be made to assume, in whole or in part, the economic burden of an accidental personal injury arising out of the trade risk of a dangerous occupation? Can the legislature say to the employer: "If for the purpose of your business you provide, and require the use of, dangerous appliances which are humanely speaking certain to result in accident, you shall not let the consequences of the accident lie where they fall, but assume your share of them?" The principle of making a common venture is not unknown to jurisprudence; in another form and application it is not unlike the principle which, under the name of general average, is familiar to the maritime law of all nations. If the common law had not developed such a principle, this simply proves that the common law is not the last word of all wisdom and justice.[177]

Because of the *Ives v. South Buffalo Railway Co.* decision, a number of states which had readied similar compulsory compensation laws did not dare to enact them and substituted elective, optional systems. The latter method of circumventing the Supreme Court's ban involved an indirect coercion of employers and employees to come under the law or else be "visited with the penalty of an unfavorable position of the recalcitrant party with regard to the common law defenses in a suit for damages." [178]

Early in 1912 a bill was introduced into Congress sponsored by the Federal Employers' Liability Commission which provided compulsory workmen's compensation coverage for employees of railroads engaged in interstate commerce. Freund noted, in an article on the subject in *Survey* that year, the possibility that the Supreme Court would pass on its validity and, if favorable, this would "settle the problem for the country outside of the state of New York"; and if not favorable, then "the agitation for making the law conformable to the demand for better justice will not stop." The proposed bill included a clause barring any plan or system which did not permit an employee to withdraw from it. Hardly any of the state compensation laws could have met this condition. Undiscouraged, Freund commented:

> In view of the fact that the system of compensation is new and experimental, and at best will involve a heavy financial burden, every effort should be made to remove such complications as must result from a concurrence of remedies operative in the same jurisdiction and frequently upon the same injury or accident.[179]

Speaking before the American Association for Labor Legislation in 1912, Freund demanded positively what he had posed for discussion the year before:

> It is considered that if an employer, for the purposes of his business, provides and requires the use of dangerous appliances which are, humanely speaking, certain to result in an accident, he ought not to let the consequences of the accident lie where they fall, but assume his share of them.[180]

All legislative commissions appointed to investigate this matter, Freund pointed out, favored the principle of compensation as distinguished from liability. In his speech he outlined six basic principles involved in workmen's compensation. These were: (1) payment for injuries or death, irrespective of fault or negligence, except when caused by wilful misconduct; (2) the benefit payable must bear a definite relation to former earning capacity; (3) payment of the benefit in periodical installments, subject to commutation in a lump sum under specific conditions; (4) denial of compensation for a brief initial period in order to eliminate the great mass of insignificant injuries, but liberal provision for medical treatment; (5) encouragement of arbitration; and (6) abrogation of the right of action at common law except where the fault of the employer is aggravated.

As a member of the American Bar Association's Committee on Compensation for Industrial Accidents and Their Prevention, Freund was the prime mover in drafting the report presented to the Association's annual meeting in August, 1912 which had a significant impact on workmen's compensation legislation throughout the country.[181] The following year Freund wrote a concise summary of the main legal considerations entering into the insurance features of workmen's compensation legislation which revealed his mastery of the subject from both domestic and international viewpoints. His philosophy of individual freedom and his concepts of the police power were expressed consistently in his opposition to adopting either the German or Norwegian plan of compulsory insurance. Both these plans constituted "a serious invasion of private right." "Every question of constitutionality ought finally to resolve itself into a question of fundamental policy and of justice, and an unjust law sustained is perhaps even a little worse than a just law declared unconstitutional." The law "must work out fairness and equity between employers as well as between employers and employees." "For the present, freedom of insurance to meet the burden of workmen's compensation should be insisted on." [182] In time Freund's views on workmen's compensation were accepted; and legislation embodying the principles he advocated was enacted at the federal and state levels and was upheld by the Supreme Court of the United States.

Industrial Hygiene

At a meeting of the American Association for Labor Legislation's General Administrative Council in Chicago in 1909 the subject of industrial hygiene was given major consideration. Freund offered a resolution, adopted unanimously, urging "all medical bodies and colleges, all bureaus of labor, boards of health, all philanthropic and charitable agencies and endowments, to take

up and carry out the scientific investigation of industrial hygiene."
Stressing the legal aspects, he cautioned: "The courts should have
before them well-worked out schedules showing what and where
protection is needed." His philosophy of labor legislation was
clearly expressed in the first sentence of the resolution: "The fundamental purpose of labor legislation is the conservation of the
human resources of the nation." Human resources, he continued,
are "of greater importance than the conservation of our natural
resources." [183]

That same year Freund wrote Governor Charles S. Deneen of
Illinois suggesting legislation dealing with industrial hygiene. Acting on Freund's proposals, the Governor introduced a bill which
the legislature passed. "The health, safety and sanitation law will
go into effect January 1, 1910 and is the best law of its kind in the
United States." [184]

Three years later the nation was aroused by the dread "phossy
jaw" or phosphorus necrosis caused by white phosphorus matches.
A bill was introduced by Rep. John J. Esch to ban such matches
by imposing a heavy tax on their manufacture. During hearings on
the bill in January, 1912 Freund testified on its legality:

> It is too late to contend that the taxing power can not be used
> for purposes other than that of producing revenue. Almost from
> the beginning of the Government the Federal revenue laws have
> been recognized as legitimate means of promoting economic ob-
> jects, and in the States all licensing laws combine the objects of
> police and revenue.
> While if the question were a new one we might be unwilling to
> urge the accomplishment of desirable policies through the taxing
> power in cases where the other Federal powers are inadequate,
> and while even under the established practice we might prefer
> other methods if feasible, yet hesitation to tax with a view to col-
> lateral effects savors of pedantry where it is a question of protect-
> ing life and health and where local sentiment of freedom from
> Federal interference is in no way involved.
> I am therefore decidedly of the opinion that the provisions of
> the Esch Bill are not subject to criticism on the ground of usurpa-
> tion of power by the Federal Government.[185]

The Esch Bill was superseded by a bill proposed by Rep. William Hughes which similarly called for a tax on white phosphorus
matches. Congress passed the latter bill and the President signed
it on April 9, 1912.

Health Insurance

By 1917 health insurance became the next big step in social legislation. Insurance companies and labor and social work organizations debated the issue and lobbied in the state legislatures. At the National Conference of Social Work which met in Pittsburgh in June that year Freund presented what was then probably the most significant paper on the constitutional and legal aspects of health insurance, in which he compared the German and English plans with those proposed in the United States. He pointed out that while workmen's compensation was linked to employers' liability with a foundation in common law, health insurance had no such linkage or foundation. With great detail Freund listed and described the "precarious constitutional status" of such plans. Allying himself with the supporters of the plans, he explained: "The strongest sympathy . . . cannot be a substitute for thorough understanding." A key to his approach is seen in point 7 of 17 points that he discussed:

> Compulsory insurance is—barring a few very minor and relatively insignificant applications—unfamiliar to our law, and some decisions seem to oppose it. It is, however, so reasonable a method of reducing the risk of pauperism and the necessity of other forms of public relief, that it ought to be regarded as a legitimate exercise of the police power. . . . The only way to settle the question is to legislate and leave the decision to the courts.[186]

ANTI-TRUST LEGISLATION

In Freund's view, the anti-trust movement would follow a course similar to that of rate regulation. The courts would find the task too highly technical and would place the responsibility on the legislature which, in turn, would delegate the work to an administrative regulatory agency. In Freund's words in 1912:

> We are reminded of the history of railroad rate regulation. After the courts had proclaimed the principle of reasonableness, they attempted to apply it; but they were not equal to the task, and eventually it had to be committed to an administrative commission. And so, in the matter of trusts, judicial regulation will merely point and open the way for regulative legislation, to be administered by way of guidance and prevention. When the his-

torian of the future comes to survey the evolution of the anti-
trust legislation in the United States, he will record the futility
and failure of the attempt to deal with difficult economic problems through criminal punishment; but he will also see therein
another illustration of the astonishing flexibility of equitable
jurisdiction, which here as so often before has anticipated statutory reform, and which has enabled the United States to cope
with certain powerful organizations at a time when all other nations stood helpless before trusts and syndicates. And he will
conclude that the framers of the Sherman act builded better than
they knew.[187]

Three years later Congress established the Federal Trade
Commission.

Freund pointed out that when American anti-trust legislation
was introduced in 1890 with the Sherman Anti-Trust Act it had
almost completely neglected to specify illegal practices with sufficient clarity and certainty. The Clayton Anti-Trust Act of 1914
attempted to remedy this by listing certain forbidden practices.
When the Federal Trade Commission was created in 1915, the
enabling act made no attempt to define prohibitable practices but
empowered the new agency to investigate and then ban activity
found contrary to the law. The Commission's orders were subject
to judicial review, and violators of these orders were punishable.
To Freund this was a rational attempt "to improve upon the
method of the anti-trust legislation, which in the matter of restraint
of trade achieved very little, if any, progress beyond the common
law." [188]

In the period from 1890 to the 1930's, the Sherman Act's most
far-reaching application was with labor organizations although
nothing in the congressional debates indicated that the law's framers
intended such an application. Furthermore, the law's enforcement was accomplished "through the power of proceeding in
equity, which," as Freund observed, "was an afterthought and,
as it were, an accident in the history of the preparation and
enactment of the law." [189]

UNIFORM STATE LAWS

Freund was a leading proponent of uniform statutes for the
different states, and served as an Illinois member of the National

Conference of Commissioners on Uniform State Laws for many years. In a survey of "Government and Law in America," published in 1900, Freund pointed out that with regard to the laws of states governing marriage, registration of deeds, insolvency, formation of corporations, and property rights of married women, for example, there was a striking lack of uniformity. While the remedy "can be found only in uniform legislation for all the States," this is "made impossible for the present by the United States Constitution, as far as most of the private law and the entire law of procedure is concerned." "Legal unity, such as now exists in Germany, is in America for a long time to come, out of the question." [190]

Sore points with Freund were the lack of assertion by private writers on the law as professional evaluators of legislation and the judiciary and the ignoring of the writings of legal thinkers by the courts in their deliberations. "Generally, the judicature of the courts is very much more representative of American jurisprudence than legislation or the treatises of law writers. The latter record and digest only the court decisions; only a few authors have independent opinions, and deference to the authority of the courts which, to a certain degree, is reasonable and necessary, sometimes goes too far." [191]

The movement for uniform state laws, Freund wrote in 1912, "represents the conviction that the Federal powers are no longer adequate for the demands of national life." "Uniform State laws are at best a poor substitute for national laws." A liberal interpretation and application of the commerce, judiciary and taxation powers of the United States Constitution may substitute national for state control in some matters. "But there does not yet appear to be an effective popular demand for an enlargement of Federal powers which would give us the possibility of a national legislation . . . ; nor would such enlargement be desirable without new guaranties of State autonomy in the administration of national laws." [192] It was not until twenty years later, the year of Freund's death, that the effective popular demand began to materialize.

In 1913 Freund was appointed by the Governor of Illinois to serve on the Illinois Commission on Marriage and Divorce; and the following year, as a member of the American Bar Associa-

tion's Committee on Marriage and Divorce, Freund drafted proposed uniform marriage and divorce legislation for consideration
by the states. However, he felt that "public opinion in America is
not ripe for complete unity in matters of marriage and divorce"
due in part to "sectional differences of sentiment" but largely because "the entire problem of the marital status is in a flux." [193]

As a member of the National Conference of Commissioners on
Uniform State Laws Freund drafted in 1922 a uniform law for the
maintenance, education, and support of illegitimate children. The
draft law deliberately omitted provisions on status rights, including
one on legitimizing the children of null and void marriages, such as
bigamous marriages or marriages of first cousins, because of the
opposition of representatives of many states.

One of the main sponsors of the proposed bill was the United
States Children's Bureau which together with other child welfare
organizations had called a conference in 1920 to draw up a legislative program leading to the drafting and enactment of such a bill
by the states. At this conference and at the one in 1921 it became
clear that a majority of the states would oppose granting illegitimate
children the right to inherit from the father. The draft bill as finally
adopted in 1922 reflected these changes. A major advancement
contained in the draft legislation made the obligation of the father
for the maintenance, education, and support of the illegitimate
child enforceable against his estate. Under then existing law such
obligation died with the father.

Freund appealed nationally to attorneys to help get the bill
adopted in as many states as possible. It was at the annual meeting
of the American Bar Association in 1921 that Freund made his
major appeal. Reported the Association's *Journal:*

> Probably the most interesting subject considered was the first
> tentative draft of an Act Relating to the Status and Protection of
> Illegitimate Children, presented to the conference by the com-
> mittee in charge thereof, through Professor Ernst Freund of
> Chicago, Chairman.
> From the very beginning the act provoked discussion from
> every angle, the most important of which was the attempt to
> define the respective rights of legitimate and illegitimate children
> in the estate of their deceased fathers. Although the subject was
> discussed at several sessions, it was passed over to next year and

the committee was instructed carefully to consider this point in the meantime.[194]

Freund had invited Mrs. Catherine Waugh McCulloch, Chairman of the Legislation Committee of the National League of Women Voters to address the meeting on the subject of guardianship of children. So impressed were the Commissioners by what she said that a resolution was adopted for the creation of a Special Committee to prepare and present in 1922 the draft of a Uniform Act for the Joint Guardianship by Parents of Their Children." In time the draft bill was enacted into law, with minor changes, by many of the states.

The Administrative Response

ADMINISTRATIVE LAW

The term "administrative law" was not first used by Frank J. Goodnow, contrary to such assertion by many writers in the field. Actually, the term originated in the United States on May 25, 1842 when United States Attorney General Hugh S. Legare, in the *Claim of Administrator to Land Scrip,* spoke of "the administration law." [195] It was next referred to on September 5, 1853 by United States Attorney General Caleb Cushing in the *Case of Spratt's Hemp Contract* in which he spoke of "the administrative law of the United States." [196]

When Frank J. Goodnow used the term "administrative law" in December, 1886, he apologized to the readers of the *Political Science Quarterly* as follows:

> Perhaps an apology and explanation should be made for the use of a term for which there is so little authority in the United States. I am trying to obtain a general classification of national public law applicable to any nation. If this classification—which is generally adopted at present in Europe—is correct, then, unless our law differs fundamentally from the law of every other state, we must on examination find in our law the rules which we have placed under the head of administrative law.[197]

The following June, Woodrow Wilson's "The Study of Administration" appeared in the same periodical with many references to administration and administrative action but none to administrative law. In comparing the province of constitutional law with that of what could have been described as administrative law, Wilson chose the term "administrative function." [198] It was, however, Freund's many articles and books referring constantly to Goodnow's term that led to the acceptance of the expression administrative law.

It was not until seven years after he first used the term that Goodnow attempted to define it. In his *Comparative Administrative Law*, published in 1893, he described administrative law in the United States as "that part of the public law which fixes the organization and determines the competence of the administrative authorities, and indicates to the individual remedies for the violation of his rights." [199] Twelve years later he modified the definition somewhat to "that part of the law which fixes the organization and determines the competence of the authorities which execute the law, and indicates to the individual remedies for the violation of his rights." [200]

In the preface to *Comparative Administrative Law,* Goodnow acknowledged his "indebtedness to . . . Doctor Ernst Freund of the New York Bar." [201] The following year, writing in the *Political Science Quarterly,* Freund called attention to Goodnow's use of the term and urged the legal profession, political scientists, and the public to become familiar with this expression, and hoped the subject would be recognized as a separate branch of public law. Freund then offered his own definition of "administrative law" as follows:

> The body of law which is thus developed regulates and limits governmental action without involving constitutional questions. Its subject matter being the administration of public affairs, as distinguished from legislation on the one side and from the jurisdiction of the courts on the other, it has been aptly called administrative law. It is to be hoped that the term will become more familiar to the public, and especially to the legal profession, than it is at present, and that the subject itself will become one of the recognized branches of public law. [202]

The line between administrative and constitutional law was not sharply fixed, Freund contended. Not only did this line fluctuate but a question in one domain from one viewpoint might be assigned to the other from another outlook. Generally, where the issue is directly between individual right and governmental power, it would be considered a question of constitutional law. However, "where merely the legality of official action is involved," or "where the fiscal rights and liabilities of the government are in issue," or "the question of remedy against the government," then these should be considered matters of administrative law.[203]

Bruce Wyman, another of the pioneers in the study of administrative law in the United States, gave the following definition in 1903 in his *The Principles of the Administrative Law Governing the Relations of Public Officers:*

> Administrative law is one of two co-ordinate branches of public law; constitutional law is the other. That is, administrative law is the complement to constitutional law; constitutional law prescribes the broad outlines of government—it describes the executive department of the government and fixes certain large limitations upon the functions of the administration. Administrative law organizes the administration—it prescribes in the minutest detail the rules which shall govern the executive department in administering the law. It is these rules which constitute the body of administrative law. Administrative law consists, as has been said, of those rules which govern the executive department in the administration of the law.[204]

In the introduction to the first edition of his *Cases on Administrative Law, Selected from Decisions of English and American Courts,* which appeared in 1911, Freund offered his definition of administrative law in the United States as follows:

> The subject of administrative law covers a number of topics, which in treatises and digests are generally divided between the law of public officers and the law of extraordinary legal remedies, but which will also be found treated incidentally under such various heads as municipal corporations, taxation, highways, elections, intoxicating liquors, nuisances, public health, public lands, etc.
> The common element, which gives the subject its unity, is the exercise of administrative power affecting private rights, and the term "administrative law" has in relatively recent times gained acceptance as the best designation for the system of legal principles which settle the conflicting claims of executive or administrative authority on the one side, and of individual or private right on the other.[205]

Freund briefly traced the development of administrative law in Europe and contrasted its status with that in the United States. He described how it became "inevitable that the common law, when applied to matters of public administration, should develop principles in many respects different from those governing ordinary private rights." It was in the area of compensatory relief for the individual by actions for damages against public officials, Freund observed, that the right to such relief, "which is the backbone of the common law, has only a very limited application in matters of public administration." As a result, extraordinary legal remedies emerged for restraining specific administrative action in violation of individual rights or for damages after such action. Such remedies "differ in important particulars from other rights of action." "They are not matter of absolute right, but are granted or refused by the courts according to a judicial discretion governed by considerations of public policy."[206]

At the state level, these extraordinary legal remedies differ from state to state resulting in a non-uniform and inadequate system of judicial control of administrative action. Every case arising out of an administrative controversy, Freund commented, "involves in the first instance the question through which of the various forms of remedies relief must be sought." [207] Where the legislature has vested in an administrative agency conclusive determination power expressly or by omitting remedies, Freund correctly foresaw the inevitable arising of the constitutional question as to whether such "final" determination satisfies the requirements of due process of law. That there is no general right to appeal to the courts on non-constitutional questions in connection with administrative decisions affecting individual rights was acknowledged by Freund.

Constantly seeking a body of general principles of administrative law, Freund early saw its linkage with legislation, particularly statutory construction and language.

> Since practically every act of exercise of administrative power must be authorized by legislation, the operation of general principles of administrative law is constantly affected, and frequently controlled, by the language of statutes. Questions of administrative law, in other words, often resolve themselves into questions of statutory construction. However, the constant recurrence of certain types of legislation has evolved principles of construction, which, in view of the rapid and enormous growth of public regulation of all kinds of interests, are as deserving of careful study as common-law principles.[208]

In concluding the introduction to the 1911 edition of his Casebook, Freund associated administrative law with political science and public administration in the broad sense that public policy and administrative efficiency were involved; but his primary approach was legalistic in that he saw administrative law as mainly concerned with the exercise of administrative power and with the protection of private rights against administrative action.

> The term "administrative law" is sometimes applied to all provisions of law regulating matters of public administration, such as civil service, elections, municipal government, schools, public revenue, or highways. In so far as such legislation involves problems of public policy and of administrative efficiency, it concerns the student of political science and of public administration. The chief concern of administrative law, on the other hand, as of all other branches of civil law, is the protection of private rights, and its subject-matter is therefore the nature and the mode of exercise of administrative power and the system of relief against administrative action. This limitation of the subject seems conformable to the prevailing usage and understanding in this country, while on the continent of Europe all positive statutory law is treated as belonging to the province of administrative law.[209]

In the second edition of his Casebook, issued in 1928, Freund introduced the volume with the following comments:

> A good deal of reflection, extending over many years in using the first edition of this casebook, has not led the author to consider fundamental changes in scope or plan to be necessary or desirable. Administrative law can be most effectively dealt with in a law school as a course on the exercise of administrative power and its subjection or non-subjection to judicial control. The three main divisions of the subject are thus administrative power and action, relief against administrative action, and administrative finality. . . .
> Administrative Law continues to be treated as law controlling the administration, and not as law produced by the administration.[210]

In his brief but pithy article on administrative law in the *Yale Law Journal* in 1916, Edward A. Harriman began by stating: "The term 'Administrative Law' has no authoritative definition in English." [211] However, after quoting Goodnow's and Freund's definitions, Harriman concluded that "Professor Freund's definition is narrower than Professor Goodnow's, and brings the subject within the scope of a purely legal treatise. . . . It will therefore be accepted as defining the scope of this article." [212]

In his address as president of the American Bar Association at its annual meeting in 1916, Elihu Root devoted the key points to administrative law. In remarks echoing Freund, he stated:

A system of administrative law must be developed, and that with us is still in its infancy, crude and imperfect. . . . If we are to continue a government of limited powers these agencies of regulation must themselves be regulated. The limits of their power over the citizen must be fixed and determined. The rights of the citizen against them must be made plain.[213]

"There is little or no dispute . . . as to what constitutes an administrative body or as to the nature of administrative law," asserted A. A. Berle, Jr. in the *Harvard Law Review* in 1917. "It seems to be assumed that the one is an executive arm of the government creating it and that the other deals with the safeguarding of private rights from such executive, and with the protection of such officials in fulfilling their task." [214] Here Berle justified his view of administrative law by quoting Freund's introduction to *Cases on Administrative Law* in which he contrasted administrative law with political science:

The chief concern of administrative law, on the other hand, as of all other branches of civil law, is the protection of private rights, and its subject-matter is therefore the nature and mode of exercise of administrative power and the system of relief against administrative action.[215]

In 1923 the Bar Association of St. Louis held a series of lectures on the growth of American administrative law, and published a volume on the proceedings. "The curtain," wrote Felix Frankfurter in his review of the book in the *Harvard Law Review* in March, 1924, "[was] raised by Professor Freund's Historical Survey." "The lawyers who heard this lecture and the readers who have thought their way through its printed pages must surely have shifted a good deal of their mental scenery of the law. . . . Professor Freund gives a just sense of the confusion and incoherence, of the rampant empiricism, which marks the present state of the cases concerning administrative law."[216]

As early as 1924 Frankfurter was critical of Freund's fear of discretionary power. Frankfurter felt that "the problem of rule *versus* discretion is far broader than its manifestations in administrative law." "In other words, Professor Freund does not sufficiently distinguish between those fields of legal control where certainty—the mechanical application of fixed rules—is the chief characteristic of law, and those fields where the law means the application of standards—a formulated measure of conduct to be applied by a tribunal to the unlimited versatility of circumstance." [217] Frankfurter contended that because of "the danger of arbitrary conduct in the administrative application of legal standards . . . our administrative law is inextricably bound up with constitutional law." [218]

J. Forrester Davison and Nathan D. Grundstein, acknowledging Freund's "pioneering work" and "the legacy of Freund," deplored in 1968 the absence of any comprehensive study updating Freund's historical survey of the growth of administrative law published in 1923.[219] Leonard D. White, in his *Introduction to the Study of Public Administration,* which appeared in 1926, agreed with Freund's approach and asserted that the major objective of administrative law was the protection of private rights while the objective of public administration was the efficient conduct of public business.[220]

In his article on "Administrative Law" in the *Encyclopaedia of the Social Sciences,* which appeared in 1930, Freund defined Continental European administrative law as the body of law "controlling the exercise of governmental power outside of traditional civil and criminal justice. . . . It covers both regulative legislation and its interpretation, and the inherent principles of official power." [221] American administrative law he described as "the law of official power and of its subjection to judicial control." [222]

Administrative law in the United States was concerned, Freund wrote, both with statutory provisions and their construction and with common law principles of remedial law, such as official liability, extraordinary legal remedies, and equitable jurisdiction. "But common law also enters into statutory construction, and legislation is controlled by the constitutional principle of due process to which the exercise of power over private rights must conform." [223]

Administrative law was concerned with problems of administrative action which were "purely" administrative and also with administrative action that involved constitutional problems. In Freund's words:

> The main problems of administrative law relate to the nature and operation of official powers (permits and orders, ministerial and discretionary, scope of discretion and legitimacy of underlying considerations), the formal and procedural conditions for the exercise of powers, official and communal liability, the specific remedies for the judicial control of administrative action (legal, equitable and statutory), jurisdictional limitations of powers and the question of administrative finality.
>
> The constitutional problems of administrative law relate to the delegability of legislative power, due process in administrative power and due process as involving subjection of administrative power to judicial control.[224]

To Freund the study of administrative organization belonged to the field of public administration, and the study of administrative powers belonged to administrative law. The former aimed at discovering "the conditions of reconciling efficiency and economy with avoidance of the drawbacks of bureaucracy," while the latter involved "the principles making for the protection of right and justice." [225]

Asserted Freund in the same article in 1930: "We are inclined to accord to the courts a law creating monopoly, and administrative law is to us primarily judicial law controlling the administration. The term might, however, also be applied to a body of principles produced by the administration; and with the growth of administrative tribunals, and particularly of a practice of publishing reports of administrative decisions and of abiding by precedents, there is every reason to suppose that such a body of commission or departmental administrative law will gradually establish itself." [226]

Freund was keenly interested in showing the extent to which management problems were legal problems involving case law, judicial control, and statutory and constitutional grants of power. In an article written for *Public Management* in 1932, Freund

traced the development of administrative law and the law of municipal corporations in the United States. The term "administrative
law," he disappointedly noted, "is even at present perhaps more
familiar to political scientists than to lawyers into whose vocabu-
lary it has barely penetrated." [227]

In January, 1933, three months after Freund's death, the *Iowa
Law Review* published a symposium on administrative law with an
introduction by Felix Frankfurter and contributors consisting of
Edwin M. Borchard, A.H. Feller, Oliver P. Field, Louis L. Jaffe,
Daniel James, Dudley O. McGovney, Maurice H. Merrill, Edwin W. Patterson, Paul L. Sayre, Arthur Suzman, John H. Wigmore, and John Willis.[228] The symposium was organized by Felix
Frankfurter in memory of Freund and included many of the leading
authorities on American administrative law.

Frankfurter's four-page introduction on the growth of administrative law in the United States is a classic in conciseness and
comprehensiveness and in the description of the interplay between theory and practice. As to Freund's role:

> A generation ago Administrative Law was outside the ken of
> the Anglo-American lawyer. Awareness of its problems was, with
> rare exceptions, even beyond the pale of scholarship. A prophe-
> tic political writer like Herbert Croly and pioneer students of
> our public law, especially Goodnow and Freund, saw the need
> for adaptation of our legal structure, and still more of our legal
> habits of thought, to the demands of what Graham Wallas called
> the Great Society, transformed, as it was becoming, by the
> cumulative influences of modern science. . . . Administrative law
> was mentioned only as a foreign inroad upon the precious
> American dogma about a government of laws and not of men,
> and as an unworthy contrast to an Englishman's passion for
> liberty secured by the Rule of Law. Soon, however, the alien
> suspect will achieve the respectability of a rubric in the Ameri-
> can Digest. Happily, Ernst Freund lived to know that his seeds
> bore fruit. Thus this volume is a tribute, in the best sense of the
> word, to Ernst Freund, for it is an unconscious memorial to the
> triumph of his insistence that the issues which are the concern
> of Administrative Law are worthy of the best scholarship be-
> cause they are matters vital to the modern state.[229]

In 1938 Frankfurter, noting the slow recognition of administrative law in the United States as a separate branch of public law,

The Administrative Response 73

wrote in an issue of the *Yale Law Journal* devoted to the growth of American administrative law:

> More than forty years ago Ernst Freund expressed the hope that the term, administrative law, "will become more familiar to the public, and especially to the legal profession, than it is at present, and that the subject itself will become one of the recognized branches of public law." To this day administrative law has no rubric in the ordinary digests, and flickering cross-references to the subject first begin to appear in 220 United States Reports. Not until 280 United States Reports does the term appear to have established itself in the index. Yet the Supreme Court has in essentials been the ultimate dispenser of administrative law as truly as the great administrative courts of the Continent.[230]

As Frankfurter observed in his foreword to a symposium in the *Columbia Law Review* in 1941 on the Attorney General's Committee on Administrative Procedure:

> Thus far our Administrative Law has largely "growed" like Topsy. The time has come for silly hostilities to cease, for us to give full acceptance to Administrative Law as an honorable and indispensable member of our legal household, instead of continuing to treat it as though it were a subverter. It may well be that the creative faculties of legislation are needed for a more sensible and secure interplay between the administrative and the judiciary. But legislation is the end of a process of understanding and not a firebell. All enduring political reform has three stages—investigation, education, and legislation. In so far as it affects Administrative Law, this rational process is at last under way.[231]

This was pure Freund.

It was to Freund that Nathan D. Grundstein in 1950 attributed the achievement of liberating administrative law from constitutional law and from the judiciary:

> The approach of Freund to American administrative law released it from bondage to the judiciary. At the same time, he identified administration with the legislature rather than with the executive. Administrative regulation was treated as a phase of legislative control operating through the delegation of legislative powers. The legislature rather than the executive was regarded as the primary instrument of policy; the hierarchical organization of the administrative apparatus was evaluated as an

indispensable prerequisite of professional administration; and the end of discretionary administrative power was interpreted as the maximum scientific standardization of delegations of legislative authority. By a quite different process of reasoning than had been followed by Goodnow, Freund had also distinguished administrative from executive power. Executive power became unstandardized power, "that residuum of government otherwise subject to law which cannot be reduced to rule." Administrative power, on the other hand, was identified with the common law ideal of the rule of law, an identification reaffirmed twenty-five years later by the Attorney General's Committee [on Administrative Procedure].[232]

Twenty years after Freund's death, Justice Robert H. Jackson declared in *Federal Trade Commission v. Ruberoid Co.*: "The rise of administrative bodies probably has been the most significant legal trend of the last century and perhaps more values today are affected by their decisions than by those of all the courts, review of administrative decisions apart.[233] Testifying before Congress in 1956, Judge David W. Peck of the Appellate Division of the Supreme Court of New York State remarked: "Undoubtedly the single most significant development of law, and perhaps even of Government, during the past quarter of a century, has been in the field of administrative law." [234] Commenting on the work of the Supreme Court in 1957, Felix Frankfurter observed: "Review of administrative action, mainly reflecting enforcement of federal regulatory statutes, constitutes the largest category of the Court's work, comprising one-third of the total cases decided on the merits." [235]

By the end of the 1950's, renewed attempts to define administrative law inevitably returned to Freund's definition. In 1958 Kenneth Culp Davis in his *Administrative Law Treatise* asserted: "Administrative law is the law concerning the powers and procedures of administrative agencies, including especially the law governing judicial review of administrative action. . . . It does not include the enormous mass of substantive law produced by the agencies." [236] This is in keeping with Freund's definition, which Davis cited together with Goodnow's definition as setting the framework of the field. In fact, Davis observed: "All the casebooks on the subject treat the subject as one of powers, procedures and judicial review." [237]

In the most recent edition of *American Jurisprudence,* the definition of administrative law given is as follows:

> In one sense the term "administrative law" embraces all the law that controls, or is intended to control, the administrative operations of government. It includes the law which provides the structure of government and prescribes its procedure, but not the substantive law which administration is supposed to apply. It embraces the law which governs the methods of legislatures, provides for the existence and operation of the courts aside from their procedure in the actual progress of litigation, establishes the executive agencies and governs their procedure, and determines personnel policies in all branches of the government. However, administrative law within the scope of this article is concerned with the protection of private rights and the problems of administrative regulation rather than those of administrative management.
>
> "Administrative law," as the term is generally used today and for the purposes of this article, is concerned with the legal problems arising out of the existence of agencies which to a noteworthy degree combine in a single entity legislative, executive, and judicial powers which, in the American system of law, were traditionally kept separate. In regard to such agencies, it is the purpose of this article to consider their creation, the powers reposed in them by the legislature, the exercise of such powers, and the extent and manner to which the agencies are subject to control by the courts or dependent upon them for fulfillment of their objectives.[238]

Admittedly, this is not fully Freund. However, Section 2 states:

> The chief concern of administrative law, as of all other branches of civil law, is the protection of private rights, and its subject matter is therefore the nature and the mode of exercise of administrative power and the system of relief against administrative action.[239]

This is strictly Freund and is so cited in the footnotes.

When one speaks of administrative law today in the 1970's, he refers to the law establishing and governing the organization, staffing, methods, and procedures by which administrative agencies carry on public business in relationship to private parties and interests and which provides for internal or external restraint on the exercise of administrative authority. In the most recent book on administrative law, Robert S. Lorch defined the term as follows:

Administrative law is law governing the legal authority of administrators to do anything that affects private rights and obligations. It limits not only the scope of authority but also the manner in which that authority is exercised. . . . Administrative law is not, by definition, the substantive rules made by administrators, nor is it the adjudicative decisions they make. If the Federal Aviation Agency makes a rule forbidding passengers on airlines to carry guns, that rule would not itself be administrative law. However, administrative law would touch on the authority of the Federal Aviation Agency to make the rule, and upon the procedure employed in making it.[240]

Again, Freund's definition prevails.

CASEBOOKS AND CURRICULA

Freund's *Cases on Administrative Law*,[241] published in 1911 and revised in 1928, was the first systematic casebook on administrative law in the United States. Frank J. Goodnow's *Selected Cases on Administrative Law*,[242] which appeared in 1906, and Bruce Wyman's *Principles of the Administrative Law Governing the Relations of Public Officers*,[243] issued earlier in 1903, were not truly casebooks as we know them. Wyman's book ignored completely legislative and judicial controls of administrative action, and devoted little attention to the organization of administrative agencies. Goodnow's gave major consideration to the organization of administrative agencies and the responsibilities, authority and control of public officers.

Freund's 1911 casebook, observed Arthur H. Kent, "had within a few years won a place for 'Administrative Law' in the curricula of virtually all the leading law schools." [244] A substantial number of changes were made in the 1928 edition, primarily in the clarification of the law, particularly regarding the nature of administrative orders and their relation to legislative and judicial action and the proof of official acts. The growth of administrative powers and agencies led Freund to add new sections on regulatory commission proceedings, the granting and refusal of licenses, and proceedings against aliens. "The subject of administrative regulations has been omitted, since the case material is inadequate for its proper understanding." [245]

Freund's 1911 and 1928 casebooks on administrative law, as

John A. Fairlie observed, "dealt with the subject from the point of view of private rights, as the law controlling the administration and not as law produced by the administration." [246] Assessing "The Literature of Administrative Law" in 1942 Shelden D. Elliott evaluated Freund's casebooks as follows:

> As a pioneer in the teaching of Administrative Law in the law school curriculum, Professor Freund directed attention primarily to problems of administrative powers and the securing of judicial relief against administrative action. His basic concern was with the matter of remedies, and he drew his materials largely from state court decisions illustrating the various actions and proceedings available to review or to obtain redress for official action affecting the individual citizen. [247]

Freund's casebooks did not explicitly recognize the separation and delegation of powers as did the casebook of Felix Frankfurter and J. Forrester Davison for example, which was published in 1932, the year of Freund's death, or the casebooks of Robert Adam Maurer in 1937, Edwin Blythe Stason in 1937, Kenneth C. Sears in 1938, Walter Gellhorn in 1940, James Hart in 1940, and Milton Katz in 1947. By the 1940's Freund's casebook appeared to be, in the opinion of Louis L. Jaffe, "a conservative picture of a system, traditional and limited, with the accent on the methods of preserving those limits. . . . Long before 1932, the impressive growth of non-traditional administrative functions had made it uncomfortably evident that the basic assumptions concerning the distribution of powers were being cruelly tried. This may not have been so obvious in 1911; furthermore, Professor Freund's genius was for organization and system rather than exploration and reorganization." [248]

The Frankfurter and Davison casebook, employing largely the decisions of the United State Supreme Court, emphasized constitutional aspects, particularly the separation and delegation of powers and judicial review of administrative action. Moreover, it discarded Freund's treatment of judicial remedies as subjects in themselves, and substituted a functional, subject matter approach. Later casebooks placed greater stress on the problems of administrative procedure and approached administrative action chronologically through its successive stages. This was especially true for the casebooks of Stason, Gellhorn, Maurer, Sears and Hart. Sears devoted special attention to the responsibilities of public officers for official action and to the problems of specific remedies. Hart gave added consideration to the powers and functions of public officers from the viewpoint of linking administrative law and public administration. Sears' casebook was originally intended to be the third edition of Freund's, but "in working upon this project it was discovered that so much had happened in that indefinite field of law known as Administrative Law that a very different selection of cases and materials would be necessary in order to present adequately the subject-matter." Acknowledgment, however, was made "of the great indebtedness . . . to Professor Ernst Freund." [249]

The test of Freund's and the others' casebooks was their analysis and treatment of the administrative process. Freund worked with a meagerness of materials at a time when licensing and taxation were viewed by the courts as routine and when the control of administration was considered as external—judicial, rather than internal—administrative. Freund devoted a major portion of his book to judicial control of administration with a detailed presentation of judicial remedies, the forms of judicial review, particularly the traditional common law writs, whereas the later casebooks assigned relatively much less space and importance to these elements, although the Frankfurter and Davison functional approach was discarded by some, including Gellhorn.

Shortly before his death Freund prepared a review of the Frankfurter and Davison casebook on administrative law for the *Harvard Law Review* in which he took issue with the two authors on the proper scope of a course in administrative law given in law schools.[250] Frankfurter and Davison viewed administrative law as being mainly concerned with the constitutional arena in which the three branches of government operated and in which judicial decisions furnished the necessary validity, coordination and integration for government generally to function. Freund conceived the administrative law course as primarily involving the study of the various categories of powers as derived from the enabling legislation, from the rules, procedures and actions of administration, and from the judicial controls and restraints provided not only by the Constitution but also by the common law remedial writs.

Freund's review was published the month following his death. Having known and worked with Frankfurter for many years, Freund recognized him to be his successor in leading the struggle to win a separate, respected status for administrative law. The review opened as follows: "Through teaching and writing, and perhaps no less by an exceptional gift of inspiring and guiding the work of others, Professor Frankfurter has placed himself in the forefront of the field of administrative law in this country, and a collection of cases of which he is the co-editor is a welcome contribution to the literature of the subject." [251]

Acknowledging the new casebook as a "substantial volume," Freund was critical of its emphasis on the separation of powers and constitutionality. "Throughout fully one-half of the book," Freund remarked, "delegated administrative powers, if they come into play at all, stand remotely in the background. In the First Part we feel that the editors' main preoccupation is with the constitutional status of the Judiciary; in the Second Part, with the legitimate or permissible share of the Executive in the process of legislation; and it is only in the Third Part that administrative action comes quite definitely to the front. Two-thirds of the book could have been fully described as cases on the separation of powers, and it is doubtful whether anywhere else an equal collection of material on that subject can be found." [252]

Freund, however, was critical also of Frankfurter's and Davison's approach to administrative powers in the Third Part. "Even where the authors give their attention entirely to delegated administrative powers," he maintained, "their interest is concentrated on problems of constitutional law, which dominate the entire book." All law schools offered courses in constitutional law and many casebooks existed on that subject, Freund observed. "On the other hand, there is in the present law school curriculum relatively little opportunity to become acquainted with the technique of administrative powers in their non-constitutional aspects." [253]

While willing to overlook the omission of the law of public officers, the organization of local government, the position of the national and local chief executives, and the administrative share in enforcement, Freund could not accept the omission of "the common-law system of remedial relief." [254] Yet, he stressed again and again that though his own approach was different, the new casebook's "range of research . . . is enormous" and "the reader moves almost constantly on a high plane of thought and expression; and a thorough study of the book under a competent leader must be a great educational experience." [255]

Freund regretted "that the non-constitutional side of administrative law receives such relatively meager treatment" [256] and had intended to resume the struggle in this area when he suddenly died in October, 1932. The truth was that Frankfurter saw more clearly than Freund at that time the shift in judicial emphasis in matters relating to administrative powers and discretion. Freund relatively neglected the significance of both the separation of powers and constitutionality.

Aptly observed Louis L. Jaffe in 1933: "The controversy is first a pedagogical and curricular one, but it has its consequence in the different type of research, both as to material and method, which the opposed conceptions are likely to beget, *e.g. cf.* Freund's own Administrative Powers Over Persons and Property with Dickinson's Administrative Justice and the Supremacy of Law (1927)." [257] The same year, Oliver P. Field criticized the Frankfurter and Davison casebook "as not a casebook on administrative law" but rather "a fine collection of cases on the separation and delegation of powers, and judicial review of administrative action" and really "a book on a highly specialized branch of constitutional law, for the most part" which omitted "most of the law of officers, as well as much of powers, liabilities and remedies." [258] As for Frankfurter's course in administrative law at Harvard University, Field stated that Frankfurter's students "studied Frankfurter, but have taught Freund." [259]

Contrasting the courses and casebooks of Freund with those of Frankfurter, Paul L. Sayre remarked in a symposium on administrative law in 1933:

> Now the casebooks by the late Professor Freund were very different. He was not concerned about the heights of constitutional law. . . . Freund did not give himself to expounding questions of legal technique or discussing the basic interests or the difficulties involved in particular cases. . . . For instance, in Frankfurter's course hardly an hour would pass when the

word "constitutional" was not used many times. But Freund could teach the whole course in administrative law and hardly mention "constitutional" once. . . . It was merely that he saw the Constitution, and the statutes, and the traditional element that we call common law, as all one system, which it was his job to adjust and to understand as best he could. For instance, where another instructor would ask about a case, "is this statute or agreement or administrative finding constitutional?" Freund would say, "Is there any sense to that?" [260]

Paul L. Sayre was not being super-critical of Freund. He studied under both Freund and Frankfurter and recognized that "the debt which legal scholarship in this country owes to Ernst Freund can hardly be overestimated. . . . Certainly his old students as long as they live will hold his memory in respect and affection." [261] Furthermore, he realized that even in 1933, administrative law was "still largely a matter of specialized constitutional law. . . . It is time," he asserted in the spirit of Freund and Frankfurter, "for administrative law to secure its complete independence, not by warfare, but by separate development of its legal content." [262]

Basically, Freund's view was that constitutions, traditions, and statutory law are part of one large system—society; and the ultimate purpose of all these elements is social harmony and order. Frankfurter viewed these elements also as interdependent but fundamentally jealous competitors for social power kept apart by the barriers of constitutionality. By the 1950's and 1960's, however, the trend was away from Frankfurter's approach and moved more towards Freund's.

As Maurice H. Merrill pointedly observed in a symposium on administrative law in 1933: "The pioneering is not all done, the lines are not yet fixed." Frank J. Goodnow's casebook "was concerned primarily with problems of structure and organization. . . . The late Ernst Freund, to whom workers in this field owe an undischargeable debt, devoted over half of his volume in 1911 to problems of judicial relief against administrative action, primarily to the methods by which relief could be secured." While Freund treated also the subjects of rule-making powers and procedure and the separation and delegation of powers, "the natural and proximate consequence of a course organized along the lines suggested by that book is to leave with the student the impression that the chief concern of administrative law must be to keep the administrator from interfering with what people want to do or to award damages for such interference if it is past prevention." [263]

Edwin Blythe Stason's casebook, containing only American cases, aimed at equipping attorneys to practice before administrative tribunals. Moving away from Freund's legal control, Stason's approach was that of "social engineering."

Felix Frankfurter and J. Forrester Davison created a casebook on administrative law from the viewpoint of constitutionality, emphasizing the separation and delegation of powers and stressing the determination of what are proper legislative, executive, and judicial functions and the degree of discretion that may properly be delegated to subordinates. Such an approach leaned a bit to Freund and hardly at all to Stason.

In breadth of knowledge, Freund's scope of English and continental European administrative law was matched only by Frankfurter and Davison. In addition, the latter dealt juristically, rather than legalistically, with the subject matter, creating a broad socio-historical environment for the student of administrative law, and posing such problems as the reconciliation of liberty with authority and the securing of social interests without unduly restricting the individual, rather than the problems of proceeding before administrative regulatory agencies. While Freund began the work of appealing to the legal scholars, law school teachers, bar leaders, and philosopher-judges to formulate the general principles and philosophical foundations for the acceptance of administrative law, it was Frankfurter who gave it the greater impetus.

By 1947, fifteen years after Freund's death, administrative law had won acceptance and the heated battle over "administrative absolutism" had largely ended with the passage of the Federal Administrative Procedure Act. A new casebook on administrative law, written by Milton Katz, appeared that year reflecting the changed environment.[264] Concentrating on two old and two new federal agencies each responsible for regulating a particular industry, the book devoted about half its space to judicial review; and adequate attention, for the first time, was given to the role of administrative agencies in the enforcement area. Still relatively untouched, however, were: (1) the historical development of the administrative process and its function in modern industrial and technological society; (2) the actual, behind-the-scene practices of administrative agencies, especially the informal procedures and dispositions; (3) organizational operations with regard to decentralization and field-central office procedures; and (4) the investigatory powers and the rights and treatment of individuals under investigation. Also largely untreated was the decision-making process, a field to which the later 1950's and the 1960's began to give concern. Yet, what was true in 1947, and even today, is that most administrative action has been occurring outside the sphere of judicial review; and here is where most casebooks on administrative law have not measured up to reality.

By the late 1940's, the field of administrative law had become so broad that doubts arose as to whether it should be taught as a single course. Just as judicial procedure occupied four or five courses in the regular law school curricula, so many experts recommended that the teaching of administrative law be divided into several courses, with the introductory course consisting of a survey of the entire administrative process and coordinated with the courses in constitutional law. Thomas I. Emerson, one of these advocates, even suggested that the courses in administrative law be supplemented by courses in public administration, including administrative management, and also in "the legal aspects of community living." [265]

In discussing the state of research in administrative law in 1964, Edwin Blythe Stason reminisced:

It is difficult for me to realize that when I started teaching administrative law at the University of Michigan Law School in 1928, there was no law casebook available as a teaching tool excepting only Ernst Freund's excellent volume predicated largely on a bygone era. There were but few courses offered in American law schools and the teachers of administrative law could be counted on one hand. Ernst Freund and Felix Frankfurter were outstanding, but the fraternity was small indeed. There was no West Publishing Company "key number" subdivision on administrative law. Yet, we were on the threshold of a striking development in American jurisprudence—namely twentieth century administrative procedure.[266]

In 1957, surprisingly, Freund's 1928 casebook was still in use in law schools, reported Harrop A. Freeman in the *Journal of Legal Education*.[267]

Observed James Willard Hurst in 1950: "The law curriculum did not bring administrative law into distinct focus until past 1900. And except for Ernst Freund's pioneering, for twenty years administrative law was restricted almost entirely to the problems of judicial review of administrative action." [268] Because of Freund's work, wrote Arthur H. Kent in 1933, "an increasing number of high-grade law schools have made the systematic study of the art of legislation a regular feature of their curricula," and thus Freund "has rendered a service to social scientists and to bench and bar the value of which it would difficult to overestimate."[269] Freund, Kent further remarked, "came upon the scene to find that the processes of legislation had been and were receiving relatively little attention from legal scholars and in the curricula of law schools, despite the fact that many vital changes in law were taking place by reason of the activities of the legislative arm." [270] While he "never depreciated the importance of the common law . . . he could not have become the legal pioneer that he was had he followed the lead of other great scholars and concentrated the powers of his clear and vigorous mind upon the judicial process." [271]

By 1933 the law schools had adopted a functional approach to law, stressing realistic jurisprudence and a close relation of law and the social sciences. "It is easy," noted Kent that year, "to underestimate the part that Professor Freund played in this." [272] With regard to the teaching of municipal corporations in the law schools, Freund observed that it consisted almost entirely of case law, and that students were rarely if ever required to go to the statute book. Branches of municipal law—municipal liability, law of streets, and municipal property—involved a complex "mingling of private and public right and of corporate and governmental capacity." To discover "legal formulae simplifying the present intricacies and fine distinctions between proprietary right and public power, contract and regulation, license and franchise, fee and easement and additional servitude, germaneness and ultra vires" and to determine whether such formulae should be evolved by legislation or judicial decision hardly seemed possible in contemporary America.[273]

To ensure that proposed legislation would be based on sound principles and conform to social needs, the legal processes and the social sciences would have to be coordinated. Just as tax and revenue laws were inseparable from public finance, so were administrative legislation and public administration intertwined. Sound administrative legislation had to be based on social science research. "In his courses," Kent wrote of Freund, "he continually emphasized this point of view. . . . He was even wont to assert that such a technical property course as 'Future Interests' might profitably be approached from the fiscal angle." [274]

In one of his last public appearances before a convocation of the graduates of the professional schools of the University of Chicago, Freund in June, 1932 spoke on the subject "Law School and University." The theme of this talk was:

Law, like other human institutions, is a working compromise, and the very fact that it is an appeal to reason demands assumptions that must not be too closely questioned. . . .
This does not mean that the inquiring spirit of the university should stop at the essentials of law, as the inquiring spirit of the church stops at the essentials of religion; but it raises the question where and by whom the inquiry should be carried on. . . .
When jurist and social scientist meet on boundary-line problems, as nowadays they often fortunately do, each will soon learn where the other has superior equipment, and sensible men will avoid quarrels over jurisdiction. Generally it will be found that the lawyer's expert qualification is more effective in a narrower range. In some issues of social legislation we are apt to be misled in this respect by the special American constitutional theory, which throws into a court problems which only statesmen can decide. The lawyer looks to the economist and the economist to the lawyer, and the Supreme Court confound both by a five to four decision. . . .
The best that a lawyer can do on the fundamental issues of social legislation is to use plausible methods of argumentation that will carry weight with the judicial mind. They leave the core of the matter untouched and merely prove that it is not only the social scientist who has a technique for dealing with unsoluble problems. The limitations of legal science can be better realized where the constitution does not come into play.[275]

This theme was expressed by Freund at the turn of the century when the University of Chicago Law School was being planned. The ideas and concepts of Freund, more than those of Joseph Henry Beale, Jr. who obtained a leave of absence from Harvard Law School for half of each of the first two years to become the Dean of the new Chicago Law School, prevailed and led to the latter school's soaring prestige. Beale, Freund and Julian William Mack were the prime movers at the Law School; but it was Freund who gave it direction and character with regard to the administrative law and legislation aspects of the curriculum, research and library holdings.[276]

Freund looked to the law school to train lawyers and legislators to study and understand history, sociology and politics and to help develop principles of administrative law and legislation based on fairness and tolerance as well as on efficiency and effectiveness. "Barring the works of Bentham," he wrote as far back as 1907, "it would be impossible to point to a book written in the English language discussing in the light of administrative and judicial experience the legal ways and means by which a given legislative policy can best be rendered effective, or the arrangements and instructions which at present serve that end." [277] Freund called this area of study and creativity "constructive jurisprudence." Reliance on lawyers alone or legislators alone to attain this goal was unrealistic. "The lawyer's treatment of the law is analytical, the legislator's constructive." [278] Both must work together; but: "A share of this work of constructive jurisprudence must fall to the universities." [279]

Thirty-seven years later, alluding to and echoing Freund, Judge Charles E. Wyzanski, Jr. of the United States District Court in Massachusetts, writing on legal education in America, stated:

> In addition to broadening the basis of instruction in specialized courses such as labor law and antitrust law, it seems of the greatest consequence to allow any undergraduate to elect, and possibly to require him to take, several courses in the fundamental norms of administrative law, of legislation and of jurisprudence. At present, in most instances, administrative law is taught primarily in the light of court cases. Such instruction overlooks the fact that what an administrator wants to know and what he expects to hear from a lawyer is not merely what he must do but what is the sound and desirable method for him to pursue.

With all their merits, the doctrine of judicial review enshrined in our constitutional system and the doctrine of the rule of law are not the only touchstones as to how an administrative process should be conducted. We need to develop for administrative law canons of fairness and tolerance, of orderliness and stability, of change and of growth—and the law school is the place to begin that development.[280]

ADMINISTRATIVE POWERS

When Frank J. Goodnow and Freund were first writing on administrative law in the last decade of the nineteenth century, the subject of administrative powers over persons and property was hardly thought about; and it was extremely unlikely anyone would foresee the magnitude of growth of such powers that was to occur in the ensuing three decades. Freund's foresight at the turn of the century is all the more remarkable in that he not only sensed this great change but began to devote himself to this subject. Acknowledging this in a symposium on administrative law in 1933, Oliver P. Field remarked:

Professor Ernst Freund's contributions to the subject of administrative law have been largely, although not exclusively, in the field of powers. Powers is an important subject. It is a technical subject and one surmises that Professor Freund has enjoyed its technicalities, despite the fact that he has always recognized the overwhelming factors of policy involved in this branch of administrative law.[281]

Louis L. Jaffe called Freund, in connection with this field of study, "the first American master of our subject." [282] Accordingly, it was not surprising that when the subject became timely in the 1920's, the scholar turned to as leading expert was Freund. In 1920 the Commonwealth Fund, allocating funds to be used for the encouragement of legal research, appointed a Legal Research Committee to recommend and carry out appropriate study projects. Members of the Committee included Justices Charles Evans Hughes and Harlan F. Stone of the United States Supreme Court; Roscoe Pound, Dean of Harvard University's Law School; Benjamin N. Cardozo, then Chief Judge of the New York State Court of Appeals; and Max Farrand, renowned historian and authority on the origin of the United States Constitution. The Committee decided to sponsor studies in administrative law which, primarily due to Freund's efforts, was rapidly gaining in importance, and selected a special Committee on Administrative Law and Practice consisting of Ernst Freund as chairman, and Felix Frankfurter, Frank J. Goodnow, and Walter L. Fisher.

In the latter Committee's opinion, a comparative survey of administrative powers in regulative legislation was sorely needed to reveal the extent to which legislation operated through administrative powers, the degree to which licenses and orders were used in the administrative process, and the relative employment of discretionary and non-discretionary action by administrative agencies. This "monumental survey," as Avery Leiserson characterized it in 1942,[283] was undertaken by Ernst Freund. Its results were published in 1928 under the title of *Administrative Powers Over Persons and Property, A Comparative Survey*.[284]

In the preface to this careful, detailed, and documented analysis of the nature and types of administrative discretion and comparison and contrast of administrative law in England, France, Germany, and the United States, Freund explained that the survey endeavored "to summarize, from the point of view of administrative powers, an era of regulation which combined respect for private right with a growing sense of the social obligations of property and business, and which fully recognized the paramount claims of public interest." [285] Charting the striking changes in the development of governmental regulative powers over private business, he maintained that government should formulate a principle of regulation which would combine the traditional, legal, political, and social respect for individual and property rights with the growing sense of social responsibilities on the part of private industry and individuals generally for the public interest.

For democratic governments to continue to be free requires a politically alert and participating public. It is not sufficient to have a democratic governmental structure. This will not, in itself, assure democracy; nor will concentration of all legislative authority in the legislature, which alone can permit delegation of rule-making power to executive agencies, automatically guarantee democracy. "The question of the superiority of one organ of regulation over another is therefore not disposed of by pointing to the popular source of all authority." [286]

Freund was admittedly fearful of the lack of popular control and supervision over the administrative process. He frankly favored "the 'political' atmosphere of parliamentary procedure with its attendant checks." [287] Although he recognized that the needs of modern, complex industrial society encourage administrative rule-making, he believed that "history shows that administrative power is not indispensable." [288] Accordingly, Freund felt that the solution lay in confining delegated legislation "to non-controversial matter of a technical character," where the best rule for desirable regulation "is a matter of technical ascertainment." [289] On the other hand, where "there is strong opposition to any regulation, or where there must be a considerable element of discretionary preference, as between different modes of regulation bearing differently on different interests, a recourse to political decision seems to be conformable to the exercise of the authoritative control over persons and property." [290].

To Freund, who felt that the fundamental issue which must be solved by contemporary America was that "between political and bureaucratic rule-making." [291] the major question with regard to administrative discretion was where to draw the line on how much discretion may properly be delegated by the legislature to administrators. On this issue of where to draw the line authorities in the field of administrative law have differed. Freund suggested that delegation should be allowed only "where there are no controverted issues of policy or opinion" or where the issues are obscured or not recognized in the public mind or in the minds of the parties affected.[292]

Accordingly, Freund felt that regulating the hours of labor of women workers in factories involved too sharp a conflict of interests and opinions to be delegated to administrative agencies, while in railroad rate regulation the factors were so obscure that the best method was to delegate such authority to administrators. In the latter event, if the legislature delegated regulative power to the administrative agency, the delegation "presupposes that regulation is conceded to be desirable, that there is agreement upon having the best rule prevail, and that the best rule is a matter of technical ascertainment." [293]

Freund's suggestion as to where to draw the line of delegation of legislative power to administration was fraught with danger, and he himself so acknowledged. Obscurity is relative. Policy is a matter of degree. Choice of methods in execution of a set program usually involves questions of policy on various levels. There are times, also, when policy determinations delegated to administrators might offer the best solution to particular problems. Nevertheless, Freund was distrustful of the latter practice, although he sympathized with the growth of administrative powers and saw its preferability, though not indispensability, at certain times. The great danger underlying the administrative process, he stressed, was that "it may be . . . that after the practice of delegation has once become as firmly established as in the regulation of public utilities, its continued and even expanded application will come to appear politically preferable to the perils of sectionally influenced legislative intervention." [294]

Freund had long known that the legislative process had become more and more complex and technical, requiring the appointment and hiring of experts to assist the politically elected legislators; nor did he gloss over the fact that delegation of legislative authority to administrative agencies was frequently resorted to in order to avoid pressures on the legislature by sectional and group interests. The solution that is accepted today by most authorities in the field of public administration and administrative law, as exemplified by J. Roland Pennock, is that the "potentialities for the abuse of administrative rule-making power can be kept fairly well in hand, while still allowing for a full utilization of the advantages of the device, by an insistence upon legislative determination and definition of policy." [295]

Acknowledging that "administrative power appears as one of the established political facts in present-day government," [296] Freund emphasized the need for democratically controlling discretion and looked to the legislature as the branch of government most politically responsive to the public to keep administration initially in check. The second source of control, often the most practical means when the legislature has delegated broad administrative powers, is the judiciary. Giving the individual his day in court might not necessarily dispense him justice, but it "affords an opportunity for protection." [297]

For Freund the courts were "keen to discover some grounds upon which the exercise of administrative power can be controlled." [298] He correctly saw in the Anglo-American writ of habeas corpus a judicial remedy of outstanding advantage over German and French remedies in their systems of administrative law. The existence of this writ enabled a person to gain access to a court whenever an administrative action allegedly resulted in infringement of personal liberty. On the other hand, Freund observed, the Continental systems' theory of state responsibility to compensate for injury inflicted in the course of official administrative action was more liberal than ours. [299]

Administrative law in the United States, Freund insisted, was not a law "outside and beyond the common law" but was "part of the common law," and "if there is need for acting outside of the rules of the common law, the action should be political, so far as such action is compatible with American constitutions." [300] Accordingly, he pointed out:

> A study of administrative law as a branch of the common law is a study on the basis of decided cases, and it is therefore natural to read the law in the light of judicial decisions. Even though it be realized that judicial law is one thing and administrative practice another, it is also true that in theory at least the practice is normally subject to judicial control, and that judicial construction is therefore a very legitimate test of the limits of discretion. A recognition of the fact that administrative practice has, so to speak, its own law, is not inconsistent with the recognition of the importance of the judicial or legal aspect of discretion, and vice versa. [301]

In a survey on "The Growth of American Administrative Law" conducted for the Bar Association of St. Louis in 1923, Freund predicted the great increase in "legislative regulation of economic activity" and with it the growth of administrative power. [302] For Freund, however, "Administrative power is defensible and desirable if it greatly aids the purposes of legislative regulation." [303] If administrative power appears to be necessary, then "the choice lies between power which merely sees to the observance of the law, and power which is intended to give definiteness to an indefinite law, i.e. between ministerial and discretionary power." [304]

Freund perceived the core question to be whether it was possible to so define and spell out the statutory requirements as to eliminate discretion. "What we cannot say of administrative power in general we can say of discretionary administrative power over individual rights, namely that it is undesirable *per se* and should be avoided as far as may be, for discretion is unstandardized power and to lodge in an official such power over person or property is hardly conformable to the 'Rule of Law.' " Therefore, "the most important point in the development of administrative law is the reduction of discretion." [305] Because of the key importance of Freund's conception of administrative discretion and the many misconceptions by later writers of his attitude, a separate section is devoted to the subject in which the matter is discussed in detail.

In *Administrative Powers Over Persons and Property,* Freund analyzed the statutory provisions conferring administrative powers on various governmental agencies, which he classified generally as enabling and directing powers and specifically and respectively licensing and permit powers, and administrative orders, examining powers, and summary powers, which are defined later in this chapter. He limited this study to powers affecting private rights and ignored administrative powers relating wholly to the management and operation of governmental agencies. One of his major recommendations was that legislatures learn to distinguish among functions which are within the "proper province of administrative power" and those which "are not appropriate to administrative control." Certain behavior areas, he argued, are not clearly distinguishable, and not all those matters which appear clearly assignable to administrative control are socially necessary or workable. Religion, politics, and the press, for example, were matters not appropriate to administrative control. Education, however, could be but in a limited way.[306]

With regard to the regulation of public utilities by administrative commissions, Freund observed in 1915 that these agencies no longer served simply as instruments of a fully expressed legislative will, but participated actively in the expression of such will. This, to Freund, was an inevitable evolutionary pattern—"from generic legislation to administrative power to carry such legislation by specific requirements." [307] It was in the particular powers of control, moreover, that Freund saw the primary element unifying the various and haphazard legislative delegations of administrative powers affecting private rights.

In discussing "powers," Freund never moved very far without bringing in "principles" and "standards." The latter two were key terms throughout all his discussions of legislative and administrative excercises of power. In tracing the development of rate regulation, for example, in England and the United States in an article appearing in the *American Bar Association Journal* in 1923, Freund asserted:

> The history of rate regulation shows that our estimate of administrative powers must take into account considerations that go beyond organization, procedure, and judicial review. There will always be the fundamental question of the standards underlying the exercise of power.[308]

If the legislature fails to set standards or leaves the working out of standards to the administrative agency then serious problems could arise. Where the matters are simple or temporary, no harm may be done; but in matters complex and technical erroneous or unworkable standards will produce unjust or harmful substantive results which even the most skillful procedural safeguards cannot prevent. In the latter event the agency exercising the administrative powers will find it hard to win or retain confidence.

Freund was not opposed to the use of administrative powers for experimenting with problems that yet appear to be unsoluble; but if we do so "we must be prepared to take the consequences. . . . We must not expect that unstandardized power can easily be harmonized with traditional notions of judicial authority. A due realization of this difficulty will be conducive to a better understanding of what appears to many as the central problem of our administrative law." [309]

Traditional liberalism regarded government as a necessary evil and sought to impose restraints on governmental power. Woodrow Wilson, whom Freund admired and was very friendly with, had expressed the liberal view that "The history of liberty is a history of the limitation of governmental power, not the increase of it." [310] Freund did not go to that extreme; and Wilson himself later modified his concept of liberty and government, stating that "law in our day must come to the assistance of the individual . . . to see that he gets fair play," that "without the watchful interference, the resolute interference, of the government, there can be no fair play," that "freedom to-day is something more than being let alone," and that "the program of a government of freedom must in these days be positive, not negative merely." [311]

Freund placed his faith in the legislature as the people's guardian of democracy but felt that, when it delegates its powers to administrative agencies to make rules of public conduct, the danger to liberty grows. However, he did not hold that the legislature should be permitted to have any and all powers that it seeks. Nor did he feel that the main danger was the expansion of official powers to restrain certain activity of people or sections of the public. "Liberty is even more curtailed by an official power to require action in the public interest than by a restraining power. The subjection of a private action to a prudential discretion represents therefore the strongest kind of government control." [312]

In reviewing Freund's *Administrative Powers Over Persons and Property,* Arthur N. Holcombe in 1929 called the study "a masterpiece of logical analysis and orderly exposition." Aptly sensing that the main problem concerning administrative powers was that of the delegation and exercise of discretion, Holcombe remarked: "Professor Freund's views concerning the relative advantages of the quasi-judicial administrative process, of the more arbitrary form of a legislative fiat, and of the system of determination by boards frankly constituted on the basis of interest representation, deserve the careful attention of every student of modern government." [313] The same year, Edward S. Corwin, in his review, characterized Freund as a conservative regarding administrative discretion, and praised the study as "especially welcome to teachers of Administrative Law for the guidance it affords to the larger aspects of the subject and its clarification of the issues both of policy and of legal principle underlying these." [314]

Freund's book was truly the first comprehensive comparative survey of regulative legislation revealing analytically the extent to which statutes operate through administrative powers, the use of licenses and orders, and discretionary and non-discretionary actions.

As of 1930, Freund was still complaining that the field of law enforcement, particularly the administrative powers dealing with prosecution and execution, "has not so far received adequate systematic treatment." [315] Freund's book was received magnificently by legal and political science circles, but it did not inspire other studies in the areas he had hoped for.

Freund's book endeavored, as Leo F. Wormser noted in 1932 at memorial services for Freund, "to summarize, from the point of view of administrative powers, an era of regulation which combined respect for private right with a growing sense of the social obligations of property and business, and which recognized the paramount claims of public interest." [316] Freund did not advocate "the imperative voice of authority" as "the most effective method" of solving economic and social conflicts.[317] He viewed the state as final resort and primarily as influencer and mediator, and the state's imperative authority should remain in the background ready to be called on to exercise its powers with right, equality and justice only when socially necessary. To devise guiding principles for such action by society and government was Freund's main life concern.

Commented Arthur H. Kent in 1933 on Freund's *Administrative Powers Over Persons and Property:*

His treatise, *Administrative Powers Over Persons and Property,* published in 1928, though it did not purport to be the comprehensive and exhaustive work on administrative law which he was so eminently qualified to produce, does represent the most important effort that has been made to provide a classification and terminology adequate to reduce this new and amorphous subject to some kind of rational order. Whatever the final judgment as to the adequacy of this classification and terminology may be, there can be no doubt that it provides the basis and point of departure for future studies in the field. To the extent that administrative law was treated by him as law controlling administration rather than as law produced by the administration, it is confessedly somewhat incomplete, and in the Introduction to the second edition of his casebook he utters a prophetic note as to the potential importance for future study of administrative practice as a source of law.[318]

The expansion of administrative powers in the depression and New Deal period of the 1930's was so great that Freund's 1928 volume on the subject was sorely outdated, but none had taken its place. Reported Charles S. Hyneman in the *Political Science Quarterly* in 1936: "No adequate survey of the spread of administrative powers has yet been made. . . . The most comprehensive effort is Ernst Freund, *Administrative Powers Over Persons and Property.*" [319] To this day no subsequent study has been published which comprehensively and systematically surveys and analyzes the gigantic mass of data which have mounted up since Freund's death.

Nearly a decade later, administrative powers were still best defined in Freund's terms as corrective intervention by government; and the enlargement of this intervention was what was meant by the growth of administrative powers. [320] Another description of the same phenomenon in that period was still in Freund's terms, the shifting from voluntary, private, corrective action to mandatory governmental action which inevitably led to the increased resort to administrative agencies. [321] To this could be added what I.L. Sharfman described as the limitation of managerial independence in contrast to freedom in internal organization. [322] If managerial independence has been restrained, it is also true that delegated powers have been redelegated internally to individual commissioners and other administrative officers with an additional control of internal review required by legislatures.

In 1940 Robert B. Hankins, writing on "The Necessity for Administrative Notice and Hearing," observed: "Most discussions of this problem in legal periodicals have been confined to a particular field of administrative action. Only a few attempts have been made to bring together a number of cases in many fields of administration. Such are in Freund, Administrative Powers Over Persons and Property." [323]

In defining administrative powers, Freund had classified five types: (1) summary powers, which governed acts not requiring ultimate judicial approval or review, (2) enabling or licensing powers, which governed acts permitting individuals or groups to carry on business; (3) dispensing powers, which governed acts exempting applicants from statutory requirements; (4) directing powers, which governed acts determining the rights and responsibilities of parties in specific cases; and (5) examining powers, which governed acts of investigation. Freund excluded rule-making powers as "legislative in substance." [324] This was in keeping with his separation of "legislative" from "administrative" powers. This separation was not fully acceptable by the end of the 1930's and early 1940's. Avery Leiserson in 1942, for example, not only added legislative powers and mediatory powers as sixth and seventh categories of administrative powers, but also expanded the definition of examining powers by going beyond Freund's restriction to acts requiring testimony and the production of books and papers.[325]

Leonard D. White turned frequently to Freund in developing his pioneering textbooks on public administration. White's sections on administrative powers and sanctions were admittedly inspired by Freund. In recommending the use of orders of individual application as a favored form of directing power, White quoted Freund in 1954: ". . . the normal function of an administrative order is to make a generic statutory prohibition or requirement definite. The directing power is given because the legislator finds himself incapable of foreseeing the precise duty of the individual." [326] Observed White: "In more and more cases the statutes do not foresee the precise duty of the individual. Discretion is vested with officials to state specifically what the legislature meant in its enactments. Exact duties and obligations are contained in orders of individual application." [327]

Freund was criticized by some later authorities in administrative law for merely posing alternatives and not recommending any definite one. A careful first-hand study of Freund's writings and lectures dispels such criticism. How appropriate then was the observation in 1933 of Evan A. Evans, Justice of the Seventh United States Circuit Court of Appeals, in reviewing Freund's *Administrative Powers Over Persons and Property* for the *American Bar Association Journal:* "In innumerable instances the author considers the possible alternatives which present themselves for coping with an administrative problem, and states the consequences attendant on each and recommends the most feasible alternative. He supplements his conclusion with valuable suggestions for the solution of existing defects." [328] Evans concluded his review with the remark, "No more comprehensive and accurate guide to a study of administrative powers can be found than in this thorough treatise." [329]

Licensing

Licensing occupied a special place in Freund's discussions on administrative powers; and an entire later generation of legislators and students of law and public administration concerned with the subject found themselves studying his ideas and recommendations regarding licensing. In his earliest writings on the police power and administrative action, Freund saw the complexities involved, such as legislative regulation, administrative approval or denial, development of standards, and governmental policy in promoting the public interest.

In his thorough, detailed analysis of licensing as a regulatory and revenue device by the City of Chicago, which appeared in 1952, Malcolm B. Parsons at the very outset stated that "Freund's expertness in this field of inquiry must be acknowledged." [330] In fact, Parsons' volume owed much to Freund's conceptions. To begin with, Freund's definition was accepted, as it is even today. Licensing was defined as "the administrative lifting of a legislative prohibition." [331] This is not to say that administrative action may permit what legislative action has denied. "The primary legislative thought in licensing is not prohibition but regulation, to be made effective by the formal general denial of a right which is then made individually available by an administrative act of approval, certification, consent or permit." [332]

Licensing is a complex administrative action which involves more than allowing or supporting activities by those who comply with certain standards. It involves also governmental policy to promote particular private activities in the public interest; it may involve organized private pressure groups interested in obtaining governmental recognition or sanction for their own ends. Licensing may become a means of limiting economic entry, supply, or substandard competition; and in the extreme, it may promote monopoly. Also involved are the politics of formulating license policy, conflict between public and private interest, and difficulties faced by the licensing agencies in resisting dominance by the very groups who are supposed to be controlled.

Freund recognized, too, the existence in licensing of the sometimes incompatible demands of liberty and authority, particularly where administrative discretion was involved. Discretion would arise in licensing generally through legislative requirements that licensing officials, in using their powers, resort "to beliefs, expectations, or tendencies instead of facts, or to such terms as 'adequate,' 'advisable,' 'appropriate,' 'beneficial,' 'competent,' 'convenient,' 'detrimental,' 'expedient,' 'equitable,' 'fair,' 'necessary,' 'practicable,' 'proper,' 'reasonable,' 'reputable,' 'safe,' 'sufficient,' 'wholesome,' or their opposites." [333]

Generally, Freund preferred the enabling powers, such as licensing or permit issuance, to the directing powers, such as order issuance. Yet he deplored the nearly unlimited discretion that sometimes accompanied the right to attach special conditions to the granting of licenses or permits. However, he felt there was a general tendency toward the reduction of administrative discretion in licensing.

Freund preferred the term "certification" to "licensing." [334] As a system of control, he saw it as follows:

> Control through licensing means an administrative advance judgment regarding the presence of legal requirements or the absence of legal objections. It is the legislative policy and hope that law observance may thus be normally and expeditiously insured by eliminating the most obvious or serious sources of future trouble that would have to be dealt with by slower remedial processes.[335]

While a system of administrative orders would provide a means of "avoiding both the stigma and the hazard of penal prosecution, a licensing system has the widest choice with reference to the freedom of official action." [336] Fearful that "discretion" could lead to "abuse of discretion," Freund observed:

> Discretion enters into the licensing power most commonly through the framing of requirements by the legislature in such a manner that some difference of question as to compliance or fulfillment is regarded as legitimate. Within the limits of this legitimate difference official judgment is respected; beyond it there is legally "abuse of discretion," with the possibility of judicial redress. Such terms as reasonable, adequate, reputable, suitable or safe, which involve value judgments or future probabilities and a lack of objective certainty, are characteristic.[337]

In licensing, administrative discretion may have profound effects on the economy. For example, the granting or refusing of a license with regard to public utilities may create or undo monopolies. Discretionary power, furthermore, may be widened by the imposition of conditions to be observed by licensees. Always alert to the protection of private rights, Freund asserted:

> Procedural provisions of licensing laws serve the purpose either of safeguarding the public interest or of preventing injustice to the applicant. The former is the more important and is achieved principally through prescribed forms of applications and notice requirements. As a matter of principle the applicant himself is equitably entitled to fair consideration; but since through his application he has automatically a chance to present his case and since he has also a common law remedy of mandamus in case of arbitrary refusal, the occasional failure of the licensing statute to make provision for hearing presents no constitutional question.[338]

In assessing the state of licensing in the United States as of 1932, Freund noted:

> Although general statements of tendency are hazardous, there seems to be evident at present a trend toward better safeguarding of the methods of licensing. This is manifested in part in a reduction or elimination of the discretionary factor, in part in an increasing attention to organization procedure and review. Where some particular branch of regulation has a long legislative history, where interests subject to regulation are strongly intrenched or where a licensing policy is politically contested, considerable attention is likely to be given to administrative detail, whereas unqualified powers are apt to accompany an unclarified legislative policy.[339]

As for the choice between a system of administrative orders and a licensing system, Freund concluded:

> As compared with the nineteenth century the present is an era of intensive governmental regulation. Even without a disposition to enhance official powers, perhaps notwithstanding a strong feeling against bureaucratic government, there are many fields in which administrative intervention and even administrative discretion are indispensable. The choice in these fields lies between administrative orders and administrative licenses. The former probably represent a more conservative exercise of public power; but with the burden of initiative thrown upon the government, the check is likely to be sporadic and confined to exceptional cases. A licensing system is the path of least resistance;

it lends itself equally to wide discretion and to non-discretion, and private interests are usually able to accommodate themselves to it without undue difficulty. It is so convenient a method of checking the observance of governmental regulations that its permanence in the economy of legislation and administration appears to be assured; but the elaboration of administrative detail with a view to the most effective reconciliation of public and private interest will necessarily be a matter of prolonged experimentation.[340]

Philanthropy

Freund's views of administrative commissions and discretion permeated the entire range of his interests, even in connection with philanthropy and its protective controls. In 1930 he wrote a chapter on the "Legal Aspects of Philanthropy" for a book, *Intelligent Philanthropy,* in which he revealed his consistent views on administrative powers and discretion:

> Experience has shown how much superior administrative commissions are to the attorney-general in availability for the protection of interests that are not backed by financial resources or inducements. It is quite possible that their powers may be made broad enough that they may serve as protectors of foundations. But it is inconceivable that their function should be solely protective in this sense; they would inevitably exercise a discretion, and intervene only if intervention would be for the public interest. If so, it would simply mean that the founder cannot have effective protection without submitting to legitimate public control.[341]

Despite the passage of over forty years since Freund's book on administrative powers appeared, few scholars have produced any systematic studies in this area. The modern tendency has been to theorize and generalize about administrative procedure to the neglect of a like concern with administrative discretion. This point was keenly made by J. Forrester Davison and Nathan D. Grundstein in 1968:

> While hypothesis and generalization concerning administrative procedure are no longer in the tentative stage, it is otherwise as respects administrative discretion. Yet it is quite likely that one would have said just the opposite a little more than a score of years ago. For then, in 1928, American administrative law had just been enriched by the publication of *Administrative*

Powers Over Persons and Property. Here, for the first time, was
a mature and comprehensive view of patterns and tendencies in
the employment of administrative powers by modern social
legislation. The lament of an eminent British authority that
English administrative law has no counterpart attests to the
value of the late Professor Ernst Freund's study of administrative
powers.[342]

Freund's studies of administrative powers led him to search for
a scientific, rational set of principles and standards producing a
system of legislative and administrative controls which would
enable administrators to use discretion and choose among alternative policies, plans and programs without offending the
individual's rights of person and property. This approach was
frequently misconstrued to imply an abhorrence of all administrative discretion. Those who knew and understood Freund rejected
such criticism.

"Lest it be thought that Professor Freund was hostile to regulative law," wrote Edwin W. Patterson in a symposium on administrative law in the *Iowa Law Review* in 1933, it should be noted
that he recognizes its superiority as an instrument for adjustment
of conflicting interests."[343] James Willard Hurst, in *The Growth
of American Law: The Lawmakers,* acknowledged this point in
1950 and characterized Freund as "sympathetic with the growth
of the administrative process, but also distrustful of the delegation
of broad policy decisions."[344] Freund himself explained why he
accepted administrative action and why he urged students of
administrative law to study this subject area:

> It is futile to denounce the extension of administrative control
> to economic interests. But we should carefully study its phases
> and qualifications, try to understand its mechanism, and appre-
> ciate differences that should have a legitimate effect upon meas-
> ures and policies. It is not for the student of administrative law
> to offer a solution for every problem in his field; but he should
> help others to understand, why some problems are as yet
> unsolved.[345]

Definiteness was one of Freund's key words. It became the
cornerstone of his ideas about administrative powers and especially
about administrative discretion. "The more indefinite the standard," Freund wrote in 1928, "the greater is obviously the temptation
to use the law as a weapon to gain economic advantage, using

the public interest as a shield." [346] This was particularly true in the United States during the depression period of the 1930's when the government asserted regulation by means of codes. The automobile, coal, and steel industries, in which stiff competition existed, were prime examples of this dangerous tendency that Freund warned about.

ADMINISTRATIVE DISCRETION

In 1894, Freund wrote an article for the *Political Science Quarterly* on "The Law of the Administration in America" in which he first formulated his ideas on administrative discretion.[347] He saw the American form of self-government as a unique administrative system unlike that of any European nation, particularly in the administration of our states:

> To the American student an acquaintance with the foreign law will reveal the interesting fact that, however diverse the systems of the European states may be, they appear almost uniform when compared to our own system. While many of our institutions may find parallels in Europe, our administrative system seems to be unique. We may, for the sake of convenience, speak of an American system; its most peculiar features, however, do not appear in the national government, but in that of the states, which in this respect are all substantially the same.[348]

What intrigued Freund the most was that here "the difference between rulers and ruled is reduced to a minimum." [349] Moreover, in our system of self-government there are a "lack of organic connection and concentration of the different offices which constitute the administration" and a lack of the same kind of coherence which characterizes the legislature and the courts. This condition "is due partly to constitutional provisions and partly to legislation." [350]

When Freund published the article in the early 1890's the state legislatures held tight reigns on the delegation of administrative powers. When such powers were delegated, the legislatures specified in great detail the framework of authority. "No discretion as to scope of action or choice of means can be allowed to subordinate officers without superior control, and the hierarchical organization necessary for such control does not exist." "The legislature must also regulate the exercise of official powers in every particular . . . because the officer has no one to look to for instruction and guidance except the letter of the statute." [351]

In Freund's outlook, the "greatest drawback of our system . . . lies in the fact that it makes no provision for the review of discretionary action—that there is no chance of reconsidering the question of expediency." As early as 1894 Freund felt that it "would be dangerous to vest such a power in the courts" and that the legislatures "will narrow as much as possible the sphere of discretionary action on the part of the administration" by fixing "precisely and completely the conditions under which the administration must act in a certain manner." [352] Here was Freund's earliest expression of his views on administrative discretion, and a comparison with his later writings reveals almost complete consistency, for even in 1894 Freund was not opposed to administrative discretion: "the progress of civilization creates new spheres of administrative action in which the exercise of discretionary powers is indispensable." [353]

Attempting to speculate how far the existing "administrative system of the states will be able to retain its peculiar features unimpaired, in view of the constant and inevitable expansion of the sphere of modern state activity," Freund predicted:

> The spirit of democracy seems at the present time to seek different methods of asserting itself from those chosen in the first half of the century; and simplicity must necessarily give way to more complicated conditions with the progress of material civilization.[354]

The basic change in state government impelled by the industrial and technological revolutions, Freund observed, was the movement away from keeping the government as weak as possible to strengthening it and expanding its functions. "With a change of the conditions that have made the present organization possible, the organization itself is liable to undergo important modifications." The new direction was indicated by the pressures for legislation regulating the economy, which would tend to centralization of administration:

> New branches or administration have developed, and the departments in whose charge they are placed show at least some degree of centralization. In newly created offices there is a mani-

fest tendency to revert from the principle of election to that of appointment; the civil service laws are putting a check upon the practice of rotation in office; above all, the changes in municipal government indicate a decided departure from the principle of loose and weak organization, and an approach to the forms of bureaucratic government; and the city only demonstrates most typically the problems characteristic of the administration of the modern state. But the growing strength of the administration incident to its more compact organization is apt to be balanced on the other side by a curtailment of its discretionary functions, so that the increase in administrative activity is likely to be greater than the increase in administrative power over the individual.[355]

Where the tasks assumed by highly civilized nations are similar, the tendencies in their developing administrative law are likewise similar. Just as it was necessary "in Germany for political reasons to offset the power of the bureaucracy by the independence of self-government, so in our system it is becoming necessary, for administrative reasons, to modify an exclusively self-governmental organization by an infusion of bureaucratic or professional elements." The result, regardless of differences in governmental systems, is a combination of the same two features. Does this development pose the danger that we would lose our self-government to a highly centralized bureaucratic administration? Freund saw "no danger at present"—this was in 1894.[356] However, as the years passed he began to think somewhat differently and looked to greater legislative and judicial action to restrain administrative discretion.

By 1914 Freund modified his views on discretion. He now recognized the need for flexibility in administrative action; however, he defined flexibility as meaning "not merely differentiation but variability of regulation." "Differentiation," he contended, "can be secured by statute as well as by administrative ruling." "Variability, on the other hand, is desirable only in very few phases of social or economic regulation, while industry needs above all permanence and continuity of policy and requirement." Accordingly, the test of a proper delegation of powers would be whether they encourage permanence or impermanence, continuity or fluctuation. In this regard, Freund felt that "the force of circumstances will impose upon commissions a proper degree of conservatism." [357]

Administrative versus legislative action was a dilemma for Freund very early in his career. While he proclaimed legislative principles and standards generally as more democratic and reliable, he acknowledged the reality of attaining a greater impartial consideration by administrative action and ultimately the probability that administrators would substitute principle for discretion:

> Weighing relative advantages, it may be expected that administrative action can be set more easily in motion than legislation, and that it can better plan a program of gradual development; that while administrative authorities have a better sense of what is practically enforceable, legislatures have a keener sense of what is politically expedient, that while the former can mix suasion with command, the latter can invest their commands with greater publicity and a higher moral authority. Administrative action will be preferred by those who believe in regulation, legislative action by those who consider regulation a necessary evil.
>
> Administrative action has however the indisputable, though incidental advantage, that it permits the process of establishing rules to be surrounded by procedural guaranties and other inherent checks which will tend to produce a more impartial consideration than the legislature is apt to give, and which should in course of time, if not immediately, substitute principle for mere discretion. Such a result would mean an enormous step in advance for our entire system of public law, and it is therefore important to inquire whether we are justified in expecting it.[358]

Not that Freund had grown fond of the vesting of discretionary power in administrative agencies. "On the contrary the history of discretionary administrative power would seem rather discouraging." As an example of "demoralization of administrative action" due to arbitrary exercise of discretion, he pointed to the valuation of property for taxation purposes. As fairer tests, however, for the operation of discretion Freund referred to the appointment and removal of public officers and the granting of licenses. These led him to generalize that "discretionary administrative powers have not been signally successful." [359] To Freund this was not surprising:

> . . . for in a government by law discretion ought to have a very limited place in administration. Its legitimate function is indicated by the organization of a chief executive power which stands for that residuum of government otherwise subject to law

which cannot be reduced to rule. Where discretion appears in inferior positions, it is either the confession of inability to discover a guiding principle, or the deliberate preference of personal influence to more objective considerations, i.e., the more or less unavowed manifestation of the shady and corrupt aspects of government.[360]

Freund saw in the development of American political institutions the strengthening of "what may be called the irresponsible elements in government," the enlargement of initiative and arbitrary discretion and the widening independence of the three branches of government from each other. The relation between discretion and self-governmental organs to Freund was that of a vicious circle, each growing as the other expanded. Underlying this basic American weakness—and Freund saw it as a weakness—was the lack of professionalism generally and in the legislature particularly. It was this absence of professionalism which tended "to retain the arbitrary type of discretion, for self-governmental organs lack the inherent checks which in professional organs evolve principle out of constantly recurrent action." [361]

The solution, Freund implied, would require basically an educated electorate sending professionals into the legislatures who would reduce the business of legislation to principle:

> The spirit of the equal protection of the law demands a firm adherence to uniform intelligible criteria of discrimination; requirements of health and safety should be standardized, and in economic adjustments there should at least be a submission to the generally accepted truths of political economy.
>
> It is not of course meant to imply that all legislation falls short of these standards, but merely that there is not the slightest assurance of uniformity of standards, and that the absence of rule inevitably results in an excessive proportion of inferior and defective measures.[362]

To Freund the legislation of Congress and New York State represented "the worst type of American legislation" at the time. Even worse, however, was the financial mismanagement of the public business by Congress and its failure to broaden the fiscal powers of the President. This was before the President was granted the authority to prepare the national budget. "But it is not beyond the range of possibility that public opinion will insist upon the executive assuming a controlling share of legislative initiative." [363]

Six years later, in 1921, Congress passed the Budget and Accounting Act which vested in the President the power to prepare the national budget.

Although steeped in constitutional law, Freund underestimated its role in public administration, a point later taken up by Felix Frankfurter to great advantage. Freund saw legislative principle as the end-all standard whereas Frankfurter viewed constitutionality in that capacity. Eventually, Frankfurter's choice prevailed. "If constitutional law looms large in our estimation," Freund asserted, "it is on account of its practical importance in litigation." As for the body of constitutional law, it cannot "provide us with principles of legislation." "The constitution-making democracy concerns itself very little with the quality of legislation." [364]

Freund recognized that not all rule-making administrative action was amenable to principle and standard in an equal degree:

> Not all government can be standardized. In the ordering of public as of private affairs, there is a legitimate place for wisdom and judgment, and even, where there are hidden or imperfectly understood forces and agencies, for speculation and chance.
>
> Even in these matters there may be a limited opportunity for applying principle. Though it be impossible scientifically to determine standards of service or of compensation, it may be possible to estimate certain considerations at their true value and give them effect accordingly. Public undertakings will probably always remain matters of discretion, but their financing can well become matter of rule. And so all along the line. Not the least valuable effect of a wise delegation of power will be that it may enable us in the light of experience to judge better the respective provinces of rule and discretion, and organize public action accordingly.[365]

Anticipating the growth of administrative discretion and sensing in it elements of danger to personal liberty and the traditional concepts of due process, Freund warned that administrative discretion must be restrained. In a paper read at a Conference on Legal and Social Philosophy at Chicago in April, 1914, whose participants included Morris Raphael Cohen, John Dewey, Thomas Reed Powell, and Roscoe Pound, he explained that the administrative commissions were created and "vested with powers of a type hitherto withheld from administrative authorities under our system, powers which are not intended to serve as instruments of a fully expressed legislative will, but which are to aid the legislature in defining requirements that on the statute book appear merely as general principles." "The course of recent legislation for the regulation of commerce, trade and industry," Freund pointed out, "has created the impression that there exists a tendency in our law to transfer powers of determination from the courts which act according to fixed principles to administrative commissions or officials vested with large discretionary powers." Normally, however, "the progress of law should be away from discretion toward definite rule." [366]

The result of this new administrative power, "though likewise in a sense discretionary, is plainly the other way: it substitutes for the more or less arbitrary judicial action—arbitrary because delegated to a jury—a fixed and responsible rule." [367] "The real significance of administrative ruling authority then does not lie in any division of genuine judicial power, but in relieving the judiciary from functions in their nature more or less legislative." [368] In areas of administrative discretion, the courts cannot be relied on either to provide a continual check on maladministration or to help develop good administration. These are matters of internal administrative organization and management. Administrative agencies should provide a hierarchal system of administrative review comparable to judicial review.

Legislative regulation of economic and social interests was not new. What was new, as Gerard C. Henderson, remarked, was the resort "to administrative instruments in the enforcement of legislative policy" for "this has greatly widened the field of discretion" and "has created, in a sharp form, new aspects of the familiar conflict in the law between rule and discretion." [369]

Freund's concept of administrative discretion as a function of the absence of definiteness and precision in legislative standards and as a danger to the rule of law led him to conclude that the ideal situation would be the defining of the most precise and definite statutory requirements possible so as to reduce administrative discretion to the point of elimination. In Freund's words:

> What we cannot say of administrative power in general we can say of discretionary administrative power over individual rights, namely that it is undesirable *per se* and should be avoided as far as may be, for discretion is unstandardized power and to lodge in an official such power over person or property is hardly conformable to the "Rule of Law." [370]

This concept, expressed at its maturest by Freund in his lecture, "Historical Survey," on the growth of administrative law delivered at a symposium on the subject conducted by the Bar Association of St. Louis and published in 1923, disturbed John H. Wigmore. In an editorial note entitled, "The Dangers of Administrative Discretion," in the *Illinois Law Review* for February, 1925, Wigmore countered:

> With this conclusion we beg leave to differ radically. The bestowal of administrative discretion, as contrasted with the limitation of power by a meticulous chainwork of inflexible detailed rules, is the best hope for governmental efficiency. What is needed only is not reduction, but *control*, of discretion. . . .
>
> Administrative discretion is so paralyzed by fixed statutory rules that the tendency is to remove all incentive for administration as a career. Our industrial efficiency is largely due to the attractiveness of high responsibility to men of great capacity for discretion. Our bureaucracy (so-called) is kept on an inferior level in many departments by the repression of free development of individualists. . . .
>
> If we can improve the personnel, we need not fear discretion. The fallacy lies in assuming that the present lack of respect for administrative officers (compared, say, to judicial officers) is normal and permanent. Instead of reducing discretion because of this state of things, why not improve the state of things and thus cease to fear discretion?
>
> The finest local government in the whole United States was that of the Canal Zone under Governor Goethals. It was a government of pure discretion, administratively, from top to bottom. . . .
>
> No doubt (since men like the one mentioned are rarely to be hoped for) administrative discretion should be subject to control—by some appropriate form of appeal or rehearing. But subsequent appeal or revision on the merits of the individual case (use or abuse of discretion) is a very different thing from prior definition of power by detailed fixed rule.[371]

Freund's reply to Wigmore appeared in the April, 1925 issue of the *Illinois Law Review* stressing the qualification that his concept applied to "discretion exercised over private rights" and also that control of discretion tends to reduce the amount of discretion otherwise exercisable:

> Discretion has many different aspects as applied to different phases of government. In my St. Louis address I spoke only of

discretion exercised over private rights. Discretion in administering governmental services presents a different problem. Mr. Wigmore's examples show that he does not distinguish the two applications. Thus, he refers to the wonders worked by discretion in Panama, but Governor Goethals did not run a normal government; he conducted a great enterprise which made all the people its beneficiaries. Besides, the discretion of martial law may likewise produce results that government by law does not attain; what conclusions are we to draw from that?

Mr. Wigmore says he wants, not reduction, but control of discretion. But every properly organized system of control, i.e., control that is not arbitrary or haphazard, inevitably tends in the long run to standardize the exercise of discretion, that is to say, to transform discretion into nondiscretion, so far as it is inherently capable of that transformation. . . .

It is claimed for discretion that it enhances the attraction of public service as a "carrière ouverte aux talents." Of official places vested with power over private rights none ever attracted men of higher caliber than the judgeships of the superior courts of Westminster. Yet I think no one can read English case law and note its almost painful submission to precedent even in such matters as the construction of wills, or its attitude toward the interpretation of statutes, without receiving the impression that the English judges abhorred discretion, whereas many a judge of the Municipal Court of Chicago is eager for its exercise.

Or, passing to public administration on its executive side, I do not think that we can ever expect to draw a better grade of men into the civil services than those who during the greater portion of the nineteenth century constituted the higher bureaucracy of England and—'pace' Mr. Wigmore—of Germany. Yet in both countries legislative policy was distinctly in favor of circumscribing or eliminating discretion in granting administrative powers over private rights.

After all, neither a few utterances of even so eminent a jurist as Dean Wigmore, nor my own poor, brief remarks, can settle this vital issue of rule versus discretion.[372]

The debate between Freund and Wigmore was not carried on any further. The two were friends, having served together for years on the Illinois Bar Association's Committee on Legal Education; and Wigmore realized that Freund's objective of achieving expertness and definiteness in formulating and drafting legislation with due regard to the rule of law was a noble goal.[373] It was Freund's aim to promote the public interest—a subject of lifelong devotion. He did not equate a governmental administrator's

112   *The Administrative Response*

subjective choices of decisions with being not in the public interest; nor did he view little or no discretion as necessarily promoting the public interest. The subject was becoming more and more complex, and Freund tended to rely on the legislature as more democratic and politically accessible and responsive to the public than the administration. If any point was singularly the cornerstone of this concept it was the reluctance of Freund to rely on the benevolence of the public administrator—a dependence that he felt was too unguardedly supported by Woodrow Wilson and John H. Wigmore.

Freund's 1928 description of administrative discretion, still quoted today, exemplified his ability to reach the core of complex problems and to venture concise, detailed explanations:

> When we speak of administrative discretion we mean that a determination may be reached, in part at least, upon the basis of consideration not entirely susceptible of proof or disproof. A statute confers discretion when it refers an official for the use of his power to beliefs, expectations, or tendencies instead of facts, or to such terms as "adequate," "advisable," "appropriate," "beneficial," "convenient," "detrimental," "expedient," "equitable," "fair," "fit," "necessary," "practicable," "proper," "reasonable," "reputable," "safe," "sufficient," "wholesome," or their opposites.[374]

Reviewing Freund's book on *Administrative Powers Over Persons and Property,* in which the above definition appeared, and which was the study referred to by Freund in his debate with Wigmore, John B. Cheadle wrote in 1930 in the *Cornell Law Quarterly:* "Here is a notable contribution to the literature on administrative law by a master in analysis and our foremost writer in this field." [375] Freund's scope of study covered the legislation of the United States Congress, New York State, Great Britain, and Germany before World War I. Dealing only with "powers determinative in their nature and exercised with regard to private rights which are in a sense of a normal character," [376] Freund's purposes were to reveal the extent to which statutes operate through powers, the relative extent of the use of licenses and orders, and the relative degree of discretionary and nondiscretionary administrative action.

A central theme is Freund's old concept that administrative

discretion is a temporary and makeshift device for solving immediate problems, but that it must eventually be replaced through a progressive process by statutory standardization. He acknowledged the great increase in the resort to discretionary powers but he deplored this growth in certain areas. Particularly, he found such extension by New York State into the insurance and banking businesses "puzzling, and perhaps not due to carefully considered policy." [377] What Freund sought was the discovery of basic principles to govern economic regulation, especially rate-fixing. Discretion to him represented an effort to discover such principles at a time when the legislature was incapable of such discovery. He was realistic enough to recognize that no dynamic nation could probably ever attain the ideal of non-discretionary administration, since this implied a static economy and society. Accordingly, he concluded that "the function of discretion would . . . not . . . be to displace rule but to prepare the way for it." [378]

Freund's view of administrative discretion as a temporary device was hardly consistent with the significance and concern he gave to the subject. That it was an experimental social factor in its early history was generally acknowledged; but Freund was unable to accept administrative discretion as a fundamental, universal, and eternal fact of life in modern, technological societies.

If the fears and prophecies of Freund have not been borne out by the three decades since his death, this does not detract from the value of his teachings. Cheadle's evaluation of *Administrative Powers Over Persons and Property* still holds true today. "The value of this book lies in the wealth of material it employs, in the patient, sustained, and consistent analysis of those materials, and in the picture presented of the functioning of administration through the use of powers in the jurisdictions chosen. . . .We shall be fortunate if other fields of administrative law may some day be covered by this author with the same thoroughness and with the same spirit of search for truth that has characterized the present work." [379]

"Administrative discretion", Freund wrote in 1932 several months before his death, "is relied upon to temper the hazard inherent in sweeping terms and to reconcile conflicting public and private interests." [380] Two years later a detailed, lengthy article on "The Problem of Apparently Unguided Administrative Discretion" appeared in the *St. Louis Law Review,* written by Lewis Allen Sigler, who opened his study by stating that his "analysis is based upon an analysis advanced by Professor Ernst Freund" in the latter's *Administrative Powers Over Persons and Property.*[381]

Sigler, guided by Freund's classifications, divided administrative discretion into four general categories: (1) prudential or quasi-legislative discretion, which is the power granted to public officers to act on the basis of expediency, such as dealing with governmental property; but the use of such discretion for controlling private action was limited; (2) mediating discretion, which is the power to act on the basis of fairness, such as fixing reasonable rates for common carriers and public utilities; (3) censorial discretion, which is the power to act on the basis of conformity, such as censorship of motion pictures and plays that do not meet standards of morality; and (4) expert or quasi-judicial discretion, which is the power to act on the basis of fitness, such as the regulation of safety, health, traffic, finance, and professional competence, or dealing with matters involving serviceability of commodities, equipment, and improvements.

In addition to these four general, qualitative categories, Freund presented a special classification of discretionary powers different from the four quantitatively in that it was based on the degree of absence of standards for the guidance of the administrative agencies. This special classification necessarily overlaps the four general ones and could involve the absence of legislatively set or administratively devised standards. Freund divided this classification of discretion into two kinds, an "unqualified" or "unguided" discretion and a "qualified" or "guided" discretion. The former, conferred by statute, makes private action dependent on official approval or disapproval but provides no standards, bases, or grounds on which such approval or disapproval is to be exercised. Absolute freedom of choice is granted; and consequently, no contesting of determinations may practically be made or successfully prosecuted by private individuals or groups. Theoretically, such absolutely unqualified discretionary power over private interests is impossible in the American system of government. The "qualified" or "guided" discretion, on the other hand, is qualified in that it must be exercised according to certain standards or guidelines which may be either expressly stated in or implied from the statute conferring the discretion. Basic to any problem arising here is the sufficiency of those standards or guidelines rather than their presence or absence.

In this context, Freund saw no real problem or question concerning the validity of absolutely unguided discretion. Problems and questions arise when the conferred discretion is insufficiently, or apparently, unguided either because no standard or guideline is specified or because the expressed standard or guideline appears to be inadequate.

Freund's use of the term "unqualified" or "unguided" discretion was based on the expression "uncontrolled discretion" asserted by the Indiana Court of Appeals in *Bessonies v. The City of Indianapolis* in 1880 in which the court stated: ". . . the granting or refusal of the license or permit is not governed by any prescribed rules, but rests, in such case, in the uncontrolled discretion of the common council and board of aldermen." [382]

Administrative discretion, Freund had written in 1928, "individualizes the exercise of public power over private interests, permitting its adjustment to varying circumstances, and avoiding an undesirable standardization of restraints, disqualifications, and particularly of requirements. Under this view, the main province would be the regulation of interests in which public policy demands both maintenance of minimum standards and the possibility of variation." [383] Two years later, in discussing administrative discretion with regard to licensing, Freund observed in the *Encyclopaedia of the Social Sciences:*

> Where as a matter of professional experience value and probability judgments are fairly standardized, discretion may be reduced to the point at which there appears to be hardly more than a question of fact; on the other hand, the range of permissible considerations and their inherent uncertainty may be such as to widen discretion to the point of substantial freedom, as where the legislative reference is to the general welfare or the public good or detriment. Ordinarily such discretion ought not to be and is not delegated where licenses are required for the exercise of private rights. It may be delegated, however, where a primary policy of prohibition is to be relaxed under conditions

of emergency or of exceptional hardship; there is then a dispensing rather than a licensing power; but modern legislative practise does not favor unregulated dispensing powers.[384]

In one of his last works, written the year of his death, Freund contended in an article in *Public Management:*

> Complex conditions require some governmental discretion, and the question is how it is to be vested. It raises the problem of the status of administrative boards in an organization the governing body of which has the habit of special legislation.[385]

In his very last study, a book entitled *Legislative Regulation: A Study of the Ways and Means of Written Law,*[386] Freund saw the legislature as the focal point of democratic government, the source of administrative discretion, and the primary arm of government in controlling administration. The volume constituted what the *American Political Science Review* characterized as "the summation of years of scholarly research and penetrating insight in this field." [387] While stressing primarily the legislative control of administrative discretion, Freund did not ignore judicial limitation, which he felt was a secondary control. In this he differed with John Dickinson, who emphasized the latter. [388]

Commented Herbert A. Simon, fifteen years after Freund's death:

> Neither Freund nor Dickinson is able to find a justification for administrative discretion except as an application of decisions to concrete instances, or as a transitory phenomenon confined to a sphere of uncertainty within which the rule of law has not yet penetrated.
>
> To be sure, the two men offer different suggestions for the gradual elimination of this area of uncertainty. Freund relies upon the legislature to restrict discretion by the exercise of its function of policy determination. Dickinson thinks that administrative discretion can gradually be replaced by general rules to be formulated by the courts, as principles gradually emerge to view from a given set of problems. Neither is willing to admit any fundamental difference between the factual and normative elements involved in law-finding, or to see in that difference a justification for discretionary action." [389]

Even today there is a lack of general agreement among authorities in the field of administrative law and public administration as to the basic difference between factual and value questions in administrative law.

Freund gave serious thought to the charge that administrative discretion was undemocratic. The argument that administrative agencies were subordinate to the legislature did not, in his opinion, constitute an adequate answer to this objection and failed "to take into account the inherent tendencies of different forms of governmental organization." [390] Legislators are responsive to public opinion and depend on politics and the ballot for election, while administrators are appointive and further removed from the direct political sphere. Consequently, administrators are much less sensitive to public opinion; moreover, special interest groups may influence administrators at the expense of the general public.

American constitutional law in general, Freund felt, "represents political action through judicial methods, dependent for success upon the ignoring, by common consent, of the political nature of the process. . . . To judge the performance of the courts by purely legal standards is to misjudge it." [391] The doctrine of judicial power owes its existence and salvation to the uncertainty of standards. Nevertheless, Freund saw that it is "a strong tribute to American constitutional law that it has been found possible to conduct government for a century and a half in war as well as in peace without recourse to 'acts of state' or to emergency powers to suspend the Constitution." [392] While the Supreme Court has occasionally aroused popular resentment by voiding politically desired legislation, "there has been substantial acquiescence in the exercise of the power and there is no disposition to doubt the soundness of the structure of which it is the cornerstone." [393]

The fact of and the necessity for delegation of legislative functions to administrative agencies are not much debated today. What is of concern is how far such delegation should go, or how much discretion is too much. The important point is that no modern legislature has the time to inquire into the volume of essential details involved in administration, nor has it the required technical competence and the ability to ensure uniform impartial treatment. As for drawing the line on administrative discretion, Freund acknowledged the difficulty but hazarded the recommendation that "with regard to major matters the appropriate sphere of delegated authority is where there are no controverted issues of policy or opinion." Equal to the absence of controverted issues is the "obscurity or non-recognition or non-formulation in the public mind or in the minds of the parties affected." Delegation, in short, pre-supposes that regulation is conceded to be desirable, that there is agreement upon having the best rule prevail, and that the best rule is technically ascertainable.[394]

Always seeking definiteness and preciseness, Freund himself could here be criticized for employing such a relative term as "obscurity." Also, what constitutes "policy" may be debatable. A whole sphere of borderline cases may arise everywhere calling for administrative discretion. In addition, political considerations may enter and make discretion more desirable in order to avoid "the perils of sectionally influenced legislative intervention." [395]

Charles Evans Hughes had asserted in 1916 that one of the primary purposes of creating discretionary administrative bodies was to introduce flexibility into the law: "The ideal which has been presented in justification of these new [administrative] agencies, and that which alone holds promise of benefit . . . is the ideal of special knowledge, flexibility, disinterestedness and sound judgment in applying broad legislative principles that are essential to the protection of the community, and of every useful activity affected, to the intricate situations created by expanding enterprise." [396] It is to the need for flexibility that the growth of administrative law is largely attributed, since flexibility is what the legislatures and the courts of law both lacked. However, flexibility is no absolute virtue and no cure-all, and, in fact, may have contributed to bringing about unnecessarily greater complexity. Not many of Freund's contemporaries appeared to sense this tendency. In the United States, Freund appeared to be accompanied only by Edward L. Metzler [397] and in England by Arthur Suzman.[398]

John B. Cheadle in 1930 recognized the "strongly individualistic tendency" running through . . . [Freund's] governmental philosophy" and aptly judged Freund's reliance on legislative standards to guide administrators. But Cheadle exaggerated Freund's fear of administrators when he concluded that Freund "would remove the responsible expert from administration and put him into the legislature.[399]

In a penetrating article on "The Role of Discretion in Modern Administration," Marshall E. Dimock in 1936 described "the unfriendly attitude toward administrative discretion" that has existed in the United States. The starting point of this attitude has been the view that "law is the monopoly of the legal profession." A corollary of this premise is that "Law is held to be inherently reasonable, while administrative discretion is by its nature arbitrary." [400] Much of Dimock's article referred to Freund's writings on this subject, and Dimock's final sentence is a quotation from Freund: "In the ordering of public as of private affairs, there is a legitimate place for wisdom and judgment, and even, where there are hidden or imperfectly understood forces and agencies, for speculation and chance." [401]

Yet, as Ralph F. Fuchs keenly noted in 1938: "In dealing with specific situations Freund at times was a defender against judicial impairment of difficult administrative fact determinations, if not of administrative discretion." [402] On the other hand, it was that "Young Turk" of the early 1900's, Roscoe Pound, who emerged as a conservative in the late 1930's on through the 1940's. After observing the growth of administrative agencies and powers during the New Deal and World War II eras, Pound became very critical of administrative law. Some of his grounds echoed the fears of Freund, particularly regarding the employment by administrators of "personal discretion rather than ascertained rule and authoritative technique." [403] However, Pound's fears were more extremist than Freund. Pound went so far as to view the decisions of administrative agencies as being determined by simply "the personal feeling of the official" [404] and that the "only checks . . . are expertness and good intentions." [405]

Louis L. Jaffe in 1965 expressed the opinion that the New Deal and World War II periods with their great expansion of administrative discretion "would have appalled" Freund.[406] "Might have" would have been more apt words to use, since Freund was far more flexible and compassionate than he has thus far been described. To Freund the delegation of legislative powers to administrative agencies was a necessary evil, whereas to Woodrow Wilson the delegation was a requirement and condition of a healthy, positive, and active administration. Freund placed reliance on the legislature, whose members were elected by the people and subject to their recall or replacement, as the source of democratically promulgated legislation, and conceded the necessary delegation of legislative power to administrative agencies but viewed the latter as less democratic than legislatures because of the nature of their status and the remoteness from control by the electorate. Wilson, on the other hand, as far back as 1887, when the federal Interstate Commerce Commission was established, asserted that "large powers and unhampered discretion seem to me the indispensable conditions of responsibility" and that "public attention must be easily directed, in each case of good or bad administration, to just the man deserving of praise or blame." [407]

While Freund's viewpoint was described by Jaffe as "demonstrably too narrow to describe legislative phenomena or to fulfill political need," [408] such evaluations tend to minimize the fundamental criticism by Freund of the remoteness of the administrator from the public and the difficulty and complexity of placing blame on specific administrators by the public. What Freund was emphasizing was the immediacy of recognition and accountability with regard to the legislator in contrast to the administrator. Wilson's view would hold up if public attention were *"easily* directed." Of the two it might very well have been Wilson who would have been appalled by the New Deal's delegation of legislative power to administrative agencies, since his postulation of easy accessibility to and accountability of the administration has never been attained. Moreover, Wilson was by nature stern with a hard inner core, whereas Freund was much softer, more compassionate, and also steeped in French and German administrative law.

Interestingly, John H. Wigmore and Roscoe Pound, who were regarded as liberal with respect to administrative discretion, were conservative on the great issues of civil liberties in the 1920's, while Freund, regarded as conservative with administrative discretion, was a civil libertarian both in theory and action. It was Freund who was a leading voice in the opposition to the "Red Raids" and the conduct of the trial of Sacco and Vanzetti, whereas Wigmore could not see excesses in the former and strongly asserted the fairness of the latter. Pound would not join Frankfurter and Freund in these and the other civil liberty cases, and later in the 1930's emerged as a complete conservative regarding administrative discretion under the New Deal.

Remedies and Controls

THE RULE OF LAW: FREUND VERSUS DICEY

Freund was not an uncompromising believer in the rule of law with its emphasis, as in Albert Venn Dicey's classic definition, on three conceptions. First, "no man is punishable or can be lawfully made to suffer in body or goods except for a distinct breach of law established in the ordinary legal manner before the ordinary Courts of the land." [409] Second, "not only that . . . no man is above the law, but . . . every man, whatever his rank or condition, is subject to the ordinary law of the realm and amenable to the jurisdiction of the ordinary tribunals." Drawn to its utmost limit, declared Dicey, "is the idea of legal equality, or of the universal subjection of all classes to one law administered by the ordinary Courts." Every official, "from the Prime Minister down to a constable or a collector of taxes, is under the same responsibility for every act done without legal justification as any other citizen." [410] Third, such general principles as the rights of personal liberty and public assembly are "the result of judicial decisions determining the rights of private persons in particular cases brought before the Courts." [411]

By the rule of law, declared John Dickinson one year before Freund's *Administrative Powers Over Persons and Property* was published, "every citizen is entitled, first, to have his rights adjudicated in a regular common-law court, and, secondly, to call into question in such a court the legality of any act done by an administrative official." [412] The recent growth of administrative rule-making and adjudication, as James Hart pointed out, "has tended to undermine the first of these features of the traditional rule of law"; but, "the second feature is preserved if judicial review is provided." [413] In Dickinson's opinion, "administrative justice exists in defiance of the supremacy of law only in so far as administrative adjudications are final and conclusive, and not subject to correction by a law court." [414]

In his *Principles of the Administrative Law of the United States,* which appeared in 1905, Frank J. Goodnow indicated that the problem comprised three major elements: the public welfare, administrative efficiency as a means of protecting the public welfare, and the immediate private interests affected by the administrative action. Primarily, the objective is to provide and adjust judicial control so as not to impede administrative efficiency and not to place private rights and interests at the unrestricted mercy of arbitrary administrative action. [415]

The distinct growth of administrative law in the United States has been impeded by the Anglo-American unwritten constitutional principle of the rule of law and the American constitutional doctrine of the separation of powers and its corollary, the non-delegation of powers. Actually, the Founding Fathers, influenced by John Locke and Montesquieu, were concerned not with a functional separation but only with a departmental division of powers. Separation was to be an insurance against tyranny and was to reduce governmental encroachment generally by employing a three-way check. The result was a separation of departments but not of functions; no distributing clause providing for a separation of functions and powers was included in the Constitution.

Core of the rule of law is that all government officials are subject to the same laws and rules of conduct as are private citizens. The superior law may have been believed to be divine or natural law, or to have been derived from natural rights themselves based on natural law, vesting the governed with the authority to determine the nature and powers of government, which could perform its governing functions only with the consent of the governed. This consent, theoretically granted by social contract, is practically manifested in the establishment of a constitution, and is today reflected in popular elections, referenda, initiative, and recall.

A central feature of this type of doctrine and social system is individualism and its thesis that beyond a certain limited area government is an oppressive evil. This concept of limited government is part of the larger, general doctrine of laissez-faire economic society operating through free competition and freedom of contract. Expansion of governmental regulation and control of economic life has been persistently resisted and impeded by this doctrinal system.

Even Dicey, let alone Freund, was not blind to realities. Dicey acknowledged that "the rigidity of the law constantly hampers . . . the action of the executive." He admitted that "from the hard-and-fast rules of strict law, as interpreted by the judges, the government can escape only by obtaining from Parliament the discretionary authority which is denied to the Crown by the law of the land." [416] The turbulence of the twentieth century has caused the modification of many economic, political, and legal concepts and doctrines of the previous century. While Dicey was expressing thanks and hopes in 1915 that the rule of law would prevent the destruction of liberty by devilish administrative law, a significant case, *Local Government Board v. Arlidge* [417] that same year jolted him into realizing that the rule of law was bending before the inevitable demands and needs of life in modern industrial society.

When the independent regulatory commissions appeared, vested with varying authority over commercial, industrial, and labor phases of our society which were traditionally subject only to the ordinary prevailing laws of liability enforced in the ordinary courts, they promulgated rules and orders imposing many new obligations, often of a highly controversial nature. Consequently, to check and control these unprecedented grants of administrative authority and discretion and the imposition of new obligations cutting deeply into the orthodox doctrines of laissez-faire, free competition, and freedom of contract, direct judicial review through enforcement proceedings initiated by the administrative agency or through appeals instituted by the administrative agency or through appeals instituted by private individuals against administrative action was generally provided by statute and in several states by constitution. In addition, the writ of certiorari to obtain judicial review of administrative action was greatly expanded. With the growth of administrative power and activity,

Freund pointed out, there expanded legislative and judicial methods of controlling administrative action.

In every modern industrial state problems arise as to determining the extent to which the laws shall govern and limit the administrators and also the extent to which the administrators may formulate laws or exercise discretionary authority. Another problem, especially true of the United States, is the extent to which the courts are to intervene in administration. Since constitutions and statutes cannot act of themselves, in the face of an arbitrary act by an administrator the law must be supported by some enforcement body which will presumably cause the law to prevail. Accordingly, in Anglo-American traditions the courts have assumed the role of special protector of the rule of law. Dicey's classic formulation of the doctrine, however, was probably never true in the rigid sense it demanded, and has long been modified in application. As a principle, nevertheless, it is still very much alive and judicially employed to direct—although many authorities in the field of public administration would say "misdirect"—the course of America's legal development.

Equality before the law with respect to the rule of law, Freund asserted, demanded that the law be administered fairly and impartially, without discrimination against, or prejudice in favor of, any political party, class, race, or religion.

The Rule of Law and Control of Administrative Action

Neither Freund nor Goodnow, remarked Nathan D. Grundstein in 1950, "acquiesced in the theory of the rule of law as expounded by Dicey, nor in its corollary of the inherent superiority of the common law over the civil law in dealing with administrative action." [418] Each, however, took a different view of how to control administrative action. Goodnow felt that with regard to the protection of private rights, the courts should prevail; for the implementation of public policy, the legislature should rule; and the attainment of governmental efficiency belonged to the administrative agencies themselves with the chief executive functioning as chief administrator.

Freund looked at the control of administrative action from the viewpoints of administrative hierarchy, administrative discretion, legislative principles, and judicial review. The first line of control was internal—the exercise of administrative authority and super- vision hierarchically. The second was the legislature, which should establish principles for the guidance of administrators and definite standards for reducing administrative discretion. As a final resort, where the others were either absent or had failed, the judiciary should assert control. In any event, as Nathan D. Grundstein ob- served: "But to Freund . . . discretionary administrative power executed by a hierarchically organized professional officialdom was less arbitrary than judicial control operating through the jury system. The administrative hierarchy emerges as the essen- tial instrument of control and policy review." [419]

Grundstein interestingly commented on two of Freund's major assumptions for the reduction of administrative discretion: (1) the tendency to develop and introduce sound administrative principles of action if professional, expert administrators staff the administrative agencies, and (2) the hope that the legislatures would draft legislation scientifically drawn by expert staffs setting clear principles and standards for the exercise of administrative power. The first assumption "has been by-passed by American administrative law and left to students of public administration. The second has only recently begun to come into its own in ad- ministrative law." [420]

Freund and Separation of Powers

Arthur H. Kent noted Freund's views on the separation of powers in these words in 1933:

> He foresaw that a breakdown of a governmental structure based upon a rigid doctrine of separation of powers was inescapable under the complex conditions with which our governments have had to deal. His chief concern from the beginning was that the nature of the changes which were taking place should be clearly understood; also that along with the growth of administrative powers there should be a concomitant development of princi- ples regulating their exercise and remedies adequate to control their arbitrary and abusive use in violation of private rights, contrary to the public interest. [421]

Administrative Finality and Jurisdictional Fact Theory

In the field of administrative law, one of the most perplexing doctrines is administrative finality, particularly with regard to jurisdictional fact theory. In his study of the subject, Forrest Revere Black in 1937 alluded frequently to Freund's many discussions of the doctrine.[422] To explain that jurisdictional fact theory has a different meaning in administrative law than in judicial proceedings, Black quoted Freund's remarks:

> Questions of fact in administrative determinations differ from like questions in judicial proceedings in two respects: in the latter, where the cause is one of general common law or equity jurisdiction, the question of fact is practically never a jurisdictional fact, but one submitted for decision, while administrative jurisdiction frequently presupposes the existence of the fact as a jurisdictional prerequisite; and notice and hearing is the normal judicial process, while administrative authorities may be authorized to proceed *ex parte,* or their action may be ministerial in the sense of being inconclusive if they proceed upon an erroneous assumption of fact. If the fact is a jurisdictional fact, if the proceeding is *ex parte,* or if the officer acts ministerially, the question of fact is open to judicial examination.[423]

That was Freund in 1928. Four years later the Supreme Court in *Crowell v. Benson* nearly echoed Freund's distinction.[424]

Freund's views on this doctrine had led him to criticize the Supreme Court's decision eight years earlier in *Ohio Valley Water Co. v. Ben Avon Borough* [425] as unworkable since it made the court an assessing authority; and, moreover, a question of value is a matter of opinion, and as long as the decision was fairly reached it should stand.[426] Eight years later Freund buttressed these arguments with another. If it is difficult to find the line between a reasonable and an unreasonable rate, it will pass the wit of commissions and courts to differentiate "unreasonably low but not confiscatory" from "so unreasonably low as to be confiscatory," assuming that the maximum rate or return in accordance with due process has never been fixed.[427]

Administrative Checks

The reliance on judicial control to limit and restrain administrative action was accepted in America from the start. Administrative checks and balances, lacking the power of the courts and limited in their spheres of activity, were not looked to here with the same status they enjoyed in Europe. The comptroller's audit, for example, strictly intended as a fiscal control, in Europe was a function of the central government and operated as a check on municipal action. Observed Freund in 1932: "There are a few indications that state administrative control over municipal action is being considered in American legislation; but there are many political obstacles to its full development. It must indeed be questioned whether self-government of the American type, with political appointment and tenure of office, can, save under very exceptional conditions, produce adequate administrative checks." [428]

TORT CLAIMS

Freund was concerned about the responsibility of the states for the errors and misconduct of their administrative officials and wrote his first study of the subject in 1893. [429] "So long as access is denied to the courts, a substantive law cannot be developed. The practice of legislative relief by special acts is an unsafe guide." State law, which appeared meager at the time, "must make the state liable for the consequences of governmental errors, particularly in the preservation of peace and the administration of justice," but this would "probably require carefully formulated measures dealing with specific conditions." [430]

If the administrative process in itself "falls short of what due process may seem to demand, the application of common law remedies (mandamus, official liability, etc.) by way of correcting the administrative process may supply the defect." Mandamus and certiorari were the main remedial writs provided by the common law; "but the courts cannot remedy every defect of the common law, and particularly the harsh operation of official liability cannot be relieved without corresponding hardship to private rights." Adequate relief, in the latter event, "may depend upon the legislative substitution of the corporate liability of municipal or state government." [431]

When the Federal Tort Claims Act was passed by Congress in 1933 after nearly ten years of effort, it carried into effect "the principles of a just and sound public policy advocated by Ernst

Freund in 1893".[432] These principles were enunciated by Freund in an article in the *Political Science Quarterly* which contained the following concluding statement:

> A tort committed in the exercise of governmental functions creates no private cause of action against the state; where a liability is demanded by justice, it must be created by statute.
>
> A tort committed in connection with private relations should give rise to a corresponding civil liability, with such statutory exceptions as may be dictated by public policy. This is not the recognized law, but seems to be demanded on general principles.[433]

Regrettably, Freund died less than a year before the Federal Tort Claims Act was passed. "It is one of the many misfortunes associated with the passing of Ernst Freund," wrote Edwin M. Borchard, "that he did not live to see the fruition of his scholarly efforts." [434]

COORDINATION OF STATE AND LOCAL ACTION

The growth of regulative legislation has not been confined to any one level of government, nor has such expansion been uniform and harmonious. In fact, state and city frequently compete with or oppose each other over administrative power. "What is needed . . . is some statutory provision for co-ordination of state and local action," wrote Freund in *Public Management* [435] in 1931 after the decision by the Supreme Court of Illinois in the case of *Chicago Motor Coach Co. v. Chicago,*[436] which involved a clash between the State of Illinois and the City of Chicago over the power to designate transportation routes and to fix terms and conditions of operation.

Control of public utilities was largely a city function in the nineteenth and early twentieth centuries; but after World War I it shifted strongly to the state, incurring the resentment of advocates of home rule. The creation or strengthening of state commissions regulating public utilities does not automatically justify the supersession of city authority, Freund contended, simply because the state stepped in at a later date. It was this chronology that served as the basis for the court's ruling. "But state control," commented Freund, "can justify itself only if the most scrupulous consideration is given to just local claims that can be reconciled with legitimate state authority." Freund's concluding remarks are still timely:

> For historical reasons, state administration and city administration operate without regard to each other. In view of changing conditions, there ought to be some organic relation between the two. The detailed working out of this relation should be regarded as one of the major problems of state and local government.[437]

HOME RULE FOR CITIES

"The movement toward home rule," Freund wrote in *Public Management* in 1932, is "a corrective of an undue limitation of power. But so long as the fundamental concept of local government remains what it is, many legal processes and legal sanctions must remain withdrawn from local control, and important legal functions will continue to be directed by state legislation." [438]

Contrasted with European systems in which general laws were supplemented by executive ordinances, in the United States the entire task was assumed by the state legislatures. "The want of powers of direction and control in higher executive authorities is thus the real cause of the administrative over-activity of our legislatures, with its attendant evils. These evils appear in their worst form in the legislative interference with local self-government, especially in cities." [439] Freund saw the need for classifying localities and to legislate for each class. That exceptionally large cities might best be classified separately and legislated for thereby individually was suggested by Freund as a practical solution short of constitutional restrictions of legislative power. The great evil to be avoided is for the legislature to become the central administrative authority of the state, for then not only might the legislature intervene in every affair of the localities but it could do so irresponsibly and without judicial redress.

Freund often stressed the need for strengthening the municipal law department as a factor in controlling local government and administrative action. In the large cities a permanent staff should be built up which would acquire special training and experience in handling problems of municipal law. "It would be easy to name well-known legal experts that have had their training in municipal service, but there are not enough of them and they do not make their influence felt as they should." [440]

Chicago's municipal charter at the turn of the century was a voluminous document containing over 600,000 words with minute details on the authority of governmental agencies and public officials. Freund severely criticized the document in lectures and writings, maintaining primarily that it impeded home rule and often rendered the city powerless to perform its essential regulatory responsibilities. Observed Freund:

> Since practically every charter, being a binding state law, constitutes in the absence of saving clauses a limitation, it follows that the volume of a charter is generally in an inverse proportion to the home rule which it bestows.[441]

This view of Freund's was incorporated into one of the major themes of Barnet Hodes' pioneering *Law in the Modern City* which appeared five years after Freund's death.[442]

The police power clause in the proposed Chicago Charter Act of 1907 reflected the influence of Freund; and the home-rule article of the Illinois Constitution of 1920 was largely drafted by Freund. In fact, when the Illinois constitutional convention convened in 1920 to revise the State constitution, the City of Chicago retained Freund as its special counsel to formulate proposals to provide for the City's future growth needs. Leo F. Wormser described Freund's participation at the convention as follows:

> After months of painstaking deliberation in drafting the portion of the constitution directly affecting Chicago, after patient discussions with groups that represented every phase of civil thought, after tolerant appraisal of all criticisms and suggestions, this man, whose gentility of manner and modesty of presence is vivid before us even now . . ., appeared before the delegates and spectators that filled the convention hall in Springfield. He proposed that Chicago should "possess for all municipal purposes full and complete power of local self-government and corporate action." Instantly he became the target of attacks. Men, spurred by sectional feeling or political aims, assailed him as an impractical visionary, derided him as a fanciful professor. He restated his views with courteous deference but with learned authority. . . . The force of his intellect, the integrity of his character, and the charm of his personality triumphed. The majority rallied to him. His provisions granting home rule to Chicago, were adopted as proposed! [443]

In 1935 Albert Lepawsky's *Home Rule for Metropolitan Chicago* was published urging new home-rule measures for Chicago. His recommendation was that "the plan of Professor Freund proposed to the Illinois Constitutional Convention in 1920" should be followed.[444]

SOME OBSERVATIONS ON CENTRALIZED AUTHORITY, ACCOUNTABILITY, AND EFFICIENCY

Freund's expertness in constitutional and legal areas led to his appointment to a score or more of governmental commissions over his lifetime. Also, because of his non-partisanship his advice was sought by a host of leaders of private organizations in many fields, particularly on proposed or enacted legislation, actions by administrative agencies, and decisions of courts on both the federal, state and local levels. The breadth and depth of his interests were evidenced, in addition, by the many references to Freund by prominent political scientists, especially in their writings on centralization of political authority, accountability of legislators and administrators, and efficiency and economy in government.

Centralization of Political Authority

In his study on *Federal Centralization* published in 1923, Walter Thompson relied heavily on Freund's writings. Noted Thompson: "A careful student of government, like Professor Freund, looks upon centralization of political authority in the United States as inevitable." [445] In fact, remarked Freund: "The consolidation of our own nation has proved our allotment of federal powers to be increasingly inadequate; and had it not been aided by liberal judicial construction, our situation would be unbearable. We live under an antiquated and intolerable system of apportionment." [446]

Accountability of Individual Legislator

Freund repeatedly cautioned that expanding government enabled the individual legislator and administrator to hide behind numbers, particularly the legislator in a two-house body. Writing on reapportionment as a political issue in Chicago and Cook County in the early 1920's, he observed: "Unfortunately, an obligation that can be carried into effect only by the action of a body is in the nature of things of imperfect operation so far as each individual member is concerned, and rests lightly upon his conscience, the more so when the body is a numerous one, and is a composite body consisting of two houses." [447]

Efficiency Versus Popular Control

Charles Grove Haines repeatedly warned of the growing conflict between the movement for efficiency in the management of political affairs and the primary American principle of popular control of government.[448] His major reliance for support in this was Freund, particularly the latter's article that appeared in the *American Political Science Review* in 1916 in which Freund wrote:

> Had a commission of economy and efficiency presided over American government from the beginning, it would tax the imagination to think of the millions that might have been saved from waste; but could there have been that spirit of individualism, that glamour of liberty, that made American institutions attractive to aliens coming to this country, and that made possible a national assimilation and consolidation which is without parallel in history? Surely, that is a political asset which no mere technical perfection of government could have won for us, and it warns us not to value the traditional essentials of American institutions too lightly.[449]

Accountability of Administration: To Legislature or Executive?

Writing on "The Law of the Administration in America" in the *Political Science Quarterly* in 1894, Freund differed with Frank J. Goodnow's view that "the centralization of local matters in the hands of an irresponsible central authority, i.e., the legislature," was due to the principle of enumeration—the absence of executive power unless statutory authority is expressly granted. Instead, Freund attributed the causes to be the principle of specialization—the "minute regulation of nearly all executive functions, so that they become mere ministerial acts" and the principle of the diffusion of executive power—the delegation of executive functions to a myriad of separate agencies.[450]

This early view of Freund's was shaped in a period when the

chief executive at the federal and state levels was not yet acknowledged to be chief administrator—when administration was held
to be accountable to the legislature rather than to the chief executive. It was not until President Theodore Roosevelt's term of
office that presidential responsibility for the administration was
asserted; but this assertion was denied and rejected by Congress.[451]
Some thirty years had to pass before Congress accepted such a
view.

Accordingly, Freund in the 1890's saw the legislature as directing administration, a position for which he felt it was "altogether
unfitted." He advocated executive direction not only because the
executive and the administrative agencies are most closely linked
by the nature of administrative action but "because the executive
authorities are subject to the control of the courts or to impeachment" while "the legislature is not amenable to any direct control." [452]

"Executive action," Freund asserted, "is in its nature responsible,
because the officer who directs is also bound to see how the
direction is carried out, and because the executive authorities
are subject to the control of the courts or to impeachment; legislative administration, however, is both legally irresponsible, because
the legislature is not amenable to any direct control, and morally
irresponsible, because it is beyond the capacity of a large body to
act intelligently on matters in which it has no interest. The only
safeguard lies in the fact that the chief executive has a voice in
legislation: as an organ of the legislative power he exercises the
functions which properly belong to his sphere, and his watchful-
ness is expected to check the action of the legislature." [453]

In administrative action the legislature "is limited to the granting
and withdrawal of powers and the imposition of duties" insofar
as its statutory power is concerned. However, the legislature
has other powers by which it can affect administration, such as
the powers of investigation, impeachment, taxation and appro-
priation. "Through these powers it exercises a strong political
control over the executive department of the government." [454]
Freund did not live long enough to see the enhancement of legislative control of administration by the power of investigation. Yet,
he foresaw the potential use of this power.

Accountability of the Counsel for An Independent Regulatory Commission

When the Interstate Commerce Commission in 1913 appointed Louis D. Brandeis to serve as special counsel in presenting the shippers' side in the case concerning the railroads' request for approval of increased rates, Freund wrote a personal letter to Brandeis expressing the hope that the latter would create a significant precedent in administrative law by making it clear that the counsel for an independent regulatory commission represents neither side of a particular economic controversy but purely the public interest. The letter, dated October 27, 1913, declared:

> I learn with great interest that the Interstate Commerce Commission has appointed you to act as counsel in the matter of the application of Eastern railroad companies for an increase of rates.
> In view of the fact that *The Commercial Chronicle* speaks of you as counsel for the opponents, and that this is, if not the first, yet the most conspicuous, instance of such an appointment, I venture to express the hope that you will set a precedent of importance in administrative law, and make it clear, whatever your conclusions, that a counsel of a quasi-judicial commission, as distinguished from counsel employed by a prosecuting department, represents not one side or the other of the controversy, but purely the public interest, which is the interest of justice to all concerned.[455]

Two and a half years later, when Brandeis was nominated by President Wilson to be an Associate Justice of the United States Supreme Court, Senator Albert Baird Cummins (Rep., Iowa) opposed the appointment on the grounds that Brandeis had admitted at the hearings conducted by the Interstate Commerce Commission in 1913 that the net revenues of the railroads were inadequate. Incensed, Freund wrote a letter to the editor of the *New York Times* criticizing Senator Cummins' position:

> Notwithstanding my admiration for Mr. Brandeis's legal ability and public spirit, I have so far not taken any part in the controversy over his appointment, since I have no first-hand knowledge of his professional activities upon which the charges against him purport to be based.
> I find, however, now that Senator Cummins supports his adverse report in the main by the position Mr. Brandeis took as

counsel for the Interstate Commerce Commission in the 5 per cent advance rate case. I quote from the report in this morning's *Chicago Daily Tribune:* "Insisting that Mr. Brandeis was employed 'to take the public side of the question,' Senator Cummins declares that his action in admitting in the closing argument that the new revenues of the railroads were inadequate was an offense against common morality and professional ethics."

Assuming this report to be correct, Senator Cummins, in my opinion, entirely misconceives the duties that were placed upon Mr. Brandeis in that connection. Having been interested in questions of administrative law for many years, I took the liberty, when Mr. Brandeis was appointed by the Interstate Commerce Commission to act in that case, to write him the following letter: [456]

Here Freund provided the full text of the letter dated October 27, 1913 and then continued:

> Senator Cummins appears to believe that Mr. Brandeis betrayed the interest that he was charged to represent. The parties to the controversy at the time were the railroad companies on the one side and the shippers on the other. The public interest was identified with neither of the two sides, but was simply the interest of justice and fair dealing, and this, I take it, was the spirit in which Mr. Brandeis conceived his duty.
>
> It would be of interest to learn the terms of Mr. Brandeis's appointment by the commission and of his acceptance, but we certainly have no right to assume that Mr. Brandeis was intended to aid the cause of the shippers any more than the cause of the railroads. If his professional record is as clear in all matters as it seems to be in this, the case against him is weak indeed.[457]

The Pursuit of Social Justice:

Involvement in Domestic Social Problems and World Affairs

CIVIL RIGHTS AND LIBERTIES

In Freund's conception of the evolution of modern legislative thought there corresponded man's own march to maturity. The highest goal and the mark of maturity was the sense of social justice and the will to act in its pursuit politically as well as economically and socially. As he saw this evolutionary process, there were five main phases: (1) the recognition of the right of personality; (2) the establishment of freedom of thought; (3) the repression of unthrift and dissipation; (4) the protection of public health and safety; and (5) the relief from social injustice.[458]

The theme of social justice repeated itself throughout Freund's life. It was not just a matter of charity, for he contributed to many charities and was a member and supporter of the Associated Jewish Charities of Chicago for about thirty years; but he also lectured at various such organizations' meetings and advised on the legal aspects of charity, child welfare, health and accident insurance, treatment of aliens, and alcoholism and drug addiction. A constant plea was that his audience, and particularly the educated, involve themselves in social causes and politics. Political careers, he decried, were much too often left to the corrupt and incompetent; it was high time for the decent and capable citizens to rid themselves of the idea that involvement in politics was incompatible with integrity and scholarship. If the state is not to be mastered by ignorance and corruption, Freund warned, it must be served by intelligence and decency.

Having been requested, from the beginning of his career, to serve on many governmental commissions under both Democratic and Republican administrations, Freund chose not to engage in partisan politics and run for political office. This decision did not prevent him, however, from pitching himself into the controversial issues of the day and anticipating other issues of the future. When Eugene V. Debs was convicted under the Espionage Act of 1917 and given a ten-year sentence that was upheld by the United States Supreme Court in 1919, Freund took issue with Justice Holmes who had delivered the Court's opinion.[459] In an article in the *New Republic* for May 3, 1919, Freund wrote:

> The cause of the government has gained nothing, while the forces of discontent have been strengthened, and have been given an example of loose and arbitrary law which at some time may react against those who have set it.[460]

In criticizing the government's case against Debs, who attacked World War I and our participation in it and was charged with the intention of obstructing military recruitment, Freund wrote in the *New Republic* in 1919: "So long as we apply the notoriously loose common law doctrines of conspiracy and incitement to offenses of a political character, we are adrift on a sea of doubt and conjecture." Always insisting on standards to avoid confusion and alienation, he asserted: "To know what you may do and what you may not do, and how far you may go in criticism, is the first condition of political liberty; to be permitted to agitate at your own peril, subject to a jury's guessing at motive, tendency and possible effect, makes the right of free speech a precarious gift." In a timely warning, Freund remarked: "Toleration of adverse opinion is not a matter of generosity, but of political prudence." [461]

Holmes read Freund's article and was hurt by the latter's severe criticism. In a letter to Sir Frederick Pollock, Professor of Jurisprudence at Oxford University, Holmes remarked that spring in Washington could have been so enchanting "if a glance at the *New Republic* had not thrown the customary gloom over life." [462]

In a hearing held on March 25, 1926 before the House Committee on Immigration, Freund appeared as one of the principal witnesses in opposition to the recommendations of Secretary of Labor James J. Davis requiring the registration of alien residents in the United States and extending the deportation laws to include many minor offenses as causes for expulsion from the country. Reported the *New York Times* the following day:

Professor Freund criticized the proposed Deportation bill, saying that to place the burden of proof of lawful entry on the alien was contrary to the traditions of British and American law, which presumed innocence until guilt was established.

He condemned the proposal to remove the present statutory limitation of five years so that aliens could be deported no matter how long they had resided in the United States, and the addition of such minor offenses as sheltering an alien subject to deportation as grounds for deportation.[463]

Three years later the Supreme Court upheld the denial of citizenship to pacifist Rosika Schwimmer.[464] Wasting no time, Freund criticized the Court's opinion on its legal reasoning and felt that it "should make a stronger appeal to militant patriots than to careful lawyers." [465]

When the government launched its raids on anarchists and communists in 1919-1920, seized, imprisoned, and tried them as criminals, and deported those among them who were aliens, Freund vigorously objected. Opposing the use of the law of October 6, 1918 to authorize such deportation, he observed that up to that time only aliens who entered illegally or who became delinquent, defective, or dependent were deportable. This "new departure in our law" permitted the deportation of any alien as a criminal, regardless of the length of his residence here, for advocating—not committing overt acts of—anarchism or communism.[466]

Shortly after Nicola Sacco and Bartolomeo Vanzetti were arrested in 1920 and charged with murder, Freund joined with Jane Addams, Felix Frankfurter, Robert Morss Lovett, and others to help secure a fair trial for the two immigrant Italian radicals. As a member of the national committee of the American Civil Liberties Union, Freund supported the New England Civil Liberties Committee which sponsored the defense of Sacco and Vanzetti. The two aliens were executed in 1927. Two years later, a survey was undertaken by the Boston magazine, *The Lantern,* to elicit the opinions of well-known attorneys, historians, philosophers, and political commentators as to whether they felt Sacco and Vanzetti were guilty and proven so in a fair trial. Freund's reply, prominently featured, was as follows:

So long as human judgment is fallible and so long as clearness of vision is liable to be warped by a conflict of loyalties, errors of justice will from time to time occur. However, the cause of justice is not lost so long as those who feel that errors have been committed will not cease to protest. The number of those who remain unconvinced of the guilt of Sacco and Vanzetti seems to be increasing rather than diminishing as time goes on. All honor, then, to those who keep the struggle for the vindication of their memory and of the integrity of Justice alive.[467]

Born in the United States but raised and educated in Germany, Freund looked on immigrants sympathetically and opposed generally restrictive immigration. "A policy of systematic restriction of immigration" he wrote in the *Social Service Review* of 1927, "is very likely to lead to legislative regulation of expulsion." [468]

Freund was equally suspicious of deportation legislation. "Deportation is at present perhaps the most conspicuous instance of the bureaucratic exercise of coercive power." [469] When a deportation bill was proposed in the 69th Congress in 1926, he maintained that it aimed to strike at anarchists and communists and extended deportation power without criminal conviction to officials below the rank of departmental secretary. "The extension of bureaucratic penal jurisdiction is not in itself a desirable thing, and it is to be hoped that Congress will not yield unduly to departmental pressure in that direction." Fearful of the vagueness of such terminology as "immoral purpose" governing the grounds for deportation, Freund warned that this "may be stretched to mean anything obnoxious to the official sense of moral or political propriety." [470] He wrote to the congressional committees concerned with the proposed legislation, pointed out various defects and recommended certain changes to eliminate ambiguity and complexity and to strengthen procedural safeguards for the individual. The "proper regard for sound standards of law and justice", he wrote, "would seem to demand a reconsideration at least of the outstanding blemishes of the proposed bill: the failure to discriminate in the definition of deportable acts; the absence of a power of remission; and the proposition to allow deportation without limit of time." [471]

These events disturbed Freund for many reasons, one of which was his lifelong urging of clear legislative standards defining the limitations of political liberties. "If political liberty had to look for its standards to the common law," he wrote in an article on "Freedom of Speech" in the *New Republic* in 1921, "it would have a precarious standing." [472] While he deplored the governmental attacks on political liberties, he nevertheless saw in those events the opportunity for the legal profession to press the legislatures to set the required standards defining the framework of such liberties. In Freund's words:

> Our legislatures . . . cannot be expected to act intelligently, unless there is abroad among the legal profession a sense of what both liberty and justice demand in the matter of political legislation. That sense was absent because there was no experience to awaken it. That experience has now come, and let it be hoped that if the inclination to repress freedom of utterance continues, it will be at least expressed in laws which advise the people of what is lawful and what is not. [473]

Freund's recommendation that legislatures spell out precisely the framework of permissible individual freedom was first expressed in 1892 in an article in *The Counsellor.* Discussing an English decision in the case of *Mogul Steamship Co. against McGregor, Gow & Co. and others,* rendered by the House of Lords in December, 1891, Freund remarked that "where . . . the statute interferes [with individual liberty] it should be in such a manner as to clearly indicate the unlawful elements of the offence and so as to avoid striking at permissible forms of combination or coercion." [474] Warning against hasty legislative intervention, particularly in the areas of civil rights and liberties, he urged, as a general principle, that legislatures study carefully and objectively the costs—economic and social—before intervening.

Freund's involvement in causes was a natural outgrowth of his economic views as a liberal. "Wealth is almost as essential to our civilization as safety, order, and morals." The acquisition of wealth is based on active individual effort, whereas safety, order, and morals can be secured by governmental restraint. Consequently, he held:

> Our economic system is essentially individualistic, and, more than that, is based upon peaceful struggle and conflict. An absolute governmental control over economic interests, similar to that over the interests of order, peace and security, would be possible only if with regard to the former as well as with regard

to the latter, equality were a desirable and practicable end, i.e.,
if the state were socialistic. Under existing conditions, governmental activity in the care and control of economic interests
must operate largely as interference and disturbance, as favoritism
or oppression.[475]

Freund was not a socialist. He believed that the society described
by socialists was a long way off:

> It may be true that ultimately there can be no conflict between
> the highest individual and the highest social interest, and the
> harmony of all interests is an ideal which every legislative
> measure professes to contemplate and to further. But until
> the conditions of that harmony are discovered, it must happen
> that genuine individual interests are made to yield not only
> to genuine social interests, but also to interests which while being
> put forward as social are not such in reality.[477]

The question then arises, according to Freund, whether the
particular action is justified as a valid exercise of the police power,
a power conceded to be constitutionally permissible only as a
means of promoting the public welfare. In our system of constitutional law the relation of private right to public welfare receives a
peculiar significance, through the power of the judiciary to
nullify legislation it regards as contrary to the Constitution.
Nevertheless, "If the fundamental law is to fulfil its purpose, it
should be flexible and yield to the changing conditions of society."
Although he insisted that liberalism's first principle must be
liberty—freedom of the individual in all his activities and relationships—he recognized that concepts of liberty varied. "What is
meant by liberty depends very much upon economic and social
ideas." [478]

Optimistic about America's democracy and educational oppor-
tunities, Freund saw that the expansion of the latter would enlarge the former. As increasing numbers of people become
educated they will demand broader and deeper freedoms of expression. As early as in 1904 he acknowledged that "the constitutional guaranty of freedom of speech and press and assembly
demands the right to oppose all government and to argue that
the overthrow of government cannot be accomplished otherwise
than by force." [479] Yet, he insisted that, if necessary, by protest
and pressure American democratic government does respond

and laws are enacted in the public interest. It was in one area of civil rights, however, that Freund was somewhat pessimistic—race. "Race alone," he wrote in 1916, "remains a sinister distinction which the law has not fully overcome." [480]

In an address delivered before the Illinois State's Attorneys Association in 1923, Freund analyzed at length the search and seizure laws of the United States, England, and Germany and also compared those of the Federal Government and various states in the United States. A question he posed then is still timely today in view of the Watergate and allied break-ins and burglaries: "Over and above all, is it not the permanent issue between maintaining law and order by sustaining convictions irregularly obtained, and maintaining law and order by insisting upon the observance of regular methods of law enforcement?" [481]

Freund's sense of social justice can be attributed, in part, to his Jewish upbringing. In an unpublished, undated, and holographic manuscript on "Jews in America," he highlighted the Jews' "respect for law," "liberality of . . . dogma," "fellowship with those struggling for emancipation," "fellowship of endeavor to relieve suffering," "intellectual force," "devotion to learning," and "traditions of democracy; no aristocracy but that of learning." In America, he observed, there is "the spirit of democracy, so essential to American institutions, for which Judaism has always stood." "Politically a good citizen of the country in which he lives," Freund pointed out, "the Jew is intellectually a citizen of the world." [482]

INTERNATIONAL LAW AND WORLD PEACE

All his professional life Freund advocated peace with honor and humanity and assailed militant, aggressive nationalism. At the end of the Spanish-American War, he wrote in the *Political Science Quarterly* in 1899:

> If the establishment of protectorates should be contemplated, it would be desirable that the treaty-making and legislative powers should adopt from the beginning a proper form in sanctioning the results of the war. It is far easier to refrain from assuming sovereignty than to relinquish sovereignty once acquired. Any phrase should, therefore, be avoided which would make the formerly Spanish islands, as Hawaii was made "a part of the terri-

tory of the United States and subject to the sovereign dominion thereof." A declaration that the "United States assumes the protection and control" of the different islands would answer the desired purpose, and would leave ample scope for the regulation of details.[483]

Four years later, in an essay on *Empire and Sovereignty,* Freund acknowledged the jealous assertion of sovereignty by all nations, but he rejected claims of "absolutely sovereign power" by any nation. All powers of government are limited, he insisted; and all nations must build up "the rule of law on the basis of compromise." [484]

In May, 1918 Freund again pleaded for a peace treaty which would take into account the realistic growth and strength of nationalism and contain sufficiently liberal provisions as to counteract militant and aggressive nationalistic impulses. "National self-determination" was less important to him than "reciprocal restraint" of nations. The latter he hoped would be "the watchword of the future." Realistic, however, he was not optimistic about nations surrendering sovereign rights after the war and creating a league of nations which would succeed in maintaining international peace. He urged that the charter of the proposed league be written to express "broad and flexible principles, rather than strict rights and obligations." [485] A year later, when the peace treaty was drafted and the League of Nations was formally proposed, Freund urged the creation additionally of an economic league of nations to neutralize the "unequality of natural resources." [486]

Analyzing Germany's new Weimar Constitution in 1920 shortly after its adoption, Freund was wary about its implementation. The provisions were socially advanced and "a positive gain to democracy," but a large section of conservative Germans would consider it too radical.[487] He was not wrong.

Freund was no easy joiner of causes and organizations. In a letter on May 18, 1922 to Mrs. E. M. Collier of the Chicago Council on Foreign Relations replying to a request to join, he wrote:

> In this day of numberless organizations appealing for adhesion, I do not join unless I am satisfied that I can be of service or that I am promoting some very useful and tangible end. . . .
> In inviting membership you should state at least something as to your fundamental principles: foreign policy issues are the most

vital and controversial with which the nation is confronted, and I should want to know in which direction the Council is steering. What is needed is not merely an open mind, but some theory of education and action.[488]

CLASSIFICATION OF CRIMES

Freund in 1915 was chairman of Committee D of the American Institute of Criminal Law and Criminology whieh prepared a pioneering report on the "Classification and Definition of Crimes." Other members of the committee were Stephen H. Allen, A. Bullard, Orrin N. Carter, William Healy, W.W. Hitchler, Joel D. Hunter, William M. Ivins, N.W. MacChesney, R.H. Marr, Adelbert Moot, and John B. Winslow. Written by Freund, the report "recognized that the proposed reclassification of crimes is too far reaching and presents too many controversial problems to constitute for the immediate future a practical legislative program; it is offered merely as a suggestion for consideration and criticism." Always urging the legislatures to seek out the advice and aid of the experts, Freund's report concluded:

A complete system of the relevant elements of guilt is . . . a prime desideratum of criminal law reform. As pointed out before, the problem of defining the elements to be specified as relevant in differentiation and of assigning to each its relative value in determining guilt and punishment is one for the solution of which the legislator must look to the trained criminologist.[489]

In his study of the classification of crimes, John W. MacDonald in 1933 repeatedly referred to Freund's writings on the subject. Particular mention was made of "Professor Freund's warning" [490] that the superiority of a written penal code over sporadic legislation "is jeopardized if there is a habit of either sporadic outside legislation dealing with crime, or of unsystematic and piecemeal code amendment." [491] This warning was ignored by many states and led to troublesome experiences.

Freund's observations on congestion in urban centers and juvenile delinquency and on the need for protecting the liberty of individuals charged with committing crimes caused him in 1915 to plead for a reclassification of crimes. He foresaw also the need for developing scientific systems of criminal statistics. However, when suggesting classification according to categories of the interest attacked or violated, his groupings did not reflect, in the opinion of Maurice Parmalee, "any consistent principle." [492] In any event, Freund's groupings were: (1) political offenses; (2) statute violations; (3) administrative crimes; (4) police offenses; (5) crimes against morality; and (6) common or ordinary crimes.[493]

Freund covered too many fields to be expert and comprehensive in all. However, this is generally true of pioneers—a point unwittingly ignored by Parmalee in his criticism of Freund's classification of crimes. The significance of Freund's effort was not that it was confused and lacked a consistent set of principles, as Parmalee observed probably correctly, but that such a necessary effort was even made at such an early date and by someone whose expertness lay elsewhere.

End of Era of
"Rugged Individualism":

Death of Freund and his Impact on the Future

TRIBUTES TO FREUND

Freund died October 20, 1932; and on Sunday afternoon, December 11, a memorial service was held at the chapel on the campus of the University of Chicago. The day was stormy with the snow blowing wildly across the campus midway, but the chapel was "completely occupied by the colleagues and friends of the honored professor of law, friends from many walks of life—former students, members of the bar, former associates in associations seeking the betterment of social conditions." [494]

Harry A. Bigelow, dean of the Law School, presided. The opening talk was delivered by Frederic Woodward, vice-president of the University; and he was followed by Jane Addams of Hull House and Leo F. Wormser. Woodward stressed the personal qualities of Freund.

> From the beginning Professor Freund was a striking figure in the school. His . . . courses gave breadth to the curriculum and his marked individuality added a delightful tang to his teaching. . . . He was frequently consulted by judges, by legislative committees, and by other public officers, who recognized not only his mastery of the law but his understanding of social problems and the disinterestedness of his service—disinterested except for his sympathy with the underprivileged and his passion for justice. [495]

Jane Addams, with whom Freund had worked closely in the social service area, then spoke of Freund as "the friend and guide of social workers," pointing out that he "had much to do with the founding of the School of Social Service Administration of the University of Chicago, the first graduate school of its kind."

147

What Freund wanted and hoped for was that the School of Social Service Administration would "engage in projects of fundamental social research which would in the end develop cooperation between legal scholars and those most cognizant of life where it presses hardest and most unfairly upon those at the bottom." "Cognizant of legal systems in all parts of the world, he looked upon the administration of the law as subject to social readjustments, and he made the social worker feel that honest work on his part was essential to the growth of progressive legal enactments." [496]

Miss Addams recounted particularly Freund's contributions to the improvement of the social and legal status of the illegitimate child and also of the alien immigrant. "He never once failed to be sensitive to injustice and preventable suffering." "Professor Freund always anticipated the day when he might see the immigration service concerned to help the friendless aliens, instead of merely trying to deport them, an anticipation which every settlement of Chicago shared." [497]

Miss Addams' concluding remarks appropriately depicted Freund:

> He was probably the finest exponent in all Chicago of the conviction that as our sense of justice widens it must be applied to new areas of human relationships or it will become stifled and corrupt. A man possessing this passion for justice, this appetite for its new applications, is a great asset to any community, but when this passion is combined, as in the case of Professor Freund, with a scholar's legal knowledge and with a mind sensitive to social growth and change, we may indeed be grateful, and consider his loss irreparable.[498]

Last speaker at the memorial service was Leo F. Wormser, a former student of Freund who was a leading member of the Chicago bar. Keenly assessing Freund's role as activist philosopher, Wormser remarked: "A philosopher may peer into other worlds but must not fail to help his own." "Ernst Freund did not treasure his learning for his own sake but as an influence in human affairs, his scholarship not as an end but as a force in the commonwealth. To him the mastery of principles of law was an incomplete accomplishment until dedicated to the progress of society." [499] The dominant conviction which permeated Freund's adult life and all his work was "that educated citizenship has an obligation to enrich human welfare and enlarge human liberty." [500]

Wormser concluded his eulogy with the following remarks:

> While many good men sit at home not knowing that there is anything to be done, nor caring to know, cultivating the feeling that politics are dirty and that government is ruled by vulgar politicians, Ernst Freund remembered that, if the government is not to be mastered by ignorance, it must be served by intelligence. He deemed no sophistry more poisonous to the state and no folly more demoralizing than the notion that education is incompatible with public service.[501]

In May, 1933, seven months after Freund's death, the University of Chicago Law School created its own law review and dedicated the first issue "to the memory of Ernst Freund." [502] Included also were two articles on Freund as a teacher of legislation [503] and his work in the field of legislation.[504] In the former, Maurice T. Van Hecke emphasized Freund's "modesty . . . old-world courtliness, his gentle kindness, his spirited gayety and quick humor, his tremendous intellectual vigor, and the universality of his scholarship." [505]

Freund's courses on statutes and administrative law were "peculiarly his own creation." He swept the students "from the German Civil Code to the English Acts of Parliament, to the Statutes at Large of the Congress and into the myriad session laws and statute books of the several states." The students "were placed in the position of legislators or draftsmen facing prospectively a problem." "Policies had to be determined, the appropriate devices discovered with which these policies could be best expressed and their administration and enforcement facilitated." Those students of his who went on to engage in drafting legislation were "grateful . . . for the master who gave the impetus and the direction." [506]

Having been a political scientist before he became a teacher of law, Freund combined the two subject areas in his courses. The exercise of power by government through its various branches and levels was his main concern. When the University of Chicago Law School was planned, its president, William Rainey Harper, desired to build it as a purely scientific school of jurisprudence for scholarly research. Freund, on the other hand, urged that it be established as a sound professional school to attract, in addition to attorneys, government officials, political scientists and social workers and to train practitioners. Freund was successful, and the emphasis on the legislative process as well as the judicial process helped lead to the school's soaring popularity and outstanding reputation.

Freund recognized the limitations of the case method of teaching law. "As early as 1915 he was saying what was then heresy but has since become a slogan: that the effectiveness of the case method of legal instruction begins to decline about the middle of the student's second year. He longed to supplement with other methods and other materials." By the 1920's and early 1930's the emphasis in the teaching of law had shifted to Freund's views and methods; but then he feared the new movement's "high-pressure salesmanship, with its blare and its extravagant pretenses." Nevertheless, he lived to see Congress and most of the state legislatures take on the services of legislative drafting experts, "only to regret that more of the draftsmen were not as expert as they were expected to be"; and he lived to see the law schools' courses and literature in statutes expand, but "he suffered because for the most part his young colleagues in the field proved incapable of seeing the woods for the trees." [507]

In his work in the field of legislation, Freund early realized "the dependence between mastery of legislative technique and understanding of social science data in the legislative process." "If only time can fully reveal the extent of his influence and the enduring values in his work," Arthur H. Kent eulogized, "none will doubt the freshness and the stimulating qualities of his mind, the thoroughness of his scholarship, his high professional ideals, his strong sense of public responsibility, and his passion for social justice. When shall we see his like again?" [508] Kent further observed in one of the few articles written on Freund, that Freund's death had "deprived American legal scholarship of a creative thinker and profound scholar. It is a loss in which all who are interested in the progress of thought and the study of human institutions must share, particularly social scientists, with whom he shared so many interests and whose achievements he so greatly valued and admired." [509]

Memorialized the *Social Service Review:*

> Professor Freund was a great legal scholar whose interest in social work had endeared him to a wide circle of the readers of this *Review*. He contributed for our first number an article entitled "Deportation Legislation in the Sixty-ninth Congress," which was so greatly in demand that it was finally reprinted for distribution among members of Congress who were then considering more stringent deportation regulations.
>
> He was sensitive to injustice and preventible suffering, and from the beginning of the movement for the protection of immigrants he was active in every effort in its behalf. . . . . He was at all times an expert counselor both on questions of national policy and on the problems of individual human beings and their difficulties. He testified before congressional committees, where his great reputation as a legal authority, his judicial temper, and his fine sense of human justice always commanded respect for the cause he advocated.[510]

William A. Robson in the English *Law Quarterly Review,* recalling his friendship with Freund, described him as "personally a most charming man: gay, humorous, open-hearted, hospitable and in every way a delightful companion." Freund's treatises, he observed, revealed "an inexhaustible industry, a remarkable capacity for inventive classification, and a power of subtle and penetrating analysis." "The works are, indeed, analytical rather than interpretive; and one sometimes wished Freund had attempted to formulate some body of conclusions at the end of his fine-spun web of conceptual exposition." [511]

Noted the *American Political Science Review:*

> A profound scholar, a distinguished authority on constitutional and administrative law and legislation, and an inspiring teacher, Professor Freund had a far-reaching influence in academic circles and on public affairs. Legislative committees, congressional committees, and constitutional conventions called on him for counsel, and his legal scholarship, judicial temper, and sense of human justice commanded respect for any cause he advocated.[512]

As W. Ivor Jennings of England acknowledged: "The great quality which Ernst Freund brought to the study of administrative law was his capacity for analysis. He was the Austin of the jurisprudence of administrative law." [513] While this was Freund's great strength, Jennings stated, it also reflected his weakness—the failure to produce conclusions for solving problems. Freund was not unaware of this, as he conceded in his *Legislative Regulation:* "The mechanism and structure of the written law is clearly a monopoly of legal science, and it is this technique which forms the subject-matter of the present study; it is not liable to be confused with other social sciences; but it can contribute little to the problem of substantive standards except in the subsidiary details of enforcement and similar provisions." [514] However, Jennings was hardly accurate in thus judging Freund, for a comprehensive study of Freund's writings and lectures indicate that he did not separate legal science from politics. He urged the coordination of legislators, political scientists, and legal philosophers and practitioners in solving problems, and he suggested solutions, many of them far ahead for his times. If any point was stressed by Freund, it was the necessity of treating the law as a whole.

In devoting more than a page to Freund's life, the *American Law School Review* remarked:

> Coupled with a keen and inquiring mind, he had a breadth of information, an individuality in point of view, and a keen feeling for social justice that made his work and contributions of unusual value. . . . His variety of interests, his understanding and sympathy, his originality of viewpoint coupled with a good humored toleration of the viewpoint of others, made him a man whose company was everywhere sought.[515]

The *Illinois Bar Journal,* which for so many years recorded the many activities of Freund especially those concerned with state and municipal affairs, asserted: "He ranked as one of the greatest American legal scholars and his passing is a great loss, both to the Law School and to legal education in general." [516]

Perhaps Justice Felix Frankfurter summed it up most appropriately in 1954 when he initiated the Ernst Freund lecture series at the University of Chicago Law School. Stressing Freund's great breadth of interests and knowledge, including music and painting, and also his "great kindliness," Frankfurter remarked:

> I have come here tonight as an act of pious gratitude to a great teacher of the law, Ernst Freund. That is the only reason, mingled as it is with my close feelings for the University of Chicago Law School—indeed, it is because Freund was the father of the Law School—that I am here tonight. . . .

I don't think I ever met anybody in the academic world who more justly merited the characterization of a scholar and a gentlemen than did Ernst Freund. . . . Unlike many scholars of courtesy and kindliness, he was a man of strong convictions. But in his case passion was behind his judgment and not in front of it. . . .

Ernst Freund was a scholar and not a pedant. His specialized competence in the field in which he was a master and . . . a pioneer was set in the context of a wide and deep culture. . . .

He was a pioneer in two domains which, until his coming, were non-existent in our legal scholarship, namely, administrative law and legislation. . . .

Ernst Freund brought to the American world of learning the realization that something was going on right under their eyes unattended to: administrative law. And, while in the beginning, for him, administrative law was the control of administrative agencies by the courts, he came soon to see that administrative law also described the controls exercised by the administrative agencies. . . .

As to both administrative law and legislation, Freund was not one of those people who thought that what is now called the "social sciences" should be added to the law. He was not for "integrating" law with the social sciences. He was aware and insisted upon the interdependence between law and the social sciences and the social sciences and law. . . .

His deep insight that law draws upon the forces of society and does not exist outside them; that law is an endeavor to accommodate these forces of society, to express them, to further them, to thwart them, more or less, in some ways, I think could easily be demonstrated by a reading of his important and influential book on the *Police Power,* published in 1904. The awareness that he then showed in construing certain provisions of the Constitution better anticipated the future than did the decision of the Supreme Court of the United States the next year in the notorious *Lochner case.* . . .

It is well worth recalling that he was one of those voices crying in the wilderness about things that we now take for granted as though they had fallen like manna from heaven. . . . Men like Holmes and Freund do not solve problems by jargon, by catchwords. They let lesser epigoni do that for them. Freund was a writer who deeply influenced the course, the current, and the forces of legal and sociological scholarship and thought and the world of adjudication, in the slow way that the world of adjudication is influenced by wisdom from without.[517]

Frankfurter's tribute was the greatest of all, for the two men whose parents were born in Europe were both in love with America's freedoms and rights and were concerned with the impact of the industrial and technological revolutions on legislation and administrative law. To Freund, the concept of social justice was even more deeply ingrained; and underlying this concept was the American ideal of equality. To Freund equality meant equal opportunity and treatment under the law; and equality was, as Wormser correctly appraised Freund's works, "the surest and in the long run, the only possible guaranty of liberty." [518]

Freund shared with Lincoln, Holmes, Brandeis, and Cardozo the vision of America as mankind's best hope on earth. As Teutonic as he was in manner and style, so was Freund democratic and American in his feelings. He felt no superiority for having been schooled in Germany. In fact, as early as 1892, in comparing the American and German bars, he asserted that while "the Bar in Germany shows a higher average of character and learning than here, . . . it is quite certain that the leaders of the German Bar are not superior, if indeed they are equal, in ability, to our foremost lawyers." [519] Never resorting to mockery, Freund could not refrain from contrasting the free, informal American style of life with the disciplined and military-oriented, ceremonial style of Germany. This he exemplified by pointing out that at the University of Munich successful candidates for the degree of *Doctor juris utriusque* would appear "girt with a sword at the final ceremony." [520]

CONCLUSION: THE POST-FREUNDIAN ERA AND THE REDISCOVERY OF FREUND

Freund died shortly before the 1932 election of Franklin D. Roosevelt to the Presidency. With the deepening of the depression, "rugged individualism" was discarded for a largely government-controlled economy; and Freund's twenty-five-year-old prediction that someday the state would take an active part in readjusting the scheme of production and consumption came true. Many new administrative agencies were created, and administrative powers were greatly enlarged and administrative discretion vastly increased. Accordingly, by 1936 political scientists were questioning Freund's prediction that in time the legislature would formulate rules to reduce and displace the discretion of administrators. Writing in the *Political Science Quarterly* that year, Charles S. Hyneman urged: "It is high time to question whether this hope of ultimate detailed statutory regulation is not largely vain and illusory." [521] Yet, three years later, concern grew over the great expansion of administrative powers and demand arose to limit and control such powers and to ensure fair procedures. At a symposium on administrative law conducted by the Law School of George Washington University in 1939, Edwin Blythe Stason praised the "inquisitorial powers of administrative agencies" for effectiveness on the one hand and warned of the need for their control on the other.[522] The following year, at a symposium on administrative law and procedure held at the Washington University School of Law, discussions heatedly posed questions and problems of administrative justice, with special emphasis on uniform administrative procedures guaranteeing due process, and raised criticism of the merging of the prosecuting and trial functions within the same administrative agencies.[523]

In the 1930's and 1940's, the emphasis in public law shifted to questions of administrative procedures, and the main battleground of administrative law literature centered on the subject of review of administrative determinations.[524] The tendency which began in the 1940's to respect administrative determinations advanced far beyond Freund's times. Notwithstanding the evidence presented by the other side, by 1941 the trend, reported J. Roland Pennock, was to uphold an administrative decision if it was supported by "substantial evidence." [525]

Also by 1941, a large section of the bar in the United States had become fearful of what Roscoe Pound called "administrative absolutism." [526] Fanned by President Franklin D. Roosevelt's veto of the Walter-Logan Bill sponsored by the American Bar Association and by publication of the *Report of the Attorney General's Committee on Administrative Procedure,* leading members of the bar expressed in extreme terms their opposition to an administrative justice separate from judicial justice. Pound led this opposition and organized a symposium on administrative law for the American Bar Association. Particularly incensed at President

Roosevelt's veto message in which he urged that the judicial process be confined to cases "appropriate for its exercise," Pound went far beyond Freund's warnings on administrative discretion and insisted that administrative tyranny would seize the country unless the judicial process prevailed in cases of administrative action. President Roosevelt further infuriated the accusers of "bureaucratic tyranny" and "administrative absolutism" by his attempt to remove the chairman of the Federal Trade Commission on grounds none other than differences in economic philosophy.[527]

In 1946, Congress passed the Federal Administrative Procedure Act which separated the legislative and judicial functions in administrative agencies. The former was termed "rule-making" and the latter "adjudication." Different procedures were prescribed for these functions with regard to questions of notice and hearing; and the investigative and prosecuting functions were separated from those of adjudication. Further, the Act extended judicial review generally to administrative action.[528]

Thomas I. Emerson in 1947 observed that the rapid development of administrative law "seems now to have reached a point of relative equilibrium." "The two major factors accounting for the growth of the administrative process—New Deal legislation and World War II—have spent their force. By and large, the judiciary has adjusted itself to the situation." [529] The demand for fair, uniform procedures guaranteeing due process had been met with the passage of the Federal Administrative Procedure Act.

By the 1950's the heated debate of the late 1930's and 1940's over the issue of administrative action and due process, "one of the most heated political controversies in our history," in the words of Ferdinand F. Stone asserted during an administrative law symposium in 1952 at the University of Miami Law School, ". . . has largely cooled." [530] "A current development like the legislative codification and standardization of administrative procedure," noted Nathan D. Grundstein in 1950, "was always implicit in Freund's analysis." [531] However, such administrative action as investigation and rule-making had achieved a far greater public acceptance by that time than had the judicial functions. As Roscoe Pound observed in 1956: "Administrative justice as a substitute for judicial justice is not the path of general reform which it was once thought to promise. But there is ample room for an American administrative law developed from experience of what bureaus and commissions and agencies have achieved and are beginning better to achieve in their regulatory functions." [532]

The pressing problem of the 1950's on into the 1970's in the administrative process has been that of the selection and retention of higher-caliber administrators. Human relations, motivation, education and training, and moral and ethical standards have become key matters in administration. This is a far cry from the early search by administrative law for legitimacy and acceptance.

The law governing the organization, procedures, interpretive rules and regulations, and policy and decision making was not stressed by Freund but is stressed today. What Freund emphasized was the law which "impinges upon, governs, and restricts agencies, and is found in constitutional, legislative, executive, and judicial pronouncements." [533] Kenneth Culp Davis noted that "the theory of separation of powers . . . has hardly any influence upon administrative arrangements or activities." The problems of delegation are tending to disappear from federal law and are of sharply diminishing importance in state law." Instead, the "heavy emphasis is now upon the administrative process itself—rule making and adjudication, and such incidental powers as investigating, supervising, prosecuting, advising, and declaring." [534] Reginald Parker wrote in 1957: "Yet, while administrative law has become an accepted part of our legal system, its necessary scope is not well settled and it appears that it never will be, since such a settlement depends on political considerations though they be clothed in legal arguments." [535]

In 1958, Charles S. Rhyne, then President of the American Bar Association, warned in a symposium on federal administrative practice and procedure held by Ohio State University's Law School that the Federal Administrative Procedure Act "has been whittled away and eroded until today it stands as a worn monument on a mighty battlefield, pockmarked by the many skirmishes which have taken place since 1946." Blaming both the administrative agencies and the courts, Rhyne charged that "this misconstruction of congressional intent" had resulted in virtually eliminating "the basic rights and guarantees of fair treatment for everyone who comes before, or into contact, or contest with federal administrative agencies." [536] The reforms recommended involved creating a new administrative code providing for more effective public information on the administrative process; improving rule-making by requiring formal hearings; tightening the rules of evidence in formal hearings; expanding and improving judicial review of agency proceedings; establishing an office of administrative practice to coordinate inter-agency rules of procedure and public information; creating a division of hearing commissioners and a division of legal services; and creating special courts, as part of the judicial system, to adjudicate administrative controversies such as labor, taxation, and combinations in restraint of trade. Rhyne's concluding remark was most appropriate in view of Freund's similar expressions as far back as the 1890's. "No lawyer," Rhyne warned, "can afford to be uninformed in the great and growing area of administrative law." [537]

In the 1930's the opposition to the expansion of administrative powers was led by those who decried substantively governmental regulation of economic and social activities. In the 1940's the opposition was led largely by attorneys who accepted such regulation but urged the judicialization of the administrative process on procedural grounds to ensure fairness. "Today," observed Melvin G. Shimm in 1961 in a symposium on administrative law conducted by Duke University's Law School, "the administrative process is once more undergoing a strenuous siege of examination and evaluation—this time, in terms of the extent to which it has, in practice, realized the hopeful expectations of its early champions. This latter-day criticism has covered a broad spectrum of charges—inefficiency, undue delay and expense, prejudgment of controversies, absence of clear rules, *ex parte* influences, capture by regulated industries, lack of expertise, excessive power of staffs, inadequate personnel, corruption, and lack of coordination." [538]

Reporting on the state of research in American administrative law, Edwin Blythe Stason pointed out in 1964 that what yet had to be done were: (1) the development of standards defining precisely the rule-making powers; (2) the formulation of standards prescribing clearly and usefully the jurisdictional limits and the factual bases of quasi-judicial decisions of administrative agencies; and (3) the setting of guiding standards which would define the terms and conditions for the exercise of administrative discretion. These needs are wholly in the spirit and letter of Freund; and when Stason clinched his remarks with the warning that the absence of "guiding standards" would lead to "opening the door to unlimited administrative discretion and to conditions that bear no relevance to the basic intent of Congress" [539] one was assured that Freund lives on.

As Francis A. Allen observed in 1965, Freund's "writing still possesses the power to stimulate thought and to illuminate contemporary issues." [540] The main reason for such "continuing relevancy" [541] was Freund's constant search for general principles and standards governing legislative and administrative action. He sought for over forty years to relate the law and administration to a broader base of rational, social theory. His primary preoccupation was not with creating practical guides for attorneys engaging in litigation. Although Freund described *The Police Power,* for example, as a "practitioner' handbook," [542] even there the theoretical concerns far outweighed the practitioner's interests and needs.

Not all of Freund's predictions have come true. His prediction that in time as the legislatures became experienced and utilized hired staffs of technical experts to help draft more precise legislation and formulate more definite standards, there would be a "gradual and rather unconscious drift . . . toward displacement of discretion" in the exercise of administrative powers [543] and they would take back their broad delegations of policy decision power from the administrative agencies has not proved true. Many decades have passed, and the administrative agencies have developed stronger than ever before. The power of the legislatures, too, has grown; and, bearing out Freund's prediction, legislatures have expanded their investigative authority and functions, strengthened their committees, increased the number of subcommittees, and enlisted permanent staffs of experts to assist in drafting bills and investigating.

Freund had counted on, as "proof" for this view, the example of navigation administration in which early discretionary power was displaced in time by ministerial authority.[544] It was in 1928, shortly before the depression and the ensuing expansion of administrative discretion, in his *Administrative Powers Over Persons and Property,* that he made his strongest assertion of his belief in the legislatures gaining sufficient experience in economic regulation to reassume leadership in policy decisions and to reduce the delegation of such power to administrative agencies.[545] By 1950, James Willard Hurst, assessing this view, concluded: "Twenty years' subsequent experience did not support his prediction. However, this did not mean that the legislature had grown weaker in that time. Rather, its partnership with the administrators had strengthened its capacity to deal with contemporary issues." [546] However, Freund's conjunctive recommendation that the legislatures should strengthen their committees and provide themselves with permanent staffs of experts to investigate and to draft bills has come true, although at the federal level it was not until 1946 that Congress recognized this need and passed the Legislative Reorganization Act.

That Freund was over-optimistic in his prediction that generally standards would gradually replace administrative discretion can be enjoyed as a present judgment. Yet, he fully believed there was a strong trend toward such standardization "with a small residual margin for flexibility which approximates the inevitable question of fact." This trend, Freund asserted, was inevitable because the very function of discretion was to prepare the way for rule rather than to replace it.[547]

Most commentators have agreed that "unguided discretion" is invalid and should be avoided as a violation of due process and equal protection. When is discretion "unguided" has not been easily defined. Apparently, the principle followed is that where the economic activity regulated is essentially lawful in character, discretion is less supportable; and where the activity is more a privilege than a property right, discretion should be reduced or eliminated. Yet, even this is disputable.[548]

Freund, wrote Arthur H. Kent shortly after the former's death, "was disqualified by temperament and innate modesty to play the part of a noisy proponent shouting from the housetops a new gospel." "He was the less showy, but not the less certain and effective, influence of the stimulating teacher firing generations of students with a new spirit, the productive and creative scholar, the efficient and public-spirited member of constitutional conventions, legislative drafting committees, and social welfare groups." [549]

"Conservative by temperament," Kent characterized Freund, "he was a vigorous and powerful supporter of some of the most forward-looking legislative measures of his day." [550] Freund's search for general principles and broad social theory prevented him from regarding law as the study of judicial behaviorism; but neither did he regard it as sterile intellectual exercising. His views were closer to those of the functionalists in his contentions that society was constantly in flux and that, as an instrument of social control, the essential purpose of law was to serve society and to help society meet the necessary changes orderly and lawfully. In order to perform this function effectively and peaceably, the law must rest on a broad, solid foundation of social reality. As for his own role in this context, Freund sought to discover and formulate a body of general principles to govern the legislature and the administration in creating law which would appropriately fulfill this social function.

Woodrow Wilson and Frank J. Goodnow distinguished between politics and administration, with the former conceived as policy making and the latter as its execution. Accordingly, the few top positions of policy making character were to be appointive on a political basis, and the lower positions, those of executory nature, were to be filled on merit, on a non-political basis, so that the occupants of the career service would perform their duty as the servants of the political will translated into policy by the political officials. This was and still is the theoretical justification of the civil service system and underlay the basic principle of unity of command which was advocated by all the congressional and executive commissions investigating the administrative agencies of the government from the Cockrell Committee in 1887 to the Hoover Commission in 1949.

Just as Wilson and Goodnow separated politics and administration, so Freund differentiated between policy and law. To Freund the desire for power inspired policy and the desire for justice inspired law. The political organization of the state itself is the resultant of these two conflicting tendencies; and the "key to the understanding of most political institutions must be found in their compromise nature." [551] Furthermore, Freund saw the electorate, administration, executive, and legislature forming a hierarchy of power with the legislature ideally at the top. In an article on presidential power and administrative law, Nathan D. Grundstein pointed out in 1950:

> The main contours of the concept of the unity of the executive power as it has developed in relation to the national administration are delineated in the early literature on administrative law, particularly in the writings of Freund and Wyman. However, these pioneer analyses concentrated not on the constitutional aspects of the administrative powers of the President, but on the significance for executive power of a hierarchically organized system of administration.[552]

Both Freund and Wyman regarded a fully integrated administrative hierarchy operating coordinately with the legislature as ideal, and measured the extent of the prevailing executive power by the degree of such hierarchy in existence.

Freund did not subordinate the legal processes to the social sciences. He saw them as each equally dependent on the other. Most of the needed social changes, he asserted, could be achieved through the law; and if they are to be timely and appropriate then the legislative process, as one of the legal processes, should be chiefly relied on. However, the legislative process is a difficult one involving many political obstacles and expediency. Here then is where the basic reforms are necessary—the improvement of the composition and operations of the legislature by alert, participating, and cooperating social scientists and attorneys.

When James Parker Hall, Dean of the Chicago Law School, died in 1928, Freund delivered the memorial address, in which he revealed his own thinking on reform. Speaking of Hall, Freund remarked: "He was open to new ideas, but was skeptical of paper schemes that had not been tried out in practice; probably he was wise in making the path of the reformer not too smooth or easy." [553] This was Freund—a reformer who felt that ideas required practical testing and had to compete for public support, and their attainment was to be sought democratically and through the law.

Freund's foresight on reform was at times phenomenal. For example, zoning, which is much in the news today and has become a battleground for civil rights issues, was recognized over forty years ago by Freund to be such a leading area of struggle. Richard F. Babcock, in *The Zoning Game,* published in 1966, made a main point of his book that zoning has been a device for protecting the homogeneous, single-family suburb from the city. To buttress this view, Babcock pointed out: "University of Chicago Law School professor, Ernst Freund, saw this thirty years ago, when he stated,[554] 'Every one knows that the crux of the zoning problem lies in the residential district, and that when we speak of amenity we have in mind residential preference.' " [555]

Oliver P. Field was an astute reviewer of Freund's writings. He truthfully and accurately found them to be "difficult to read" and to assume "a great deal of knowledge of specific details, on the part of the reader." "The points are almost as difficult to see as they are worth while seeing, once discovered. For this reason, it is doubtful whether they will have the influence which they deserve, unless someone is able to put into simple and understandable language the major theoretical contributions which Professor Freund made to law and political science." Field noted one exception to this assessment—Freund's book on *The Police Power,* "a book which had a tremendous influence, in the sense that it was widely read, quoted, and cited, by students, teachers, courts, and lawyers." Field felt *The Police Power* "was not a great book," an opinion that Freund himself frequently expressed. The three greatest works of Freund, according to Field, were the *Standards of American Legislation, Administrative Powers Over Persons and Property,* and *Legislative Regulation.*[556]

What Freund had hoped but did not live to do was a comprehensive study on the procedure of legislative bodies in the United States and Europe in transforming ideas into legislation. No one has yet fulfilled the task. As Justice Evan A. Evans of the Seventh United States Circuit Court of Appeals remarked in the *American Bar Association Journal* shortly after Freund's death: "Ernst Freund was a pioneer; he has pointed out the paths for others to go further, but so well has his task been done, that it will take time and another giant intellect to approach his accomplishment." [557] It is taking a long time. Perhaps, the days of struggle for recognition and acceptance of administrative law made it possible for such giants as Goodnow, Freund, and Frankfurter to emerge.

For Freund the greatest problem of American public law in his time was that of controlling unrestrained administrative discretion. Today, as has been noted by many observers of the modern administrative scene, the judicial work of the courts is far surpassed by the huge volume of adjudication by administrative agencies. The problem of preventing or reducing injustice to the individual from the exercise of discretionary power by administrators is ever greater than in Freund's days. Kenneth Culp Davis, echoing Freund, recommends that the unnecessary power be cut back and that the necessary power be properly confined, structured and checked.[558] Similarly, the problem exists at the state governmental level. In 1965 Frank E. Cooper, in his comprehensive treatise on state administrative law, recalled Freund as "a prophet in the wilderness" predicting that administration of regulatory laws would gravitate from discretion to rule and that standards would be imposed by the legislatures and the courts to curtail unguided or uncontrolled administrative discretion.[559] In one of the most recent books on administrative law, which appeared in 1972, Bernard Schwartz and H. W. R. Wade concluded: "The key problem in judicial review today appears to be that of the control of administrative discretion." [560]

An allied problem, which is still with us and which Freund often discussed, was that of the creation of specialized administrative courts, particularly in such broad economic areas as labor, taxation, and trade. In 1971 the Advisory Council on Executive Organization, popularly known as the Ash Council, considered the problem and studied the dilemma posed by Freund of making a regulatory agency simultaneously independent, responsive and accountable—guaranteeing due process for those regulated while providing proper protection of the interests of the general public.[561] Not only the Ash Council appeared to get nowhere; a year later a symposium in the *Public Administration Review* on the same subject was aptly subtitled, "Are We Getting Anywhere?" The answer was, and still is, in the negative.[562]

In recent articles, such well-known political scientists as C. Herman Pritchett and Robert G. Dixon, Jr. have bemoaned the decline of interest of political scientists in public law.[563] Ironically, this has been occurring at a time when public law professors and attorneys are becoming increasingly interested in political science. Martin Shapiro attributes the decline to the definition of administrative law "not as the law made by administrators for the governance of the citizenry, but as the law made by courts for the judicial review of administrative proceedings and the internal rules by which the agencies govern themselves." Had the definition included the former, Shapiro maintains, administrative law would have been accepted as a popular, respected discipline in political science.[564]

Shapiro's conclusion is debatable. The more likely reason is that for the past thirty-five years the emphasis in administrative law has been on procedure. In the future, as Peter Woll predicts, "agencies will not be permitted to hide behind procedural curtains to avoid meeting problems that confront society." Administrative law has already begun to swing from its long preoccupation with preventing or curtailing particular action by the regulatory agencies in the areas of industry, commerce, and agriculture to concern with social and community welfare and interests and with compelling effective governmental action in these areas; and the courts are spearheading this trend. Consequently, substantive administrative law will become as important as procedural law; and political scientists, if they are to be a concerned discipline, must encourage interest and enthusiasm in the study of administrative law. Woll concluded his study of the current state of administrative law by asking a question which could well have been posed by Freund were he alive: "Is the inductive case-by-case approach producing the kinds of results we need, or is it necessary to develop new mechanisms of decision making which will emphasize a broader and more deductive and analytical approach?" [565] While Freund had predicted that an educated public would swing governmental action to social legislation he did not foresee the increasingly active and forceful pressure by various sections of the public, especially through public interest action suits.

Although he favored the progressive democratization of our institutions, Freund feared that this process might shift the balance of legislative power from the legislature to the executive. For him the responsibility of a legislator was greater than that of an administrator. Creating law was next to godliness; and a good legis-

lator should be a combination of lawyer, sociologist, economist
and political scientist since he must learn the limits of attain-
ability. Accordingly, he must know not only the economic needs
of people but also their customs, habits and traditions and their
ethnic, religious and nationalistic feelings. All these factors must
be taken into account in the legislative process. Otherwise, legislatures cannot effectively define the limitations of legal and illegal
behavior. How timely is Freund's admonition of 1917 regarding
vagueness and generality in criminal statutes: ". . . the generality
of the prohibition is not only unjust to the defendant, but disadvan-
tageous to the prosecuting government, not only because it will
make convictions difficult, but because it will diminish the vigor
and confidence of official enforcement." [566]

Acknowledging that an advancing technological society requires
administrators who are technical experts, Freund persisted in warning that leaving it to such experts could be politically harmful and
dangerous to individual rights and liberties. Administrators too
frequently are blind followers of orders from their chiefs and will
subvert good ends by illegal or unethical methods. The current
Watergate Affair is a prime example of this condition. Appointed
officials need checking by elected officials other than those who
make such appointments. The best check on the administrators,
Freund urged, was electing legislators who themselves are technical experts and providing legislators with advisory staff experts.

As much as Freund warned of administrative misconduct, he did
not foresee the eventually urgent need for a comprehensive and
stringent code of ethics for public officers, for a set of standards to
ensure the selection of competent, effective and responsible administrators, for a body of rules governing the conduct of administrative investigations, and for guidelines to encourage informal adjudication. Neither did Frankfurter, for that matter; and
neither foresaw the expansion of administrative tribunals as a
means of relieving judicial court congestion and delay. Nor did
they anticipate the possibility of the indigents' need for representation before administrative as well as judicial agencies; and
neither was practically involved with expanding the accessibility
of administrators to the public.

Time erodes many issues and problems. However, some matters

defy time and cling to a society which is either not ready for a certain change or is fearful of the probable effects. As of this date, for example, there is no uniform marriage and divorce law in the United States. The National Conference of Commissioners on Uniform State Laws has been working on such an act for many years. Freund, one of the Conference's earliest members and prime movers, had advocated such a law during the first three decades of this century.

While the trend in the 1930's to the early 1950's appeared to be in the direction of constitutionalism and its advocates, such as Frankfurter and Davison, were in ascendancy, the trend of the late 1950's through the present is away from constitutionality to administrative independence and responsibility and the controlling of administrative discretion; and consequently, we may soon see a revival of Freund and a revisiting by the bench, bar, and the social sciences to the old master.[567]

Bibliography:
THE PUBLISHED WRITINGS
OF ERNST FREUND

Books and Pamphlets

The Legal Nature of Corporations. University of Chicago Studies in Political Science. Chicago. University of Chicago Press. 1897. 83 pp. Ph.D. Thesis. Columbia University Faculty of Political Science. November, 1896.

Empire and Sovereignty. University of Chicago Decennial Publication. Chicago. University of Chicago Press. 1903. First Series, Vol. IV, Sec. VII. Pp. 257–88.

The Police Power: Public Policy and Constitutional Rights. Chicago. Callaghan and Co. 1904. 819 pp.

Co-editor with William E. Mikell and John H. Wigmore. *Select Essays in Anglo-American Legal History.* Compiled and edited by a Committee of the Association of American Law Schools. Boston. Little Brown and Co. 3 Vols. 1907–09.

Constitutional Aspects of the Ten Hour Law. Bulletin, Bureau of Labor Statistics, Illinois. Springfield, Ill. Illinois State Journal Co. State Printers. 1909. 6 pp.

Labor Legislation in the Forty-Sixth General Assembly of Illinois. Bureau of Labor Statistics, Illinois. Springfield, Ill. Illinois State Journal Co. State Printers. 1909. 202 pp.

Cases on Administrative Law Selected from Decisions of English and American Courts. St. Paul. West Publishing Co. 1911. 681 pp.

Das Oeffentliche Recht der Vereinigten Staaten von Amerika. Tübingen. J. C. B. Mohr. 1911. 387 pp.

Labor Legislation in the Forty-Seventh General Assembly of Illinois. Co-authored with Luke Grant. Chicago. Illinois Association for Labor Legislation. 1911. 16 pp.

Elements of Law: Syllabus and Illustrative Material. Chicago. University of Chicago Press. 1912. 33 pp.

Legislative Drafting. Indianapolis, Ind. Mellett Printing Co. 1916. 15 pp.

Standards of American Legislation: An Estimate of Restrictive and Constructive Factors. Chicago. University of Chicago Press. 1917. 327 pp.

"Scientific Method in Legislative Drafting." Chapter XIII in *Science of Legal Method: Select Essays by Various Authors.* Introduction by Henry N. Sheldon and John W. Salmond. Boston. Boston Book Co. 1917. Pp. 558–86.

Illegitimacy Laws of the United States and Certain Foreign Countries. Washington. Government Printing Office. 1919. 260 pp. U. S. Department of Labor. U. S. Children's Bureau. Legal Series No. 2. Bureau Publication No. 42.

Uniform Illegitimacy Laws. Report to the Children's Bureau of the United States Department of Labor. Washington. Government Printing Office. 1922.

"Historical Survey." In Ernst Freund, Robert V. Fletcher, Joseph E. Davies, Cuthbert W. Pound, John A. Kurz and Charles Nagel (co-editors). *The Growth of American Administrative Law.* St. Louis. Thomas Law Book Co. 1923. 190 pp. At pp. 9–41.

Administrative Powers Over Persons and Property: A Comparative Survey. Chicago. University of Chicago Press. 1928. 620 pp.

Cases on Administrative Law Selected from Decisions of English and American Courts. St. Paul. West Publishing Co. 1928. Second edition. 745 pp.

"Legal Aspects of Philanthropy." In Ellsworth Faris, Ferris Laune, and Arthur J. Todd (editors). *Intelligent Philanthropy.* Chicago. University of Chicago Press. 1930. Pp. 149–81.

Legislative Regulation: A Study of the Ways and Means of Written Law. New York. The Commonwealth Fund. 1932. 458 pp.

Articles

"The Effect of the Norman Conquest on English Law." *Columbia Law Times.* Part 1: Vol. I, No. 7. April, 1888. Pp. 232–40; Part 2: Vol. II, No. 8. May, 1888. Pp. 257–62.

"Contracts and Consideration in Roman Law." *Columbia Law Times.* Vol. II, No. 5. February, 1889. Pp. 167–78.

"The Proposed German Civil Code." *American Law Review* Vol. XXIV. March-April, 1890. Pp. 237–54.

"Historical Jurisprudence in Germany." *Political Science Quarterly.* Vol. V, No. 3. September, 1890. Pp. 468–86.

"The Study of Law in Germany." *The Counsellor.* Vol. I, No. 5. February, 1892. Pp. 131–35.

"A Recent Case on the Law of Conspiracy." *The Counsellor.* Vol. I, No. 8. May, 1892. Pp. 220–29.

"Private Claims against the State." *Political Science Quarterly.* Vol. VIII, No. 4. December, 1893. Pp. 625–52.

"The Law of the Administration in America." *Political Science Quarterly.* Vol. IX, No. 3. September, 1894. Pp. 403–25.

"Malice and Unlawful Interference." *Harvard Law Review.* Vol. XI, No. 7. February 25, 1898. Pp. 449–65.

"The Control of Dependencies through Protectorates." *Political Science Quarterly.* Vol. XIV, No. 1. March, 1899. Pp. 19–38.

"The New German Civil Code." *Harvard Law Review.* Vol. XIII, No. 8. April, 1900. Pp. 627–37.

"Government and Law in America." *American Law Review.* Vol. XXXIV, January-February, 1900. Pp. 16–27.

"Jurisprudence and Legislation." Congress of Arts and Science. Universal Exposition. St. Louis. 1904. Vol. VII. Edited by Howard J. Rogers. Boston. Houghton, Mifflin and Co. Pp. 619–35.

"Limitation of Hours of Labor and the Federal Supreme Court." *Green Bag.* Vol. XVII, No. 7. July, 1905. Pp. 411–17.

"Limitation of Hours of Labor and the Supreme Court." *Journal of Political Economy.* Vol. 13, No. 7. September, 1905. Pp. 597–99.

"Recent Illinois Decisions Regarding Injunctions Issued in the Course of Strikes." *Journal of Political Economy.* Vol. 14, No. 1. January, 1906. Pp. 43–46.

"On the Legality of A Boycott in Germany." *Journal of Political Economy.* Vol. 14, No. 9. November, 1906. Pp. 573–74.

"Constitutional Aspects of Employers' Liability Legislation." *Green Bag.* Vol. XIX, No. 1. January, 1907. Pp. 80–83.

"The Problem of Intelligent Legislation." *Proceedings of the American Political Science Association.* Vol. IV, 1907. Pp. 69–79.

"Some Legal Aspects of the Chicago Charter Act of 1907." *Illinois Law Review.* Vol. II, No. 7. February, 1908. Pp. 427–39.

"Federal Employers' Liability Act." *Charities,* Vol. 19. March 7, 1908. Pp. 1662–64.

"Can the States Cooperate for Labor Legislation?" *Survey.* Vol. XXII, June 12, 1909. Pp. 409–11.

"Discussion [on Administrative Control of Corporations and Administrative Courts for the United States]." *Proceedings of the American Political Science Association.* 1909. Pp. 58–62.

"Constitutional Limitations and Labor Legislation." *Third Annual Meeting, American Association for Labor Legislation, New York, N. Y., Dec. 28-30, 1909: Proceedings—Reports—Addresses.* New York. American Association for Labor Legislation. 1910. Pp. 51–71.

"Constitutional Limitations and Labor Legislation." *Illinois Law Review,* Vol. IV, No. 9. April, 1910. Pp. 609–23.

"A Proposed Uniform Marriage Law." *Harvard Law Review.* Vol. XXIV, No. 7. May, 1911. Pp. 548–62.

"Court of Appeals Decision." *Survey.* Vol. XXVI, April 29, 1911. Pp. 195–96.

"Constitutional Status of Workmen's Compensation." *Illinois Law Review*. Vol. IV, No. 7. February, 1912. Pp. 433–46.

"Constitutional Status of Workmen's Compensation." *American Labor Legislation Review*. Vol. II, No. 1. February, 1912. Pp. 43–59.

"Unifying Tendencies in American Legislation." *Yale Law Journal*. Vol. XXII, No. 1. November, 1912. Pp. 96–113.

"The Federal Workmen's Compensation Act." *Survey*. Vol. 27. February 3, 1912. Pp. 1670–71.

"The Enforcement Provisions of the Sherman Law." *Journal of Political Economy*. Vol. 20, No. 5. May, 1912. Pp. 462–72.

"Insurance Aspects of Workmen's Compensation." *American Labor Legislation Review*. Vol. III, No. 2. June, 1913. Pp. 273–75.

"Problems of the Police Power." *Case and Comment*. Vol. 20, No. 5. October, 1913, Pp. 301–04.

"Problems of the Police Power." *Chicago Legal News*. Vol. XLVI, No. 13. November 1, 1913. Pp. 104–05.

"Constitutional Aspects of Hour Legislation for Men." *American Labor Legislation Review*. Vol. IV, No. 1. March, 1914. Pp. 129–31.

"Supplemental Acts: A Chapter in Constitutional Construction." *Illinois Law Review*. Vol. VIII, No. 8. March, 1914. Pp. 507–17.

"Uniform Marriage and Divorce Legislation." *Case and Comment*. Vol. 21, No.1. June, 1914. Pp. 7–9.

"The Problem of Adequate Legislative Powers under State Constitutions." *Proceedings of the Academy of Political Science*. Vol. V. October, 1914. Pp. 98–126.

"The Substitution of Rule for Discretion in Public Law." *International Journal of Ethics*. Vol. XXV, No. 1. October, 1914. Pp. 100–02.

"Classification and Definition of Crimes." *Journal of the American Institute of Criminal Law and Criminology*. Vol. V, No. 6. March, 1915. Pp. 807–26.

"The Substitution of Rule for Discretion in Public Law." *American Political Science Review*. Vol. IX, No. 4. November, 1915. Pp. 666–76.

"Social Legislation and Charity." *Associated Bulletin of the Associated Jewish Charities of Chicago*. January, 1916. Pp. 21–22.

"Principles of Legislation." *American Political Science Review*. Vol. X, No. 1. February, 1916. Pp. 1–19.

"Principles of Legislation." *Chicago Legal News*. Vol. XLVIII, No. 31. March 2, 1916. Pp. 243–44, 246.

"Tendencies of Legislative Policy and Modern Social Legislation." *International Journal of Ethics*. Vol. XXVII, No. 1. October, 1916. Pp. 1–24.

"The Correlation of Work for Higher Degrees in Graduate Schools and Law Schools." *Illinois Law Review*. Vol. XI, No. 5. December, 1916. Pp. 301–10.

"Constitutional and Legal Aspects of Health Insurance." *Proceedings of the National Conference of Social Work.* At the Forty-Fourth Annual Session Held in Pittsburgh, Pennsylvania June 6-13, 1917. Chicago. National Conference of Social Work. 1917. Pp. 553–58.

"Interpretation of Statutes." *University of Pennsylvania Law Review.* Vol. 65, No. 3. January, 1917. Pp. 207–31.

"The Outlook for International Law." *New Republic.* Vol. XV, No. 185. May 18, 1918. Pp. 80–82.

"Prolegomena to A Science of Legislation." *Illinois Law Review.* Vol. XIII. May, 1918. Pp. 264–92.

"Judicial Doctrines Defined." *Lawyer and Banker and Southern Bench and Bar Review.* Vol. XII, No. 1. January-February, 1919. Pp. 440–58.

"The Debs Case and Freedom of Speech." *New Republic.* Vol. XIX, No. 235. May 3, 1919. Pp. 13–15.

"The Treaty and International Law." *New Republic.* Vol. XXI, No. 263. December 17, 1919. Pp. 74–77.

"Burning Heretics." Letter to the *New Republic.* Vol. XXI, No. 269. January 28, 1920. Pp. 266–67.

"Three Suggestions Concerning Future Interests." *Harvard Law Review.* Vol. XXXIII, No. 4. February, 1920. Pp. 526–41.

"A Course in Statutes." *American Law School Review.* Part 1: Vol. 4, No. 5. February-March, 1917. Pp. 273–75; Part 2: Vol. 4. No. 9. April, 1920. Pp. 503–05.

"The New German Constitution." *Political Science Quarterly.* Vol. XXXV, No. 2. June, 1920. Pp. 177–203.

"Three Suggestions concerning Future Interests." *Law Times.* Vol. 150, No. 4038. August 21, 1920. Pp. 125–27; Vol. 150, No. 4039. August 28, 1920. Pp. 136–38.

"Freedom of Speech and Press." *New Republic.* Vol. XXV, No. 324. February 16, 1921. Pp. 344–46.

"Legislative Problems and Solutions." *American Bar Association Journal.* Vol. VII. December, 1921. Pp. 656–58.

"The Right to a Judicial Review in Rate Controversies." *West Virginia Law Quarterly.* Vol. XXVII, No. 3. March, 1921. Pp. 207–12.

"The Use of Indefinite Terms in Statutes." *Yale Law Journal.* Vol. XXX, No. 5. March, 1921. Pp. 437–55.

"The Teaching of Statute Law." *North Carolina Law Review.* Vol. One, No. Two. November, 1922. Pp. 104–110.

"A Uniform Illegitimacy Law." *Survey.* Vol. XLIX. October 15, 1922. Pp. 104, 127 and 129.

"A New Constitution for Illinois." *New Republic.* Vol. XXXIII, No. 419. December 13, 1922. Pp. 67–69.

"Commission Powers and Public Utilities." *American Bar Association Journal.* Vol. IX, No. 5. May, 1923. Pp. 285–88.

"Search and Seizure." *Chicago Legal News.* Vol. LVI, No. 27. January 24, 1924. Pp. 211–12, 214–15.

"Administrative Discretion: A Reply to Dean Wigmore." *Illinois Law Review.* Vol. XIX, No. 8. April, 1925. Pp. 663–64.

"Administrative Law—Appeal from Administrative Decision—[United States]." *Illinois Law Review.* Vol. XXI, No. 4. December, 1926. P. 378.

"Administrative Law—Due Process in the Revocation of Licenses." *Illinois Law Review.* Vol. XXI, No. 5. January, 1927. Pp. 493–94.

"Deportation Legislation in the Sixty-ninth Congress." *Social Service Review.* Vol. I, No. 1. March, 1927, Pp. 46–57.

"The Product of the Fifty-Fifth General Assembly." *Illinois Law Review.* Vol. XXII, No. 5. January, 1928. Pp. 473–79.

"James Parker Hall: Dean of the Law School." *University Record.* University of Chicago. Vol. XIV, No. 2. April, 1928. Pp. 110–11.

"Some Inadequately Discussed Problems of the Law of City Planning and Zoning." *Illinois Law Review.* Vol. XXIV, No. 2. June, 1929. Pp. 135–49.

"United States v. Schwimmer." *New York University Law Quarterly Review.* Vol. VII, No. 1. September, 1929. Pp. 157–59.

"Operation of the Rule Against Perpetuities." *Illinois Law Review.* Vol. XXIV, No. 6. February, 1930. Pp. 727–28.

"Administrative Law." *Encyclopaedia of the Social Sciences.* New York. The Macmillan Co. 1930. Vol. One. Pp. 452–55.

"Co-ordinating State and Local Action." *Public Management.* Vol. XIII, No. 1. January, 1931. Pp. 12–13.

"Legislative Standardization." *State Government.* Vol. 4 No. 2. February, 1931. Pp. 15–18.

"Power of Zoning Boards of Appeals to Grant Variations." *National Municipal Review.* Vol. XX. No. 9. September, 1931. Pp. 537–39.

"United States v. Macintosh." *Illinois Law Review.* Vol. XXVI, No. 4. December, 1931. Pp. 384–95.

"Zoning—Power of Board to Vary." *Illinois Law Review.* Vol. XXVI, No. 5. January, 1932. Pp. 575–77.

"The Law Back of Public Management." *Public Management.* Vol. XIV, No. 2. February, 1932. Pp. 57–60.

"Law School and University." *University Record.* University of Chicago. Vol. XVIII, No. 3. July, 1932. Pp. 143–52.

"Legislation." *Encyclopaedia of the Social Sciences.* New York. The Macmillan Co. 1933. Vol. Nine. Pp. 347–54.

"Licensing." *Encyclopaedia of the Social Sciences.* New York. The Macmillan Co. 1933. Vol. Nine. Pp. 447–51.

"Responsibility of the State in Internal (Municipal) Law." *Tulane Law Review.* Vol. IX, No. 1. December, 1934. Pp. 1–16. Posthumously published. Originally prepared as a report for the International Congress of Comparative Law at The Hague, August 2–6, 1932.

Notes

Introduction

1. Felix Frankfurter, "The Task of Administrative Law," *University of Pennsylvania Law Review,* Vol. 75, No. 7 (May, 1927), pp. 614–21, at 616.
2. Arthur T. Vanderbilt, "One Hundred Years of Administrative Law," in *Law: A Century of Progress* (New York: New York University Press, 1937), Vol. One, pp. 117–44, at 120.
3. Frederic Woodward, "Ernst Freund," *University Record,* University of Chicago, Vol. XIX, No. 1 (January, 1933), pp. 39–42, at 39.
4. Ernst Freund, "Law School and University," *University Record,* University of Chicago, Vol. XVIII, No. 3 (July, 1932), pp. 143–52, at 149.
5. *Ibid.,* p. 152.
6. *American Bar Association Journal,* Vol. XIX, No. 1 (January 1, 1933), p. 56.
7. Ernst Freund, "A Constitution for Illinois," *New Republic,* Vol. XXXIII, No. 419 (December 13, 1922), pp. 67–69.
8. See Henry Steele Commager, *The American Mind* (New Haven: Yale University Press, 1950), p. 376, in which Commager characterized Freund's *The Police Power* as "a remarkable analysis . . . which elaborated and vindicated the institutions of Holmes."
9. 208 U.S. 412 (1908).
10. "Ernst Freund, 1864–1932," *Social Service Review,* Vol. VI, No. 4 (December, 1932), p. 651.
11. For biographical sketches of Ernst Freund, see Isaac Landman (ed.), *The Universal Jewish Encyclopedia* (New York: The Universal Jewish Encyclopedia, Inc., 1941), Vol. 4, p. 444; Isidore Singer (ed), *The Jewish Encyclopedia* (New York: Funk and Wagnalls Co., 1925), Vol. V, p. 509; Cyrus Adler and Henrietta Szold (ed.), *American Jewish Year Book 5665* (Philadelphia: The Jewish Publication Society

of America, 1904), p. 97; *The National Cyclopaedia of American Biography* (New York: James T. White & Co., 1937), Vol. XXVI, pp. 98–99; Frank W. Price and Charles P. Barry (editors), *Collier's Encyclopedia* (New York: P.F. Collier & Son, 1950), Vol. 8, p. 457; *Who's Who in Government* (New York: The Biographical Research Bureau, Inc., 1932), Vol. II, p. 525; Albert Nelson Marquis (ed.), *Who's Who in America 1932-1933* (Chicago: A. N. Marquis Co., 1932), Vol. 17, p. 887; *Chicago Daily Tribune*, October 21, 1932, p. 9; *New York Times*, October 21, 1932, p. 21; *New York Herald Tribune*, October 22, 1932, p. 13; *United States Law Review*, Vol. LXVI, No. 11 (November, 1932), p. 635; and *American Political Science Review*, Vol. XXVI, No. 6 (December, 1932), pp. 1103–04.

12. Ernst Freund, "Judicial Doctrines Defined," *The Lawyer and Banker and Southern Bench and Bar Review*, Vol. XII, No. 1 (January-February, 1919), pp. 440–58, at 454.

13. Edward L. Metzler, "The Growth and Development of Administrative Law," *Marquette Law Review*, Vol. XIX, No. Four (June, 1935), pp. 209–27, at 212.

14. Ernst Freund, *Administrative Powers Over Persons and Property: A Comparative Survey* (Chicago: University of Chicago Press, 1928), p. 578; and Ernst Freund, *Legislative Regulation: A Study of the Ways and Means of Written Law* (New York: The Commonwealth Fund, 1932), pp. vii–ix.

15. Leo M. Alpert, "Suits against Administrative Agencies under N.I.R.A. and A.A.A.," *New York University Law Quarterly Review*, Vol. XII, No. 3 (March, 1935), pp. 393–438, at 437.

16. Forrest Revere Black, "The 'Jurisdictional Fact' Theory and Administrative Finality," *Cornell Law Quarterly*, Part I: Vol. XXII, No. 3 (April, 1937), pp. 349–78, at 78.

17. Woodrow Wilson, "The Study of Administration," *Political Science Quarterly*, Vol. II, No. 2 (June, 1887), pp. 197–222, at 212.

18. Roscoe Pound, "Some Parallels from Legal History," *American Bar Association Journal*, Vol. X, No. 8 (August, 1924), pp. 547–53, 564, at 553.

19. James Willard Hurst, *The Growth of American Law: The Law Makers* (Boston: Little, Brown and Co., 1950), pp. 269–70.

20. William Seagle, *The Quest for Law* (New York: Alfred A. Knopf, 1941), p. 420.

21. Joseph P. Chamberlain, review of Freund's *Legislative Regulation* in *American Political Science Review*, Vol. XXVI. No. 5 (October, 1932), pp. 938–40, at 938.

22. James Hart, *An Introduction to Administrative Law, With Selected Cases* (New York: Appleton-Century-Crofts, 1950), 2d edition, pp. 9–10. Justice Holmes stated in his dissent in *Springer v. Philippine Islands* in 1928: "It is said that the powers of Congress cannot be delegated, yet Congress has established the Interstate

Commerce Commission, which does legislative, judicial and executive acts, only softened by a *quasi . . ."* 277 U.S. 189, 210 (1928).

23. Harlan B. Phillips, *Felix Frankfurter Reminisces* (New York: Doubleday & Co., Anchor Books, 1962), p. 206.

24. Francis A. Allen, "Preface to the 1965 Edition," in Ernst Freund, *Standards of American Legislation* (Chicago: University of Chicago Press, 1965), p. vii.

25. Vanderbilt, *supra* note 2, p. 121.

26. Ernst Freund, *The Police Power: Public Policy and Constitutional Rights* (Chicago: Callaghan and Co., 1904), p. 721.

27. Felix Frankfurter, *The Ernst Freund Lecture: Some Observations on Supreme Court Litigation and Legal Education* (Chicago: University of Chicago Press, 1954), 20 pp., at 12.

28. Ernst Freund, *The Legal Nature of Corporations,* University of Chicago Studies in Political Science (Chicago: University of Chicago Press, 1897), p. 5.

29. Allen, *supra* note 24, p. ix.

30. Felix Frankfurter, in a three-page "Foreword" to W. Ivor Jennings, "Courts and Administrative Law—The Experience of English Housing Legislation," *Harvard Law Review,* Vol. XLIX, No. 3 (January, 1936), pp. 426–54, at 427.

31. Ernst Freund, "The Law of the Administration in America," *Political Science Quarterly,* Vol. IX, No. 3 (September, 1894), pp. 403–25, at 405.

32. *Cornell Law Quarterly,* Vol. XVIII, No. 4 (June, 1933), pp. 645–46, at 646.

33. *Ibid.,* p. 645.

The Police Power

34. Leo F. Wormser, "Legal Learning Dedicated to the Progress of Society," *University Record,* University of Chicago, Vol. XIX, No. 1 (January, 1933), pp. 45–47, at 45.

35. Joseph P. Chamberlain in *American Political Science Review,* Vol. XXVI, No. 6 (December, 1932), p. 1103. "The best definition of the 'police power' is still that of Ernst Freund." "Freund's work, *The Police Power* (1904), may be regarded as the constitutional classic of this period." Seagle, *The Quest for Law, op. cit.,* pp. 416–17. By 1908 many opinions of various state courts of highest appeal were rendered with allusions to Freund to indicate "the weight of authority." Judge Glen H. Worthington of the Maryland Court of Appeals in *Cochran v. Preston,* 108 Maryland Reports 220, 228 (1908).

36. Freund, *The Police Power, op. cit.,* p. 17.

37. 12 Wheaton 419 (1827).

38. 11 Peters 102 (1837).

39. 5 Howard 504, 583 (1847).

40. 200 U. S. 561, 592 (1906).
41. 219 U. S. 104, 111 (1911).
42. *Harvard Law Review,* Vol. XVII, No. 8 (June, 1904), pp. 592–93, at 592.
43. I. L. Sharfman, *The Interstate Commerce Commission: A Study in Administrative Law and Procedure* (New York: The Commonwealth Fund, Four Parts, 1931–1937), Part Two (1931), p. 193.
44. Freund, *The Police Power, op. cit.,* p. iii.
45. *Ibid.,* p. 3.
46. *Ibid.,* p. iii.
47. *Ibid.,* p. iv.
48. *Ibid.,* p. iii.
49. *Ibid.,* p. iv.
50. *Ibid.,* p. 63.
51. *Ibid.,* p. 6.
52. *Harvard Law Review, supra,* p. 593.
53. Freund, *The Police Power, op. cit.,* p. 3. See also, Ernst Freund, "Problems of the Police Power," *Case and Comment,* Vol. 20, No. 5 (October, 1913), pp. 301–04.
54. John Dickinson, *Administrative Justice and the Supremacy of Law in the United States* (Cambridge: Harvard University Press, 1927), p. 28.
55. *Loc. cit.*
56. *Annals of the American Academy of Political and Social Science,* Vol. XXIV, No. 3 (November, 1904), pp. 140–41, at 141. "Those who have known Professor Freund," wrote James Wilford Garner, "have recognized in him a scholar of unusual promise in the fields of public law and jurisprudence. . . . The treatise which he has now given us on the police power is truly a *magnum opus.* Other works on the police power have appeared in the past . . . but they have either lacked the elements of scientific treatment and arrangement or comprehensiveness of treatment. We have in Professor Freund's treatise the work of a public lawyer trained in American and Continental schools of jurisprudence and consequently his work is marked by a breadth of view which does not characterize the older treatises." *Ibid.,* pp. 140–41. See also, Walter Wheeler Cook's review in which he stated: ". . . the book is . . . far and away the best yet offered to the wanderers in the mazes of this branch of our constitutional law and is therefore an indispensable guide, alike for practitioner and student." *Political Science Quarterly,* Vol. XIX, No. 4 (December, 1904), pp. 687–90, at 690.
57. Morris R. Cohen, *Law and the Social Order: Essays in Legal Philosophy* (New York: Harcourt, Brace and Co., 1933), p. 179.
58. Morris R. Cohen, "A Critical Sketch of Legal Philosophy in America." in *Law: A Century of Progress 1835-1935* (New York: New York University Press, 1937), Vol. Two, pp. 266–317, at 316.
59. *Ibid.,* pp. 316–17.

60. Thomas Reed Powell, *The Supreme Court and State Police Power 1922–1930* (Charlottesville, Va.: The Michie Co., 1932).

61. Ruth Locke Roettinger, *The Supreme Court and State Police Power: A Study in Federalism* (Washington, D.C.: Public Affairs Press, 1957).

Principles and Standards of Legislation

62. *University of Pennsylvania Law Review,* Vol. 81, No. 7 (May, 1933), p. 890.

63. Ernst Freund, "The Problem of Intelligent Legislation," *Proceedings of the American Political Science Association at Its Fourth Annual Meeting Held at Madison, Wisconsin, December 27-31, 1907,* Vol. IV, 1907 (Baltimore: The Waverly Press, 1908), pp. 69–79, at p. 69.

64. *Ibid.,* pp. 70–71.

65. *Ibid.,* p. 71.

66. *Ibid.,* p. 77. Ten years later, Freund offered the following definition: "Principle as applied to legislation . . . is something that in the long run will tend to enforce itself by reason of its inherent fitness, or, if ignored, will produce irritation, disturbance, and failure of policy." Written during World War I, this second definition was accompanied by a remark revealing some cynicism as to the relative strength of reason versus prejudice: "Perhaps the best criterion of principle is that reasonable persons can be brought to agree upon the correctness of a proposition, though when they are called upon to apply it their inclinations or prejudices may be stronger than their reason." Ernst Freund, *Standards of American Legislation* (Chicago: University of Chicago Press, 1917, Second edition 1965 with a Preface by Francis A. Allen), p. 218.

67. Freund, "Judicial Doctrines Defined," *op. cit.,* pp. 457–58. A similar assertion was made by Freund two years earlier in *Standards of American Legislation, op. cit.,* p. 214. For Freund the objective of such study of legislation was the discovery of principles which would not only contribute to the effectiveness of statutory law but also provide it with a foundation of legitimacy and validity. "So long as legislation claims to produce law it must also strive to realize in its product that conformity to principle from which law derives its main sanction and authority." *Standards of American Legislation, op. cit.,* p. 215.

68. Freund, "The Problem of Intelligent Legislation," *op. cit.,* pp. 78–79.

69. Freund, *Legislative Regulation, op. cit.,* p. 7.

70. Ernst Freund, "Principles of Legislation," Presidential Address, Twelfth Annual Meeting of the American Political Science Association, *American Political Science Review,* Vol. X, No. 1 (February, 1916), pp. 1–19, at 17.

71. Freund, *Standards of American Legislation, op. cit.*, p. 2.
72. *Ibid.*, p. 22.
73. *Ibid.*, pp. 42 and 48.
74. *Ibid.*, p. 218.
75. *Ibid.*, p. 286.
76. *Ibid.*, p. 312.
77. *Ibid.*, p. 21.
78. *Ibid.*, p. 104. Remarked Arnold Bennett Hall in 1921 regarding Freund's discussion of principles of legislation: "Professor Freund has given a very excellent statement of what he means by principle in legislation which will help us to understand the technical nature of the task imposed upon those who undertake the formulation of statutes." Arnold Bennett Hall, *Popular Government: An Inquiry into the Nature and Methods of Representative Government* (New York: The Macmillan Co., 1921), p. 134.
79. Ernst Freund, "Interpretation of Statutes," *University of Pennsylvania Law Review,* Vol. 65, No. 3 (January, 1917), pp. 207–31, at 31.
80. Charles Grove Haines, "The Law of Nature in State and Federal Judicial Decisions," *Yale Law Journal,* Vol. XXV, No. 8 (June, 1916), pp. 617–57, at 648.
81. Freund, *The Police Power, op. cit.*, p. 15.
82. Arthur N. Holcombe, Review of *Administrative Powers Over Persons and Property,* in *Political Science Quarterly,* Vol. XLIV, No. 2 (June, 1929), pp. 265–67, at 265.
83. Ernst Freund, "Legislative Problems and Solutions," *American Bar Association Journal,* Vol. VII (December, 1921), pp. 656–58, at 658.
84. Freund, "Principles of Legislation," *American Political Science Review, op. cit.*, p. 7.
85. Leo F. Wormser, "Legal Learning Dedicated to the Progress of Society," *op. cit.*, pp. 45–47, at 46.
86. Ernst Freund, "The Use of Indefinite Terms in Statutes," *Yale Law Journal,* Vol. XXX, No. 5 (March, 1921), pp. 437–55, at 454.
87. Freund, *Legislative Regulation, op. cit.*, p. 225.
88. *Ibid.*, p. 4.
89. Freund, "Principles of Legislation," *American Political Science Review, op. cit.*, p. 19.
90. Ernst Freund, "Jurisprudence and Legislation," *Congress of Arts and Science,* Universal Exposition, St. Louis, 1904 (Boston: Houghton, Mifflin and Co., 1906), Vol. VII, pp. 619–35, at 627.
91. *Ibid.*, p. 634.
92. *Ibid.*, p. 635.
93. *Ibid.*, pp. 631–32.
94. Freund, *Standards of American Legislation, op. cit.*, p. 48.
95. Ernst Freund, "Power of Zoning Boards of Appeals to Grant

Variations," *National Municipal Review,* Vol. XX, No. 9 (September, 1931), pp. 537–39, at 537.
96. 344 Illinois Reports 82, 176 North Eastern Reporter 333 (1931).
97. Freund, "Power of Zoning Boards of Appeals to Grant Variations," *op. cit.,* p. 539.
98. *Ibid.,* p. 538.
99. *Iowa Law Bulletin,* Vol. III, No. 4 (November, 1917), pp. 253–56, at 256.
100. Ernst Freund, "Legislation", *Encyclopaedia of the Social Sciences* (New York: The Macmillan Co., 1933), Vol. Nine, pp. 347–54, at 347.
101. *Ibid.,* p. 348.
102. *Ibid.,* p. 353.
103. *Ibid.,* p. 348.
104. *Ibid.,* p. 349.
105. *Ibid.,* p. 351.
106. *Cornell Law Quarterly,* Vol. XV, No. 3 (April, 1930), p. 510.
107. Woodward, "Ernst Freund," *University Record, op. cit.,* p. 41.
108. Freund, *Standards of American Legislation, op. cit.,* pp. 320–21.
109. Nathan Isaacs, "The Schools of Jurisprudence: Their Places in History and Their Present Alignment," *Harvard Law Review,* Vol. XXXI, No. 3 (January, 1918), pp. 373–411, at 409.
110. Charles E. Wyzanski, Jr., "The Trend of the Law and Its Impact on Legal Education," *Harvard Law Review,* Vol. LVII, No. 4 (April, 1944), pp. 558–64, at 563.

Legislative Regulation

111. Freund, *Legislative Regulation, op. cit.,* p. viii.
112. *Ibid.,* p. ix.
113. *Loc. cit.*
114. *Ibid.,* p. 3.
115. Since Freund did not spell out this point concisely and pointedly, "appears" is appropriately used here.
116. Freund, *Legislative Regulation, op. cit.,* p. 3.
117. *Ibid.,* pp. 55–56.
118. *Ibid.,* p. 9. Freund expressed the view that "As the law becomes more socialized, the demand for qualified, in preference to absolute, rights, increases; and in satisfying this demand, the uncompromising logic of the courts has proved inferior to legislation." *Ibid.,* p. 10.
119. Edwin W. Patterson, "Legislative Regulation and the Unwritten Law," *Iowa Law Review,* Vol. XVIII, No. 2 (January, 1933), pp. 193–97, at 195.

120. Freund, "Legislation," *Encyclopaedia of the Social Sciences, op. cit.*, p. 350.
121. Ernst Freund, "Administrative Law," *Encyclopaedia of the Social Sciences,* (New York: The Macmillan Co., 1930), Vol. One, pp. 452–55, at 454.
122. Freund, "Legislation," *Encyclopaedia of the Social Sciences, op. cit.*, p. 349.
123. *Ibid.*, p. 352.
124. *Loc. cit.*
125. *American Political Science Review,* Vol. XXVI, No. 5 (October, 1932), pp. 938–40, at 938.
126. *West Virginia Law Quarterly,* Vol. XXXIX, No. 4 (June, 1933), pp. 373–76, at 375–76.
127. *Columbia Law Review,* Vol. XXXIII, No. 3 (March, 1933), pp. 554–55, at 555.
128. *Tulane Law Review,* Vol. VII, No. 4 (June, 1933), pp. 639–41, at 639.
129. *Ibid.*, p. 640.
130. *Ibid.*, p. 641.
131. *Journal of the American Institute of Criminal Law and Criminology,* Vol. XXIV, No. 2 (July–August, 1933), pp. 466–69, at 466.
132. *Temple Law Quarterly,* Vol. VIII, No. 3 (April, 1934), pp. 441–43, at 443.
133. *American Bar Association Journal,* Vol. XIX, No. 2 (February, 1933), pp. 111–12, at 111.
134. *Indiana Law Journal,* Vol. VIII, No. 3 (December, 1932), pp. 206–09, at 209.
135. W. Ivor Jennings, Review of *Legislative Regulation* in the *Law Quarterly Review,* Vol. XLIX, No. CXCVI (October, 1933), pp. 588–89.
136. *Canadian Bar Review,* Vol. X, No. 9 (November, 1932), pp. 612–14, at 612–13.
137. *Minnesota Law Review,* Vol. XVII, No. 6 (May, 1933), pp. 684–86, at 684–85.
138. *West Virginia Law Quarterly, supra,* p. 373.
139. See particularly, Freund, *Legislative Regulation, op. cit.*, p. 70.

Legislative Drafting

140. "Report of the Special Committee on Legislative Drafting," *American Bar Association Journal,* Vol. II, No. 3 (July, 1916), pp. 454–86, at 454. The text of the draft manual was appended to the Report, at pp. 456–86. See also, *American Bar Association Journal,* Vol. V, No. 3 (July, 1919), pp. 416–39, for the text of the revised

182   *Notes*

draft of the manual. Actually, the American Bar Association's Special
Committee on Legislative Drafting originated in 1912. In December,
1915 a group met, at Freund's suggestion, during the annual convention of the American Political Science Association to discuss the
problems of reform in bill drafting and decided to organize as a bill
drafting conference and to meet alternately with the American
Bar Association and the American Political Science Association for
developing a program and a manual. The first such meeting was held
in Chicago on August 29, 1916 which the directors of several state
legislative reference and drafting bureaus and a large number of others
interested in bill drafting attended. Freund presented the first address
which was published as a pamphlet: *Legislative Drafting* (Indianapolis,
Ind.: Mellett Printing Co., 1916), 15 pp.

The Special Committee on Legislative Drafting of the American
Bar Association, formed in 1912, included Louis D. Brandeis, Thomas
I. Parkinson, Samuel Untermyer, and William Draper Lewis among
its early members; and its final report was approved at the Bar Association's annual meeting in 1921. The Committee was then disbanded
and its work connected with uniform legislation was transferred to the
National Conference of Commissioners on Uniform State Laws.
Freund was a member of both the Special Committee and the National Conference. *American Bar Association Journal,* Vol. 7, No.
9 (September, 1921), p. 478. See *American Bar Association Reports,*
Vol. 46 (1921), p. 68 for the text of the final report. The manual was
attached thereto as an appendix. Commented the American Bar
Association: "We are glad to say that it is now generally recognized
that legislative bodies should have expert drafting assistance." *Ibid.,*
p. 68.

141. Arthur H. Kent, "Ernst Freund (1864–1932)—Jurist and Social Scientist," *Journal of Political Economy,* Vol. 41, No. 2 (April,
1933), pp. 145–51, at 148.

142. Bertram M. Gross, *The Legislative Struggle: A Study in Social
Combat* (New York: McGraw-Hill Book Co., 1953), p. 198.

143. Freund, "Legislation," *Encyclopaedia of the Social Sciences,*
op. cit., pp. 347–48.

144. *Ibid.,* p. 348.

145. *Ibid.,* p. 352.

146. *Loc. cit.*

147. *Ibid.,* p. 353.

148. Ernst Freund, "Legislative Standardization," *State Government,* Vol. 4, No. 2 (February, 1931), pp. 15–18, at 15.

149. *Loc. cit.*

150. *Ibid.,* p. 16. See also, Ernst Freund, "The Problem of Adequate
Legislative Powers under State Constitutions", *Proceedings of the
Academy of Political Science,* Vol. V (October, 1914), pp. 98–126,
at 109.

151. Freund, "Legislative Standardization", *op. cit.,* pp. 16–17.

152. *Ibid.*, p. 17.
153. *Ibid.*, pp. 17–18.
154. *Ibid.*, p. 18.
155. *Loc. cit.*, See also, Ernst. Freund, "The Use of Indefinite Terms in Statutes," *Yale Law Journal*, Vol. XXX, No. 5 (March, 1921), pp. 437–55.
156. Alfred F. Conard, "New Ways to Write Laws," *Yale Law Journal*, Vol. 56, No. 3 (February, 1947), pp. 458–81, at 458.
157. Wormser, "Legal Learning Dedicated to the Progress of Society," *op. cit.*, p. 46.
158. Kent, "Ernst Freund (1864–1932)—Jurist and Social Scientist," *supra* note 141, pp. 148–50.
159. *West Virginia Law Quarterly*, Vol. XXXIX, No. 4 (June, 1933), p. 374.
160. *American Political Science Review*, Vol. XXVI, No. 5 (October, 1932), pp. 938–40. Reviewing Freund's *Legislative Regulation* in 1933, Joseph P. Chamberlain stated that it was "of great value to the legislative draftsman to have at his elbow a volume like this . . . which gives him in convenient compass not only a large number of legislative devices, but citations to statutes and cases in which they have been tried out." In his discussion of the definiteness of terms and of the choice of phrases and terms, Chamberlain said of Freund, "the author gives a very valuable collection of statutes and of cases which illustrate the importance of definite and clear provisions in legislation." *University of Pennsylvania Law Review*, Vol. 81, No. 7 (May, 1933), pp. 890–93, at 892.
161. *Cornell Law Quarterly*, Vol. XVIII, No. 4 (June, 1933), pp. 645–46, at 646.
162. *Journal of the American Institute of Criminal Law and Criminology*, Vol. XXIV, No. 2 (July–August, 1933), pp. 466–69, at 466.

Labor Legislation

163. Freund, *The Police Power, op. cit.*, pp. 298–99.
164. 198 U.S. 45 (1905).
165. Ernst Freund, "Limitation of Hours of Labor and the Supreme Court," *Journal of Political Economy*, Vol. 13, No. 7 (September, 1905), pp. 597–99, at 599.
166. Ernst Freund, "Limitation of Hours of Labor and the Federal Supreme Court," *Green Bag*, Vol. XVII, No. 7 (July, 1905), pp. 411–17, at 417.
167. Ernst Freund, "Recent Illinois Decisions Regarding Injunctions Issued in the Course of Strikes," *Journal of Political Economy*, Vol. 14, No. 1 (January, 1906), pp. 43–46, at 46.
168. *W. C. Ritchie & Co. v. John E. W. Wayman*, 244 Illinois

509 (1910). Greatly impressed with Brandeis' brief, Freund urged Brandeis to send a copy to Roscoe Pound, then professor of law at the University of Chicago Law School. See Melvin I. Urofsky and David W. Levy, *Letters of Louis D. Brandeis* (Albany: State University of New York Press, Vol. II, 1972), p. 299. The relationship of Freund and Brandeis grew closer, particularly in labor legislative and legal circles. Both were elected to serve in 1911 on the American Association for Labor Legislation's Committee on One Day of Rest in Seven.

169. Ernst Freund, "Can the States Co-operate for Labor Legislation?," *Survey*, Vol. XXII (June 12, 1909), pp. 409–11.

170. *Ibid.*, p. 411.

171. Ernst Freund, *Constitutional Aspects of the Ten Hour Law* (Springfield, Ill.: Illinois State Journal Co., State Printers, 1909), 6 pp., at 5. Issued as Bulletin, Bureau of Labor Statistics, Illinois.

172. Ernst Freund, "Constitutional Limitations and Labor Legislation," *Illinois Law Review*, Vol. IV, No. 9 (April, 1910), pp. 609–23, at 623.

173. Ernst Freund, "Constitutional Aspects of Hours Legislation for Men," *American Labor Legislation Review*, Vol. IV, No. 1 (March, 1914), pp. 129–31, at 131.

174. Ernst Freund, "Constitutional Aspects of Employers' Liability Legislation," *Green Bag*, Vol. XIX, No. 1 (January, 1907), pp. 80–83, at 83. The first workmen's compensation bill to be introduced in the United States was in New York State in 1898 but it was not passed. Four years later Maryland adopted such legislation but it was declared unconstitutional.

175. 201 New York Reports 271, 94 North Eastern Reporter 431 (1911). The 1911 law was replaced by Chap. 816, Laws of 1913, incorporating a voluntary plan.

176. Ernst Freund, "Court of Appeals Decision," *Survey*, Vol. XXVI (April 29, 1911), pp. 195–96, at 195.

177. *Ibid.*, pp. 195–96.

178. Ernst Freund, "The Federal Workmen's Compensation Act," *Survey*, Vol. 27 (February 3, 1912), pp. 1670–71, at 1670. See also, Ernst Freund, "Constitutional Status of Workmen's Compensation," *Illinois Law Review*, Vol. IV, No. 7 (February, 1912), pp. 432–46. Substantially the same article appeared with the same title as the latter in *American Labor Legislation Review*, Vol. II, No. 1 (February, 1912), pp. 43–59.

179. *Loc. cit.*

180. *The Common Cause*, Vol. 1, No. 3 (March, 1912), p. 110.

181. An outline of this report was written by Freund for the *American Labor Legislation Review*, Vol. II, No. 4 (December, 1912), pp. 566–67.

182. Ernst Freund, "Insurance Aspects of Workmen's Compensation," *American Labor Legislation Review*, Vol. III, No. 2 (June, 1913), pp. 273–75, at 75.

183. *Report of the General Administrative Council Meeting of the American Association for Labor Legislation Held at Chicago, Illinois, April 10, 1909* (Madison, Wisconsin: American Section of the International Association for Labor Legislation, April 1909), 13 pp., at 11–13. Among those attending the meeting were Jane Addams, John B. Andrews, John R. Commons, Alice Hamilton, Frederick N. Judson, Julian William Mack, and Charles Edward Merriam.

184. American Association for Labor Legislation, *Third Annual Meeting, New York, N. Y., Dec. 28-30, 1909: Proceedings—Reports —Addresses* (New York: American Association for Labor Legislation, 1910), pp. 24–26, at 24.

185. *White Phosphorus Matches,* Hearings Before the Committee on Ways and Means of the House of Representatives, Sixty-second Congress, Second Session, on H. R. 2896, January 10, 1912 (Washington: Government Printing Office, 1912), 110 pp., at 61–62. See also, *Phosphorus Poisoning* (New York: American Association for Labor Legislation, Leaflet No. 6, 1912), 8 pp., at 8.

186. Ernst Freund, "Constitutional and Legal Aspects of Health Insurance," *Proceedings of the National Conference of Social Work, At the Forty-Fourth Annual Session Held in Pittsburgh, Pennsylvania June 6–13, 1917* (Chicago: National Conference of Social Work, 1917), pp. 553–58, at 555.

In January, 1916 Freund spoke on "Social Legislation and Charity" at a meeting of the Associated Jewish Charities in Chicago. "So vital was the discussion," it was reported, "that the waiters engrossed in their interest neglected to disturb the speaker with the usual clatter of the dishes." Freund pointed out that social legislation up to that time was confined to granting special benefits to working women and children, but that soon legislation would extend benefits to male employees. "Workmen's compensation, old age pensions, insurance against sickness, industrial diseases are . . . steps in that direction." These will be spurred on by "the changed industrial conditions brought about by the war." Further, he predicted, "The state may also take an active part in readjusting the scheme of production and consumption." Ernst Freund, "Social Legislation and Charity," *Associated Bulletin of the Associated Jewish Charities of Chicago.* January, 1916, pp. 21–22, at 22.

In an address on "The Living Law" delivered before the Chicago Bar Association on January 3, 1916, Louis D. Brandeis observed that with the deepening of American democracy a shift had occurred from legal justice to social justice, and coincidentally a waning respect for law. Many different causes were involved and many different remedies were advanced. "The causes and the remedies have received perhaps their most helpful discussion from three lawyers whom we associate with Chicago: Professor Roscoe Pound; . . . Professor Wigmore; and Professor Freund." *Illinois Law Review,* Vol. X, No. 7 (February 1916), pp. 461–62.

Anti-Trust Legislation

187. Ernst Freund, "The Enforcement Provisions of the Sherman Law," *Journal of Political Economy,* Vol. 20, No. 5 (May, 1912), pp. 462–72, at 471–72.

188. Freund, *Standards of American Legislation, op. cit.,* p. 75.

189. *Ibid.,* p. 223. In an interesting letter on December 17, 1931 to Gilbert H. Montague, who had requested Freund's opinion on certain proposals to amend the Sherman Act, Freund wrote: "I have . . . come myself to think that politically, (if that term may be applied to economics) the Sherman Law has achieved almost the status of inviolability and that it is looked upon in many quarters as the great charter of economic liberty." Box III, "Ernst Freund Papers" (unprocessed), Department of Special Collections, Joseph Regenstein Library, University of Chicago.

Uniform State Laws

190. Ernst Freund, "Government and Law in America," *American Law Review,* Vol. XXXIV (January–February, 1900), pp. 16–27, at 27.

191. *Ibid.,* pp. 26–27.

192. Ernst Freund, "Unifying Tendencies in American Legislation," *Yale Law Journal,* Vol. XXII, No. 1 (November, 1912), pp. 96–113, at 112–13. See also, Freund, "The Problem of Adequate Legislative Powers under State Constitutions," *op. cit.,* pp. 120–22.

193. Ernst Freund, "Uniform Marriage and Divorce Legislation," *Case and Comment,* Vol. 21, No. 1 (June, 1914), pp. 7–9, at 9.

194. *American Bar Association Journal,* Vol. 7, No. 9 (September, 1921), p. 486. See also, Ernst Freund, "A Universal Illegitimacy Law," *Survey,* Vol. XLIX (October 15, 1922), pp. 104, 127 and 129; and Ernst Freund, *Illegitimacy Laws of the United States and Certain Foreign Countries* (Washington: Government Printing Office, 1919), 260 pp. Issued as U. S. Department of Labor, U. S. Children's Bureau, Legal Series No. 2, Bureau Publication No. 42. In the study for the U. S. Children's Bureau, Freund acknowledged the practical limitations of social conditions and concepts in attempting to legislate equal status for illegitimate children. "Everything should undoubtedly be done that is within the legislative power, to alleviate the hardship and stigma of illegitimacy, but the limits of practical legislative power should be considered." However, legislatures should try to advance social conditions and concepts. "Where legislation can affect social sentiment it should do so; and even such a matter of terminology should not be neglected." Here Freund suggested the elimination from law of the words "illegitimate" and "bastard," and recommended the substitution of the term "natural child" to correspond to the terminology of the law of citizenship. *Ibid.,* p. 58.

Administrative Law

195. 4 Opinions of the United States Attorneys General 37 (1842).
As Kenneth Culp Davis so aptly observed in 1958: "Administrative
law existed long before the term 'administrative law' came into use.
The first federal administrative law was embodied in the 1789 statutes."
Kenneth Culp Davis, *Administrative Law Treatise* (St. Paul: West
Publishing Co., 1958), Vol. 1, p. 24. Likewise, administrative agencies
have existed since the very first Congress in 1789.

196. 6 Opinions of the United States Attorneys General 99–103,
at 99 (1853).

197. Frank J. Goodnow, "The Executive and the Courts: Judicial
Remedies Against Administrative Action." *Political Science Quarterly*,
Vol. I, No. 4 (December, 1886), pp. 533–59, at 535.

198. Wilson, "The Study of Administration," *op. cit.*, p. 212.

199. Frank J. Goodnow, *Comparative Administrative Law* (New
York: G.P. Putnam's Sons, 2 Vols. 1893), Vol. I, pp. 8–9.

200. Frank J. Goodnow, *The Principles of the Administrative Law
of the United States* (New York: G.P. Putnam's Sons, (1905), p. 17.

201. Goodnow, *Comparative Administrative Law, op. cit.*, Vol. I,
p. vi.

202. Freund, "The Law of the Administration in America," *op.
cit.*, p. 404.

203. *Loc. cit.*

204. Bruce Wyman, *The Principles of the Administrative Law
Governing the Relations of Public Officers* (St. Paul, Minn.: Keefe-
Davidson Co., 1903), p. 23.

205. Ernst Freund, *Cases on Administrative Law Selected from
Decisions of English and American Courts* (St. Paul: West Publishing Co., 1911), p. 1.

206. *Ibid.*, p. 2.

207. *Ibid.*, p. 3.

208. *Loc. cit.*

209. Ernst Freund, *Cases on Administrative Law* (St. Paul: West
Publishing Co., 1928), 2d ed., p. v.

210. *Ibid.*, p. vi.

211. Edward A. Harriman, "The Development of Administrative
Law in the United States," *Yale Law Journal*, Vol. XXV, No. 8
(June, 1916), pp. 658–65, at 658.

212. *Ibid.*, p. 659.

213. Elihu Root, "Public Service by the Bar," *American Bar
Association Journal*, Vol. II, No. 3 (July, 1916), pp. 736–55, at 750.

214. A. A. Berle, Jr., "The Expansion of American Administrative
Law," *Harvard Law Review*, Vol. XXX, No. 5 (March, 1917), pp.
430–48, at 432.

215. Freund, *Cases on Administrative Law, op. cit.*, Introduction,
p. 3.

216. *Harvard Law Review,* Vol. XXXVII, No. 5 (March, 1924), pp. 638–42, at 640.

217. *Ibid.,* pp. 640–41.

218. *Ibid.,* p. 641.

219. J. Forrester Davison and Nathan D. Grundstein, *Administrative Law and the Regulatory System* (Washington, D.C.: Lerner Law Book Co., 1968), Rev. ed., pp. 1–20.

220. Leonard D. White, *Introduction to the Study of Public Administration* (New York: The Macmillan Co., 1926), p. xvi.

221. Freund, "Administrative Law," *Encyclopaedia of the Social Sciences, op. cit.,* p. 452.

222. *Ibid.,* p. 454.

223. *Loc. cit.*

224. *Loc. cit.*

225. *Ibid.,* p. 455.

226. *Ibid.,* pp. 454–55.

227. Ernst Freund, "The Law Back of Public Management," *Public Management,* Vol. XIV, No. 2 (February, 1932), pp. 57–60, at 57.

228. "A Symposium on Administrative Law, Based Upon Legal Writings 1931–33," *Iowa Law Review,* Vol, XVIII, No. 2 (January, 1933), pp. 129–248.

229. Felix Frankfurter, "Introduction," *ibid.,* pp. 129–132, at 130–31.

230. Felix Frankfurter, "Foreword," *Yale Law Journal,* Vol. 47, No. 4 (February, 1938), p. 5.

231. Felix Frankfurter, "Foreword," *Columbia Law Review,* Vol. XLI, No. 4 (April, 1941), pp. 585–88, at 586–87.

232. Nathan D. Grundstein, "Presidential Power and Administrative Law," *George Washington Law Review,* Vol. 18, No. 3 (April, 1950), pp. 285–326, at 325–26.

233. *Federal Trade Commission v. Ruberoid Co.,* 343 U.S. 470, at 487.

234. Testimony of Judge David W. Peck, Special Subcommittee of the Committee on Rules, House of Representatives, 84th Congress, 2d Session, under Authority of House Resolution 462, 1956, page 26.

235. Felix Frankfurter, "The Supreme Court in the Mirror of Justices," *University of Pennsylvania Law Review,* Vo. 105, No. 6 (April, 1957), pp. 781–96, at 793.

236. Davis, *Administrative Law Treatise, op. cit.,* Vol. 1, pp. 1–2.

237. *Ibid.,* p. 3.

238. 1 American Jurisprudence 2d, *Administrative Law,* Sec. 4, 806.

239. *Ibid.,* 807.

240. Robert S. Lorch, *Democratic Process and Administrative Law* (Detroit: Wayne State University Press, 1969), pp. 59–60.

Casebooks and Curricula

241. Freund, *Cases on Administrative Law, Selected from Decisions*

of English and American Courts, op. cit. In reviewing Freund's first Casebook in 1912, Thomas Reed Powell prophetically commented: "The study of administrative law is indebted to this compilation of Professor Freund's for a service even more important than that rendered to the law of trusts by the case-book of Dean Ames. The subject matter of the collection still receives but slight recognition in the law school curriculum. . . . Professor Freund's interest seems to lie more particularly in developing the subject from the point of view of individual private right. His selection and arrangement of cases merits unqualified approval not only because it provides an admirable case-book for the class-room and thus promotes the study of an important subject, but because it aids materially in securing a more definite conception of what are still ill-defined categories of legal principles." *Columbia Law Review,* Vol. XII, No. 6 (June, 1912), pp. 570–571, at 570.

242. Frank J. Goodnow, *Selected Cases on American Administrative Law* (Chicago: Callaghan & Co., 1906). Goodnow acknowledged Freund's placing at his disposal a collection of cases on administrative law from which he chose a number of cases for inclusion in his book. (p. iv) ". . . Goodnow's greatest contribution was to the field of political science, whereas Freund's writings more definitely set the direction for the study of administrative law as it would be taught in the law school." "Ernst Freund—Pioneer of Administrative Law," in "Comments," *University of Chicago Law Review,* Vol. 29, No. 4 (Summer, 1962), pp. 755–81, at 756.

243. Bruce Wyman, *Principles of the Administrative Law Governing the Relations of Public Officers, op. cit.*

244. Kent, *supra* note 141, p. 150.

245. Ernst Freund, *Cases on Administrative Law* (St. Paul: West Publishing Co., 1928), 2d ed., p. vi. Walter F. Dodd recognized Freund's insights and goals in his review in 1929 of the second edition of the Casebook: "The author of this volume is primarily responsible for the attention now given to the important problems of administrative law in the law schools of this country. His volume . . . has determined the scope of law school courses in this field; and his activities as chairman of the special committee on Administrative Law and practice of the Commonwealth Fund have largely determined the character of special investigations in this field. By the present volume he has still further increased the debt which all students of our legal system owe to him." *Illinois Law Review,* Vol. XXIII, No. 6 (February, 1929), pp. 623–24, at 623.

246. John A. Fairlie, "Public Administration and Administrative Law," in *Essays on the Law and Practice of Governmental Administration: A Volume in Honor of Frank Johnson Goodnow,* edited by Charles G. Haines and Marshall E. Dimock (Baltimore: The Johns Hopkins Press, 1935), pp. 28–29.

247. Shelden D. Elliott, "The Literature of Administrative Law,"

Mississippi Law Journal, Vol. XIV, No. 3 (April, 1942), pp. 412–24, at 418–419.

248. Louis L. Jaffe, Review of *Cases and Comments on Administrative Law* by Walter Gellhorn, *Harvard Law Review,* Vol. LIV, No. 2 (December, 1940), pp. 368–69.

249. Kenneth C. Sears, *Cases and Materials on Administrative Law* (St. Paul: West Publishing Co., 1938), p. vii.

250. *Harvard Law Review,* Vol. XLVI, No. 1 (November, 1932), pp. 167–71.

251. *Ibid.,* pp. 167–69.

252. *Ibid.,* pp. 168–69.

253. *Ibid.,* p. 169.

254. *Ibid.,* p. 170.

255. *Ibid.,* p. 171.

256. *Ibid.,* p. 170.

257. Louis L. Jaffe, "The Contributions of Mr. Justice Brandeis to Administrative Law," *Iowa Law Review,* Vol. XVIII, No. 2 (January, 1933), pp. 213–27, at 213.

258. Oliver P. Field, "The Study of Administrative Law: A Review and A Proposal," *Iowa Law Review,* Vol. XVIII, No. 2 (January, 1933), p. 236.

259. *Ibid.,* p. 235.

260. Paul L. Sayre, "A Common Law of Administrative Powers," *Iowa Law Review,* Vol. XVIII, No. 2 (January, 1933), pp. 241–48, at 242–43.

261. *Loc. cit.*

262. *Ibid.,* p. 247.

263. Maurice H. Merrill, "Three Possible Approaches to the Study of Administrative Law," *Iowa Law Review,* Vol. XVIII, No. 2 (January, 1933), pp. 228–32, at 228.

264. Milton Katz, *Cases and Materials on Administrative Law* (St. Paul: West Publishing Co., 1947).

265. Thomas I. Emerson, Review of *Cases and Materials on Administrative Law* by Milton Katz, in *Harvard Law Review,* Vol. LXI, No. 1 (November, 1947), pp. 199–203, at 200.

266. Edwin Blythe Stason, "Research in Administrative Law," *Administrative Law Review,* Vol. 16 (Winter-Spring, 1964), pp. 99–107, at 99.

267. Harrop A. Freeman, "Administrative Law in the First-Year Curriculum," *Journal of Legal Education,* Vol. 10, No. 2 (1957), pp. 225–31, at 230.

268. Hurst, *The Growth of American Law, op. cit.,* p. 270.

269. Kent, *supra* note 141, p. 148.

270. *Ibid.,* p. 147.

271. *Ibid.,* p. 146.

272. Freund, "The Law Back of Public Management," *op. cit.,*

p. 58. See also, Ernst Freund, "The Study of Law in Germany," *The Counsellor*, Vol. I, No. 5 (February, 1892), pp. 131–35.

273. Freund, "The Law Back of Public Management," *op. cit.*, p. 59. Freund did not recommend the elimination of the case method of instruction in the law schools. He insisted it should not be the only method. This reflected his broader view that law professors and legal scholars generally did not adequately study or concern themselves with social problems and policy.

274. Kent, *supra* note 141, p. 149.

275. Freund, "Law School and University," *op. cit.*, pp. 151–52.

276. "Upon Professor Beale, Professor Freund, and Professor Mack chiefly devolved the labor of successfully meeting, in the brief time allowed, the many problems of organization and administration, the creation of the Faculty, and the acquisition of the Library." Also, plans were made for the Law School's new building which was occupied in May, 1904. "The University of Chicago Law School," *University Record*, University of Chicago, Vol. XII, No. 3 (January, 1908), pp. 100–07, at 101.

At first, Freund and Beale clashed, from a number of viewpoints— the new school's purpose and curriculum and also because of legal philosophy. Beale, supporting the policy of Dean James Barr Ames of Harvard Law School excluding from its curriculum any subject considered not to be pure law, opposed Freund's recommendation that two-ninths of the courses leading to the law degree should consist of subjects then generally taught in the departments of political science and sociology, such as criminology, railroad transportation, banking, government and industry, accounting and psychology. Also, Freund had proposed admitting to the law faculty professors of political science and sociology, whereas Harvard permitted only attorneys who were professors of law to teach in its law school. Furthermore, since Harvard had been enlisted to supervise the establishment of the Chicago Law School, Beale insisted on the case method of teaching, in which Freund did not believe. In a letter to President Harper, Beale wrote on April 2, 1902: "We should have assumed that everybody in Chicago was of the same mind, if it had not been for the ideas Mr. Freund expressed here. I dislike to speak of this matter, because Mr. Freund personally made such an agreeable impression upon me. . . . Such a school as Mr. Freund has in mind differs from ours in almost every one of these particulars." In a letter, dated April 7, 1902 Beale wrote Freund that "Ames was more disturbed than I by what he (and I) consider your heretical views about law."

Freund compromised and agreed to forgo all the non-legal courses but won out on the teaching of international law by members of the political science faculty and on retaining his own course in administrative law. At the time, only Columbia and Chicago taught courses in administrative law, at the undergraduate level, with Goodnow at

Columbia and Freund at Chicago. On the other hand, Harvard did not introduce such a course until 1911 with Wyman teaching it at the graduate level. "Ernst Freund—Pioneer of Administrative Law," in "Comments," *op. cit.,* pp. 763–70.

By the time Beale completed his two year term as dean, however, the two were friendly, intellectual opponents. In fact it was Freund whom Beale asked to introduce him as the university convocation orator in June, 1904 upon his departure from the Law School. Ernst Freund, "Introduction of the Convocation Orator: the Fifty-First University Convocation," *University Record,* University of Chicago, Vol. IX, No. 2 (June, 1904), pp. 41–42. Eventually, however, Freund's views prevailed, and the Chicago Law School took on the legal personality of Freund.

277. Freund, "The Problem of Intelligent Legislation," *op. cit.,* p. 78.

278. *Ibid.,* p. 79.

279. *Loc. cit.*

280. Wyzanski, "The Trend of the Law and Its Impact on Legal Education," *op. cit.,* p. 563.

Administrative Powers

281. Oliver P. Field, "The Study of Administrative Law: A Review and A Proposal," *Iowa Law Review,* Vol. XVIII, No. 2 (January, 1933), pp. 233–40, at 234–35.

282. Louis L. Jaffe, *Judicial Control of Administrative Action* (Boston: Little, Brown and Co., 1965), p. 34.

283. Avery Leiserson, *Administrative Regulation, A Study in Representation of Interests* (Chicago: University of Chicago Press, 1942), p. 56.

284. Freund, *Administrative Powers Over Persons and Property, op. cit.*

285. *Ibid.,* p. viii.

286. *Ibid.,* p. 220.

287. *Ibid.,* p. 221.

288. *Ibid.,* p. 578.

289. *Ibid.,* p. 221.

290. *Loc. cit.*

291. *Ibid.,* p. 220.

292. *Ibid.,* p. 218.

293. *Ibid.,* p. 221.

294. *Ibid.,* p. 219.

295. J. Roland Pennock, *Administration and the Rule of Law* (New York: Rinehart & Co., 1941), pp. 52–53.

296. Freund, *Administrative Powers Over Persons and Property, op. cit.,* p. 584.

297. *Ibid.,* p. 194.

298. *Ibid.*, p. 233.
299. *Loc. cit.*
300. *Ibid.*, p. 101.
301. *Ibid.*, p. 95.
302. Ernst Freund, "Historical Survey," in *The Growth of American Administrative Law* (St. Louis: Thomas Law Book Co., 1923), pp. 9–41, at p. 20. Freund was co-editor of this study with Robert V. Fletcher, Joseph E. Davies, Cuthbert W. Pound, John A. Kurz and Charles Nagel.
303. *Ibid.*, p. 21.
304. *Loc. cit.*
305. *Ibid.*, pp. 22–24.
306. Freund, *Administrative Powers Over Persons and Property, op. cit.*, pp. 23, 437 and 583.
307. Ernst Freund, "The Substitution of Rule for Discretion in Public Law," *American Political Science Review,* Vol. IX, No. 4 (November, 1915), pp. 666–76, at 666.
308. Ernst Freund, "Commission Powers and Public Utilities," *American Bar Association Journal,* Vol. IX, No. 5 (May, 1923), pp. 285–88, at 288. See also, Freund, "Historical Survey," in *The Growth of American Administrative Law, op. cit.*, pp. 38–40.
309. Freund, "Commission Powers and Public Utilities," *op. cit.*, p. 288.
310. Woodrow Wilson, Speech at the New York Press Club, September 9, 1912, *New York Tribune,* September 10, 1912, p. 4.
311. Woodrow Wilson, *The New Freedom* (New York: Doubleday, Doran & Co., 1933), p. 284.
312. Freund, *Administrative Powers Over Persons and Property, op. cit.*, p. 74.
313. Holcombe, Review of *Administrative Powers Over Persons and Property, op. cit.*, pp. 266–67.
314. Edward S. Corwin, Review of *Administrative Powers Over Persons and Property* in *Public Management,* Vol. XI, No. 12 (December, 1929), p. 701.
315. Freund, "Administrative Law," *Encyclopaedia of the Social Sciences, op. cit.*, p. 455.
316. Wormser, "Legal Learning Dedicated to the Progress of Society," *op. cit.*, pp. 46–47.
317. Freund, *Administrative Powers Over Persons and Property, op. cit.*, p. 584.
318. Kent, *supra* note 141, p. 151.
319. Charles S. Hyneman, "Administrative Adjudication: An Analysis," *Political Science Quarterly,* Vol. LI, No. 3 (September, 1936), Part I, pp. 383–417, at 388.
320. Freund, *Administrative Powers Over Persons and Property, op. cit.*, p. 583.

321. *Ibid.,* p. 580.

322. Sharfman, *The Interstate Commerce Commission, op. cit.,* Part One, p. 4.

323. Robert B. Hankins, "The Necessity for Administrative Notice and Hearing," *Iowa Law Review,* Vol. XXV, No. 3 (March, 1940), pp. 457–84, at 457.

324. Freund, *Administrative Powers Over Persons and Property, op. cit.,* pp. 14–15, 80–84, 196–206.

325. Leiserson, *Administration Regulation: A Study in Representation of Interests, op. cit.,* p. 56. See also, F.F. Blachly and M.E. Oatman, *Federal Regulatory Action and Control* (Washington: Brookings Institution, 1940), pp. 13–37 for a different classification of administrative powers.

326. Freund, *Administrative Powers Over Persons and Property, op. cit.,* p. 148.

327. White, *Introduction to the Study of Public Administration, op. cit.,* p. 481.

328. *American Bar Association Journal,* Vol. XIX, No. 2 (February, 1933), pp. 112–13, at 112.

329. *Ibid.,* p. 113.

330. Malcolm B. Parsons, *The Use of the Licensing Power by the City of Chicago* (Urbana, Ill.: The University of Illinois Press, 1952), p. 3.

331. Ernst Freund, "Licensing," *Encyclopaedia of the Social Sciences* (New York: The Macmillan Co., 1933), Vol. Nine, pp. 447–51, at 447.

332. *Loc. cit.*

333. *Ibid.,* p. 448, and Freund, *Administrative Powers Over Persons and Property, op. cit.,* p. 71.

334. Freund, "Licensing," *op. cit.,* p. 447.

335. *Ibid.,* pp. 447–48.

336. *Ibid.,* p. 448.

337. *Loc. cit.*

338. *Ibid.,* p. 449.

339. *Ibid.,* pp. 450–51.

340. *Ibid.,* p. 461.

341. Ernst Freund, "Legal Aspects of Philanthropy," in Ellsworth Faris, Ferris Laune, and Arthur J. Todd (editors), *Intelligent Philanthropy* (Chicago: University of Chicago Press, 1930), pp. 149–81, at 180–81.

342. Davison and Grundstein, *Administrative Law and the Regulatory System, op. cit.,* p. 11.

343. Edwin W. Patterson, "Legislative Regulation and the Unwritten Law," in "A Symposium on Administrative Law, Based Upon Legal Writings 1931–33," *Iowa Law Review,* Vol. XVIII, No. 2 (January, 1933), pp. 193–97, at 195.

344. Hurst, *The Growth of American Law: The Law Makers, op. cit.,* p. 411. As John Preston Comer observed in 1927: "Professor Freund endeavored to set forth the advantages resulting from the new administrative activities of a legislative character." John Preston Comer, *Legislative Functions of National Administrative Authorities* (New York: Columbia University Press, 1927), p. 15.
345. Freund, "Historical Survey," in *The Growth of American Administrative Law, op. cit.,* p. 41.
346. Freund, *Administrative Powers Over Persons and Property, op. cit.,* p. 583. See also, Marvin B. Rosenberry, "Administrative Law and the Constitution," *American Political Science Review,* Vol. XXIII, No. 1 (February, 1929), pp. 32–46, at 32. In 1914 Freund, as chairman of the American Bar Association's Committee on Taxation, issued a report on the new federal income tax law which stated: "It is extremely undesirable that administrative powers of regulation not strictly warranted by law, and loose construction, should be demanded and condoned on the plea that the law as written is unworkable or contrary to justice and good sense. . . . We ought to strive for a law that can be executed to the letter without injustice or unnecessary burden." Report of the Committee on Taxation of the American Bar Association Presented at American Bar Association October 20-22, 1914, *Chicago Legal News,* Vol. XLVII, No. 11 (October 17, 1914), pp. 82–84 and 86, at 86.

Administrative Discretion

347. Freund, "The Law of the Administration in America," *op. cit.,* pp. 403–25.
348. *Ibid.,* p. 406.
349. *Ibid.,* p. 407.
350. *Ibid.,* p. 408.
351. *Ibid.,* p. 410.
352. *Ibid.,* p. 419.
353. *Loc. cit.*
354. *Ibid.,* p. 424.
355. *Ibid.,* pp. 424–25.
356. *Ibid.,* p. 425.
357. Freund, "The Substitution of Rule for Discretion in Public Law," *op. cit.,* pp. 668–69.
358. *Ibid.,* p. 669.
359. *Ibid.,* p. 670.
360. *Loc. cit.*
361. *Ibid.,* pp. 671–72.
362. *Ibid.,* p. 672.
363. *Ibid.,* p. 674.
364. *Ibid.,* pp. 674–75

365. *Ibid.*, p. 676.
366. *Ibid.*, p. 666.
367. *Ibid.*, p. 667.
368. *Ibid.*, p. 668.
369. Gerard C. Henderson. *The Federal Trade Commission: A Study in Administrative Law and Procedure* (New Haven: Yale University Press, 1924), p. v–vi.
370. Freund, "Historical Survey," in *The Growth of American Administrative Law, op. cit.*, p. 22.
371. John H. Wigmore, "The Dangers of Administrative Discretion," *Illinois Law Review*, Vol. XIX, No. 6 (February, 1925), pp. 440–41.
372. Ernst Freund, "Administrative Discretion: A Reply to Dean Wigmore," *Illinois Law Review*, Vol. XIX, No. 8 (April, 1925), pp. 663–64.
373. See Julius Stone, *Social Dimensions of Law and Justice* (Stanford, Cal.: Stanford University Press, 1966), p. 717.
374. Freund, *Administrative Powers Over Persons and Property, op. cit.*, p. 71.
375. *Cornell Law Quarterly,* Vol. XV, No. 3 (April, 1930), pp. 507–10, at 507.
376. Freund, *Administrative Powers Over Persons and Property, op. cit.*, p. vii.
377. *Ibid.*, p. 80.
378. *Ibid.*, p. 102.
379. *Cornell Law Quarterly, supra,* p. 510.
380. Freund, "Legislation", *Encyclopaedia of the Social Sciences, op. cit.*, pp. 350–51.
381. Lewis Allen Sigler, "The Problem of Apparently Unguided Administrative Discretion," *St. Louis Law Review*, Vol. XIX. No. 4 (June, 1934), pp. 261–321, at 262.
382. 71 Indiana Reports 189, 197–98 (1880).
383. Freund, *Administrative Powers Over Persons and Property, op. cit.*, p. 97.
384. Freund, "Licensing," *Encyclopaedia of the Social Sciences, op. cit.*, p. 448.
385. Freund, "The Law Back of Public Management," *op. cit.*, p. 59.
386. Freund, *Legislative Regulation, op. cit.*
387. *American Political Science Review*, Vol. XXVI, No. 6 (December 1932), p. 1103.
388. Dickinson, *Administrative Justice and the Supremacy of Law in the United States, op. cit.*
389. Herbert A. Simon, *Administrative Behavior* (New York: The Macmillan Co., 1947), pp. 55–56.
390. Freund, *Administrative Powers Over Persons and Property, op. cit.*, p. 220.

391. Freund, "Administrative Law," *Encyclopaedia of the Social Sciences, op. cit.,* p. 254.

392. *Loc. cit.*

393. *Loc. cit.*

394. Freund, *Administrative Powers Over Persons and Property, op. cit.,* pp. 218–21.

395. *Ibid.,* p. 219.

396. Charles Evans Hughes, "Some Aspects of the Development of American Law," New York State Bar Association Proceedings of the Thirty-Ninth Annual Meeting Held at New York, January 14–15, 1916, *Report of New York State Bar Association* (Albany: The Argus Co., 1916), Vol. XXXIX, pp. 266–88, at 270.

397. Metzler, "The Growth and Development of Administrative Law," *op. cit.,* pp. 209–27.

398. Arthur Suzman, "Administrative Law in England: A Study of the Report of the Committee on Ministers' Powers," *Iowa Law Review,* Vol. XVIII, No. 2 (January, 1933), pp. 160–86.

399. *Cornell Law Quarterly,* Vol. XV, No. 3 (April, 1930), p. 510.

400. Marshall E. Dimock, "The Role of Discretion in Modern Administration," in John M. Gaus, Leonard D. White, and Marshall E. Dimock, *The Frontiers of Public Administration* (New York: Russell & Russell, 1936), p. 55.

401. *Ibid.,* p. 65.

402. Ralphs F. Fuchs, "Concepts and Policies in Anglo-American Administrative Law Theory," *Yale Law Journal,* Vol. 47, No. 4 (February, 1938), pp. 538–76, at 547. See also, Ernst Freund, "The Right to a Judicial Review in Rate Controversies," *West Virginia Law Quarterly,* Vol. XXVII, No. 3 (March, 1921), pp. 207–12.

403. Roscoe Pound, *The Task of the Law* (Lancaster: Franklin and Marshall College, 1944), 94 pp., at p. 34.

404. *Ibid.,* pp. 22–23.

405. *Ibid.,* p. 59.

406. Jaffe, *Judicial Control of Administrative Action, op. cit.,* p. 37.

407. Wilson, "The Study of Administration", *op. cit.,* p. 197.

408. Jaffe, *supra* note 406, p. 34.

The Rule of Law

409. Albert Venn Dicey, *Introduction to the Study of the Law of the Constitution* (London: The Macmillan Co., 1915), 8th edition, pp. 183–84.

410. *Ibid.,* pp. 189–90.

411. *Ibid.,* p. 191.

412. Dickinson, *Administrative Justice and the Supremacy of Law in the United States, op. cit.,* p. 35.

413. Hart, *An Introduction to Administrative Law, With Selected Cases, op. cit.,* p. 14.

414. Dickinson, *supra,* pp. 37–38.
415. Goodnow, *The Principles of the Administrative Law of the United States. op. cit.,* pp. 367–73.
416. Dicey, *supra,* p. 406.
417. A. C. 120 (1915).
418. Grundstein, *supra* note 232, p. 321.
419. *Ibid.,* p. 324.
420. *Ibid.,* p. 325. Marshall E. Dimock wisely appraised the problem of judicial control of administration: "The burden of the judiciary, therefore, is to balance in the right proportions the legitimate needs of social efficiency and individual liberty. In relation to social efficiency Ernst Freund commented that the protection of private rights from the possibility of official error, partiality, or excess of zeal is at least important as carrying out some governmental policy. And Frank J. Goodnow, the first of the great writers on administrative law, believed that the importance of and need for administrative efficiency should receive due emphasis as against the inherent natural rights of the individual because effective social control depends on that efficiency." Marshall Edward Dimock and Gladys Ogden Dimock, *Public Administration* (New York: Holt, Rinehart and Winston, Inc., 3d ed., 1964), pp. 382–83.
421. Kent, *supra* note 141, p. 150.
422. See Black, "The 'Jurisdictional Fact' Theory and Administrative Finality," *op. cit.;* see also, A. Martin Tollefson, "Administrative Finality," *Michigan Law Review,* Vol. XXIX, No. 7 (May, 1931), pp. 839–49.
423. Freund, *Administrative Powers Over Persons and Property, op. cit.,* p. 293.
424. 285 U.S. 22 (1932).
425. 253 U.S. 287 (1920).
426. Ernst Freund, "The Right to a Judicial Review in Rate Controversies," *West Virginia Law Quarterly,* Vol. XXVII, No. 3 (March, 1921), pp. 207–12, at 205.
427. Freund, *Administrative Powers Over Persons and Property, op. cit.,* p. 298.
428. Freund, "The Law Back of Public Management," *op. cit.,* p. 59. Admiring the self-government aspects of American society, Freund in 1903 asserted that "the idea of consent negatives that of power and authority." "The failure of authority at some point should, however, not be regarded as the failure of the idea of law, for the ultimate resort and support of the law is, in all modern states, the voluntary consent and submission on the part of the majority subject to its rule. The power of the law is the power of numbers, and numbers derive their power from consent." Ernst Freund, *Empire and Sovereignty* (Chicago: University of Chicago Press, 1903), First Series, Vol. IV, the Decennial Publications, Sec. VII, p. 287.

Tort Claims

429. Ernst Freund, "Private Claims against the State," *Political Science Quarterly,* Vol. VIII, No. 4 (December, 1893), pp. 625–52. See also Ernst Freund, "Malice and Unlawful Interference," *Harvard Law Review,* Vol. XI, No. 7 (February 25, 1898), pp. 449–65, in which he discussed the right of trade unions to interfere between employers and employees in England.

430. Ernst Freund, "Responsibility of the State in Internal (Municipal) Law," *Tulane Law Review,* Vol. IX, No. 1 (December, 1934), pp. 1–16, at 16. This article, published posthumously, was prepared as a report for the International Congress of Comparative Law at The Hague, August 2–6, 1932.

431. Freund, "Administrative Law," *Encyclopaedia of the Social Sciences, op. cit.,* p. 454. See also, Ernst Freund, "Discussion [on Administrative Control of Corporations and Administrative Courts for the United States]," *Proceedings of the American Political Science Association at Its Sixth Annual Meeting, 1909* (Baltimore: The Waverly Press, 1910), pp. 58–62.

432. Edwin M. Borchard, "The Federal Tort Claims Bill", *University of Chicago Law Review,* Vol. 1, No. 1 (May, 1933), pp. 1–12, at p. 1.

433. Freund, "Private Claims against the State," *op. cit.,* p. 652.

434. Borchard, *op. cit.,* p. 12.

Coordination of State and Local Action

435. Ernst Freund, "Co-ordinating State and Local Action," *Public Management,* Vol. XIII, No. 1 (January, 1931), pp. 12–13, at 13.

436. 337 Illinois Reports 200, 169 North Eastern Reporter 22 (1930).

437. Freund, "Co-ordinating State and Local Action," *op. cit.,* p. 13.

Home Rule for Cities

438. Freund, "The Law Back of Public Management," *op. cit.,* p. 59.

439. *Ibid.,* p. 412.

440. *Ibid.,* p. 60.

441. Ernst Freund, "Some Legal Aspects of the Chicago Charter Act of 1907," *Illinois Law Review,* Vol. II, No. 7 (February, 1908), pp. 427–39. In 1906 Freund was selected by the Chicago Charter Convention's Subcommittee of Six "to draft a digest of the various propositions before the convention for the use of the subcommittee and committee in preparing the report on which a bill for a new charter is founded." "The subcommittee . . . considered Professor Freund the best obtainable person for the important work of digesting and presenting to the convention the ideas that have been presented." *Chicago Record-Herald,* October 23, 1906, p. 5. Freund was no passive digester

or reporter. He presented many of his own views and suggestions; and the Subcommittee of Six, of which his friend and colleague, Charles E. Merriam, was a member, adopted a number of them.

442. Barnet Hodes, *Law in the Modern City* (Chicago: Reilly and Lee, 1937).

443. Wormser, "Legal Learning Dedicated to the Progress of Society," *op. cit.*, p. 47.

444. Albert Lepawsky, *Home Rule for Metropolitan Chicago* (Chicago: University of Chicago Press, 1935), p. 178.

Some Observations on Centralized Authority, Accountability and Efficiency

445. Walter Thompson, *Federal Centralization: A Study and Criticism of the Expanding Scope of Congressional Legislation* (New York: Harcourt, Brace and Co., 1923), p. 10.

446. Ernst Freund, "The New German Constitution," *Political Science Quarterly*, Vol. XXXV, No. 2 (June, 1920), pp. 177–203, at 181, 183–84.

447. Ernst Freund, "Reapportionment—a political issue [in Chicago and Cook County]," unpublished holographic manuscript, undated [c. 1921], 9 pp., at 3. Box I, Folder 1, "Papers of Ernst Freund" (processed), Department of Special Collections, Joseph Regenstein Library, University of Chicago.

448. Charles Grove Haines and Bertha Moser Haines, *Principles and Problems of Government* (New York: Harper and Bros., 1926), pp. 488–90.

449. Freund, "Principles of Legislation," *American Political Science Review, op. cit.*, p. 2. Freund was referring to the Taft Commission on Economy and Efficiency (1910-1913). Two years earlier he wrote: "Clearly the greatest problem of American public law is how to assert against unrestrained legislative discretion the legitimate claims of principle. One way would be the according of a larger and perhaps a controlling influence to the initiative of the executive power. This has been the burden of the recommendations of President Taft's Commission for Economy and Efficiency in the important field of public finance." Ernst Freund, "The Substitution of Rule for Discretion in Public Law," *International Journal of Ethics*, Vol. XXV, No. 1 (October, 1914), pp. 100–02, at 102.

450. Freund, "The Law of the Administration in America," *op. cit.*, pp. 410–12.

451. Oscar Kraines, "The President Versus Congress: The Keep Commission, 1905–1909, First Comprehensive Presidential Inquiry into Administration," *Western Political Quarterly*, Vol. XXIII, No. 1 (March, 1970), pp. 5–54.

452. Freund, *supra* note 450, p. 413.

453. *Loc. cit.*

454. *Ibid.*, pp. 413–14.

455. *New York Times,* April 6, 1916, p. 12. See also, Alpheus Thomas Mason, *Brandeis: A Free Man's Life* (New York: The Viking Press, 1946), p. 337.

456. *Loc. cit.*

457. *Loc. cit.*

Civil Rights and Liberties

458. Ernst Freund, "Tendencies of Legislative Policy and Modern Social Legislation," *International Journal of Ethics,* Vol. XXVII, No. 1 (October, 1916), pp. 1–24, at 5.

459. *Debs v. United States,* 249 U. S. 211 (1919).

460. Ernst Freund, "The Debs Case and Freedom of Speech," *New Republic,* Vol. XIX, No. 235 (May 3, 1919), pp. 13–15, at 13.

461. *Ibid.,* pp. 14–15.

462. Mark DeWolfe Howe (ed.), *Holmes-Pollock Letters* (Cambridge: Harvard University Press, 1941), Vol. II, p. 14. See also, Max Lerner (ed.), *The Mind and Faith of Justice Holmes* (New York: Random House, Inc., the Modern Library, 1954), pp. 298–301 and 326–27.

463. *New York Times,* March 26, 1926, p. 20.

464. *United States v. Schwimmer,* 49 U. S. 448 (1929).

465. Ernst Freund, "United States v. Schwimmer," *New York University Law Quarterly Review,* Vol. VII, No. 1 (September, 1929), pp. 157–59, at 157.

466. Ernst Freund, "Burning Heretics," Letter to *New Republic,* Vol. XXI, No. 269 (January 28, 1920), pp. 266–67. In June, 1919 a bomb exploded outside United States Attorney General A. Mitchell Palmer's home, killing only the bomb bearer who was never identified. The Department of Justice thereupon launched its "Red Raids" against "dangerous aliens." Incensed by the illegal break-ins and burglaries, mail thefts, wiretapping and recording, falsification of evidence, perjury and other illegal and unethical behavior of Department of Justice and immigration authorities, Freund spoke at many public meetings confining himself to pointing out the unconstitutional and illegal acts performed by governmental officials. See postcard notice, "Recent Raids and Deportations," announcing a meeting to be held on January 23, 1920 at the Chicago Y.M.C.A., whose speakers were to be Edward F. Dunne, Ernst Freund, Frank H. McCulloch, and others. Box IV, "Ernst Freund Papers" (unprocessed), Department of Special Collections, Joseph Regenstein Library, University of Chicago.

A committee of twelve leading attorneys was formed to conduct an inquiry into the practices of the Department of Justice relating to the treatment of aliens. The twelve were R. G. Brown, Zechariah Chafee, Jr., Felix Frankfurter, Ernst Freund, Swinburne Hale, Francis Fisher Kane, Alfred S. Niles, Roscoe Pound, Jackson H. Ralston, David

Wallerstein, Frank P. Walsh, and Tyrell Williams. See United States Senate, "Charges of Illegal Practices of the Department of Justice," *Congressional Record,* 67th Congress, 4th Session, February 5, 1923, pp. 3005–27. In testifying against the charges of the committee of twelve, all that Attorney General Palmer could say about Freund was that he, Frankfurter, and Walsh were "identified with the American Civil Liberties Union." *Ibid.,* p. 3022.

467. *Lantern,* Vol. II, No. 3 (August, 1929), p. 4. Freund and Wigmore found themselves once again on opposite ends of controversy during the Sacco-Vanzetti Case. Joined by Frankfurter, Freund felt the trial had been unfair, whereas Wigmore defended its fairness. For details of the bitter ensuing exchange between Frankfurter and Wigmore, see Francis Russell, *Tragedy in Dedham: The Story of the Sacco–Vanzetti Case* (New York: McGraw-Hill Book Co., 1962), pp. 371–73.

Interestingly and consistently, Wigmore objected to the Senate committee which investigated the "Teapot Dome Scandal" in 1923-24 as "senatorial debauch . . . poking into political garbage cans" and encroaching on the powers of the executive. John H. Wigmore, "Legislative Power to Compel Testimonial Disclosure," *Illinois Law Review,* Vol. XIX, No. 6 (February, 1925), pp. 452–54. Frankfurter and Freund, on the other hand, defended the investigation.

468. Ernst Freund, "Deportation Legislation in the Sixty-ninth Congress," *Social Service Review,* Vol. I, No. 1 (March, 1927), pp. 46–57, at 46.

469. *Ibid.,* p. 47.

470. *Ibid.,* p. 52.

471. *Ibid.,* p. 57.

472. Ernst Freund, "Freedom of Speech," *New Republic,* Vol. XXV, No. 324 (February 16, 1921), pp. 344–46, at 346.

473. *Loc. cit.* While Freund felt that the legislatures had failed generally to define the frameworks of legality and illegality, he believed that obscenity had been adequately defined by legislation.

474. Ernst Freund, "A Recent Case on the Law of Conspiracy," *The Counsellor,* Vol. I, No. 8 (May, 1892), pp. 220–29, at 228.

475. Freund, *The Police Power, op. cit.,* p. 8.

476. Shortly after the Russian Revolution of October, 1917 Freund jotted down several questions in handwritten notes under the heading, "Bolshevism": "Can we conceive of guarantees of liberty equal to those afforded by present polit[ical] system?" Is the present polit[ical] system inconsistent with econ[omic] revolution?" "Which promises a saner econ[omic] gov[ernmen]t?" One page, undated, in Box III, "Ernst Freund Papers" (unprocessed), Department of Special Collections, Joseph Regenstein Library, University of Chicago.

477. Freund, *The Police Power, op. cit.,* p. 12.

478. *Ibid.,* pp. 16–17.

479. *Ibid.,* p. 513.
480. Freund, "Tendencies of Legislative Policy and Modern Social Legislation," *op. cit.,* p. 9.
481. Ernst Freund, "Search and Seizure," *Chicago Legal News,* Vol. LVI, No. 27 (January 24, 1924), pp. 211–12, 214–15, at 215.
482. Ernst Freund, "Jews in America," holographic manuscript, undated, 39 pp. Box II, "Ernst Freund Papers" (unprocessed), Department of Special Collections, Joseph Regenstein Library, University of Chicago.

International Law and World Peace

483. Ernst Freund, "The Control of Dependencies through Protectorates," *Political Science Quarterly,* Vol. XIV, No. 1 (March, 1899), pp. 19–38, at 38.
484. Freund, *Empire and Sovereignty, op. cit.,* pp. 287–88.
485. Ernst Freund, "The Outlook for International Law," *New Republic.,* Vol. XV, No. 185 (May 18, 1918), pp. 80–82.
486. Ernst Freund, "The Treaty and International Law," *New Republic.,* Vol. XXI, No. 263 (December 17, 1919), pp. 74–77, at 77. In a letter to Freund on November 14, 1919 Herbert Croly, editor of the *New Republic,* acknowledged receipt of the manuscript and explained why there would be a delay in publishing the article: "No matter how intolerant the state of mind of the public is becoming in other respects, it is daily becoming more tolerant in respect to Germany, and they will consider an argument such as yours with less prejudice after the Treaty has been ratified in some form by the Senate and before the reserved ratification has been accepted by the European Powers than it would now." Box IV, "Ernst Freund Papers" (unprocessed), Department of Special Collections, Joseph Regenstein Library, University of Chicago.
487. Freund, "The New German Constitution," *op. cit.,* p. 203.
488. Letter, dated May 18, 1922, to Mrs. E. M. Collier, Box IV, "Ernst Freund Papers" (unprocessed), Department of Special Collections, Joseph Regenstein Library, University of Chicago.

Classification of Crimes

489. Ernst Freund, "Classification and Definition of Crimes," *Journal of the American Institute of Criminal Law and Criminology,* Vol. V, No. 6 (March, 1915), pp. 807–26, at 826.
490. John W. MacDonald, "The Classification of Crimes," *Cornell Law Quarterly,* Vol. XVIII, No. 4 (June, 1933), pp. 524–63, at 531.
491. Freund, *Legislative Regulation, op. cit.,* pp. 10–11.
492. Maurice Parmalee, *Criminology* (New York: The MacMillan Co., 1918), p. 269.
493. Freund, "Classification and Definition of Crimes," *op. cit.,* p.

322. In one of the most penetrating articles published recently on the purpose and scope of the criminal law in the United States with regard to "victimless crimes," Norval Morris, Professor of Law and Criminology at the University of Chicago, pointedly referred to Ernst Freund and his inquiry into the subject and observed that Freund's warnings had not been heeded. Freund had begun his study with the caution: "Not every standard of conduct that is fit to be observed is also fit to be enforced." Norval Morris, "The law is a busybody: Crimes without victims," *New York Times Magazine,* April 1, 1973, pp. 10–11, 58–62, at 11.

Tributes to Freund

494. University of Chicago, *University Record,* Vol. XIX, No. 1 (January, 1933), p. 43.
495. *Ibid.,* pp. 39–42.
496. Jane Addams, "The Friend and Guide of Social Workers," *ibid.,* pp. 43–45, at 43–44.
497. *Ibid.,* p. 44.
498. *Ibid.,* pp. 44–45.
499. Wormser, "Legal Learning Dedicated to the Progress of Society," *op. cit.,* p. 45.
500. *Loc cit.*
501. *Ibid.,* p. 47.
502. *University of Chicago Law Review,* Vol. 1, No. 1 (May, 1933), p. 1.
503. Maurice T. Van Hecke, "Ernst Freund as A Teacher of Legislation," *University of Chicago Law Review, ibid.,* pp. 92–94.
504. Arthur H. Kent, "The Work of Ernst Freund in the Field of Legislation," *ibid.,* pp. 94–96.
505. Van Hecke, *op. cit.,* p. 92.
506. *Ibid.,* p. 93.
507. *Ibid.,* pp. 93–94.
508. Kent, *supra* note 504, pp. 95–96.
509. Kent, "Ernst Freund (1864–1932)—Jurist and Social Scientist," *supra* note 141, p. 145.
510. "Ernst Freund, 1864–1932," *Social Service Review, op. cit.,* pp. 650–51.
511. W. A. Robson, "Notes," *Law Quarterly Review,* Vol. XLIX, No. CXCIV (April, 1933), p. 177.
512. *American Political Science Review.* Vol. XXVI. No. 6 (December, 1932), pp. 1103–04.
513. W. Ivor Jennings, *supra* note 135, p. 588.
514. Freund, *Legislative Regulation, op. cit.,* p. 113.
515. "Notes and Personals," *American Law School Review,* Vol. 7, No. 7 (December, 1932), pp. 667–68.
516. *Illinois Bar Journal,* Vol. 21, No. 2 (October, 1932), p. 19.

517. Frankfurter, *The Ernst Freund Lecture: Some Observations on Supreme Court Litigation and Legal Education, op. cit.,* pp. 1–4. Holders of the lectureship, following Frankfurter, have included Walter V. Schaefer, Charles E. Wyzanski, Jr., Lord Denning of Whitchurch, Lord Parker of Waddington, Wilber G. Katz, John Marshall Harlan, Sir Kenneth Diplock, and Carl McGowan.
518. Wormser, "Legal Learning Dedicated to the Progress of Society," *op. cit.,* p. 46.
519. Freund, "The Study of Law in Germany," *op. cit.,* p. 135.
520. *Ibid.,* p. 134.

Conclusion: The Post-Freundian Era and the Rediscovery of Freund

521. Charles S. Hyneman, "Administrative Adjudication: An Analysis," *Political Science Quarterly,* Vol. LI, No. 4 (December, 1936), Part II, pp. 516–37, at 519.
522. E. Blythe Stason, "Study and Research in Administrative Law," *George Washington Law Review,* Vol. 7, No. 6 (April, 1939), pp. 684–702, at 691–92.
523. See particularly, A. H. Feller, "Administrative Procedure and the Public Interest—The Results of Due Process," *Washington University Law Quarterly,* Vol. XXV, No. 3 (April, 1940), pp. 308–20. See also, Arthur W. Macmahon, "The Ordeal of Administrative Law," *Iowa Law Review,* Vol. XXV, No. 3 (March, 1940), pp. 424–56.
524. See Carl McFarland, *Judicial Control of the Federal Trade Commission and the Interstate Commerce Commission 1920–1930: A Comparative Study in the Relations of Courts to Administrative Commissions* (Cambridge: Harvard University Press, 1933).
525. J. Roland Pennock, *Administration and the Rule of Law* (New York: Rinehart & Co., 1941), p. 170.
526. Roscoe Pound, "The Place of the Judiciary in a Democratic Polity," *American Bar Association Journal,* Vol. 27, No. 3 (March, 1941), pp. 133–39.
527. *Humphrey's Executor v. United States,* 295 U.S. 602 (1935).
528. 60 Stat. 237, 5 U.S.C. Sec. 1001 (1946).
529. Emerson, *supra* note 265, p. 199.
530. Ferdinand F. Stone, "An Introduction to the Administrative Process," *Miami Law Quarterly,* Vol. 6, No. 3 (April, 1952), pp. 281–98, at 294.
531. Grundstein, *supra* note 232, p. 325.
532. Roscoe Pound, "Foreword," *Federal Bar Journal,* Vol. XVI, No. 4 (October-December, 1956), pp. 445–52, at 451.
533. Morris D. Forkosch, *A Treatise on Administrative Law* (Indianapolis: The Bobbs-Merrill Co., 1956), p. 2.
534. Davis, *Administrative Law Treatise, op. cit.,* pp. 5–6.

535. Reginald Parker, "Why do Administrative Agencies Exist?" A Reappraisal," *Georgetown Law Journal*, Vol. 45, No. 3 (Spring, 1957), pp. 331–63, at 333.

536. Charles S. Rhyne, "Foreword: Proposed Changes in Federal Administrative Practice and Procedure," *Ohio State Law Journal*, Vol. 19, No. 3 (Summer, 1958), pp. 377–79, at 377–78.

537. *Ibid.*, p. 379.

538. Melvin G. Shimm, "Foreword," *Law and Contemporary Problems*, Vol. 26, No. 2 (Spring, 1961), pp. 179–80, at 179.

539. Stason, "Research in Administrative Law," *op. cit.*, p. 105.

540. Allen, "Preface to the 1965 Edition," *Standards of American Legislation*, p. viii.

541. *Loc cit.*

542. Van Hecke, *supra* note 503, p. 92.

543. Freund, "Historical Survey," in *The Growth of American Administrative Law*, *op. cit.*, p. 23.

544. Freund, *Administrative Powers Over Persons and Property*, *op. cit.*, p. 581.

545. *Ibid.*, pp. 578–85.

546. Hurst, *The Growth of American Law: The Law Makers*, *op. cit.*, p. 411.

547. Freund, *Administrative Powers Over Persons and Property*, *op. cit.*, p. 102.

548. Parsons, *supra* note 330, p. 7. See also, Gellhorn, *Administrative Law, Cases and Comments*, *op. cit.*, pp. 331–460.

549. Kent, *supra* note 141, p. 146.

550. *Loc. cit.*

551. Freund, "Historical Survey", in *The Growth of American Administrative Law*, *op. cit.*, p. 40.

552. Grundstein, *supra* note 232, p. 287.

553. Ernst Freund, "James Parker Hall: Dean of the Law School," *University Record*, University of Chicago, Vol. XIV, No. 2 (April, 1928), pp. 110–11, at 110.

554. Richard F. Babcock, *The Zoning Game: Municipal Practices and Policies* (Madison: University of Wisconsin Press, 1966), p. 3.

555. Freund, "Some Inadequately Discussed Problems of the Law of City Planning and Zoning," *op. cit.*, p. 142.

556. *Minnesota Law Review*, Vol. XVII, No. 6 (May, 1933), p. 685.

557. *American Bar Association Journal*, Vol. XIX, No. 2 (February, 1933), p. 112.

558. Kenneth Culp Davis, *Discretionary Justice* (Urbana: University of Illinois Press, 1971).

559. Frank E. Cooper, *State Administrative Law* (Indianapolis: The Bobbs-Merrill Co., Inc., 1965), Vol. One, pp. 20–21.

560. Bernard Schwartz and H. W. R. Wade, *Legal Control of Government: Administrative Law in Britain and the United States*

(Oxford: Clarendon Press, 1972), p. 315. See also, *Law and Contemporary Problems,* Vol. 37, No. 1 (Winter, 1972) devoted entirely to "Administrative Discretion."

561. President's Advisory Council on Executive Organization, *A New Regulatory Framework—Report on Selected Independent Regulatory Agencies* (Washington, D. C.: U. S. Government Printing Office, 1971).

562. Michael D. Reagan (ed.), "A Symposium—Regulatory Administration: Are We Getting Anywhere?" *Public Administration Review,* Vol. XXXII, No. 4 (July/August, 1972), pp. 283–310.

563. C. Herman Pritchett, "Public Law and Judicial Behavior," *Journal of Politics,* Vol. 30, No. 2 (May, 1968), pp. 480–509; and Robert G. Dixon, Jr., "Who is Listening? Political Science Research in Public Law." *PS,* Vol. IV, No. 1 (Winter, 1971), pp. 19–26.

564. Martin Shapiro, "From Public Law to Public Policy, or The 'Public' in 'Public Law,' " *PS,* Vol. V, No. 4 (Fall, 1972), pp. 410–18, at 416.

565. Peter Woll, "Administrative Law in the Seventies," *Public Administration .Review,* Vol. XXXII, No. 5 (September/October, 1972), pp. 557–64, at 563–64.

566. Freund, *Standards of American Legislation, op. cit.,* p. 225.

567. See the recent issue of the *University of Chicago Law Review* with a section on "Ernst Freund and the First Amendment Tradition" in which Harry Kalven, Jr. contributed an article, "Professor Ernst Freund and *Debs v. United States,*" containing an account of Judge Learned Hand's joining with Freund in opposition to Justice Holmes' decision. Kalven's theme is that Holmes' opinion happily is no longer the law and is not likely to become law again; and that when taken together with Freund's criticism it provides us with "important clues to the intellectual history of the first amendment tradition, a history we had better understand if we are to hang on to the tradition today." Vol. 40, No. 2 (Winter, 1973), pp. 235–47, at 235.

Index

Abortion, 27
Abbott, Grace, 5
Accessibility of administrators, 166
Accident and sickness insurance, 50, 52, 59, 136, 185
Accountability of administration, 132-136, 200-201; of individual legislator, 132-133, 200-201; of counsel for an independent regulatory commission, 135-136
Addams, Jane, 139, 147-148, 185, 204
Adjudication, administrative. *See* Administrative adjudication
Administration. *See* Bureaucracy, Management, and Public administration
Administrative absolutism, 82, 155-156
Administrative action, 8-9, 11, 35, 44, 46-48, 66-76, 79, 98, 105-106, 108, 112, 118-120, 123, 125, 130, 134, 156, 159. *See also* Administrative discretion, Administrative powers, Administrative procedures, and Rule-making
Administrative adjudication, 10, 122-129, 158-160, 164, 166, 193, 205; formal, 158-159; informal, 158-159, 166; legislation v. adjudication, 158; notice and hearing, 28, 127; orders, 48; procedural due process, 158-159; sanctions, 138-140, 148, 151
Administrative authority v. individual rights, 66-76, 82, 103-121
Administrative code, 158
Administrative courts, 71, 82, 123, 158, 164, 166, 170, 199
Administrative crimes, 146
Administrative discretion, 9, 11, 13-

14, 33, 37, 40, 70-71, 80, 88-89, 92, 94, 97-98, 102-121, 124-125, 154, 159-160, 164, 167, 171, 173, 193, 195-197, 200, 206-207; abuses of, 14, 94, 99, 106-108; broad v. narrow, 119-120; censorial, 114; discretion as unstandardized power, 92, 108-109, 112-113; discretion v. regulation, 40, 46, 108-109, 160, 200, expansion of, 9, 104, 160; Freund-Wigmore debate on, 14, 110-112, 173, 196; Freund's changed views on, 105; mediating discretion, 114; prudential or quasi-legislative discretion, 114; qualified or guided, 114-115; quasi-judicial, 114, 159; relation between discretion and self-governmental organs, 103-107; remedies against, 14; rule v. discretion, 70, 92, 107, 109-111, 113, 160, 200; Sigler's classification of 114-115; substitution of principle for discretion, 14, 92, 107, 110-111, 160, 200; uncontrolled, unqualified or unguided, 14, 33, 114-115, 160
Administrative efficiency, 68, 123, 125, 158, 198
Administrative finality. *See* Finality
Administrative hearings, 44
Administrative hierarchy, 126, 162
Administrative independence, 167
Administrative justice. *See* Administrative adjudication, Administrative courts, Administrative procedures, and Justice
Administrative justice v. judicial justice, 123
Administrative law, 1, 6, 8-11, 14-15, 21, 36, 40, 43, 64-103, 105, 116-

Kraines, Oscar.
        World and ideas of Ernest
Freund.